Dakota Women's Work

Dakota Women's Work

Creativity, Culture, and Exile

Colette A. Hyman

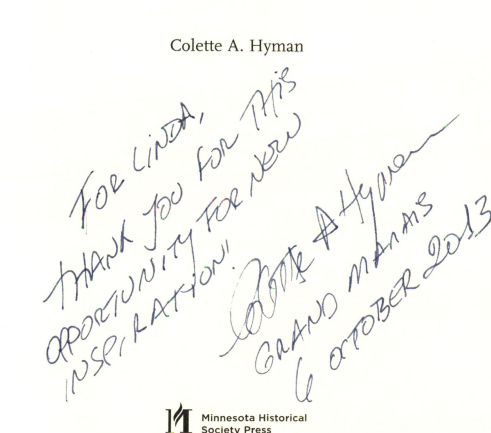

For Linda,
Thank you for this
opportunity for new
inspiration!
Colette A Hyman
Grand Marais
6 October 2013

M Minnesota Historical
Society Press

CLEAN
WATER
LAND &
LEGACY
AMENDMENT

The publication of this book was supported in part by the
Ken and Nina Rothchild Fund for Business and Women's History.

www.mhspress.org
The Minnesota Historical Society Press is a member of the
Association of American University Presses.

Manufactured in [the United States of America/Canada]

10 9 8 7 6 5 4 3 2 1

♾ The paper used in this publication meets the minimum requirements
of the American National Standard for Information Sciences—Permanence for
Printed Library Materials, ANSI Z39.48–1984.

International Standard Book Number
ISBN: 978-0-87351-850-5 (paper)
ISBN: 978-0-87351-858-1 (e-book)

Library of Congress Cataloging-in-Publication Data

Hyman, Colette A. (1958–)
Dakota Women's Work : Creativity, Culture, and Exile / Colette A. Hyman.
p. cm.
Includes bibliographical references and index.
ISBN 978-0-87351-850-5 (pbk. : alk. paper) — ISBN 978-0-87351-858-1 (e-book)
1. Dakota women—History. 2. Dakota women—Social conditions.
3. Dakota women—Economic conditions. 4. Dakota Indians—Industries.
5. Dakota beadwork. 6. Indian leatherwork. 7. Quillwork. I. Title.
E99.D1 H96 2012
978.004/975243
2011047752

For
WILLIAM BEANE,
the late EDITH BICKERSTAFF,
and their families

CONTENTS

Dakota Women's Work

Women, Work, and Survival

WHEN LILLIAN BEANE WAS BORN IN 1911, her great-aunt Mary Eastman Faribault made her a pair of deerskin moccasins beaded with a floral design characteristic of their people, the Eastern Dakota. These carefully protected moccasins have remained in the family for more than a century. They honor the memory of the woman who made them and the generations that they represent, connecting Lillian's grandmothers to her children, her grandchildren, and her great-grandchildren.

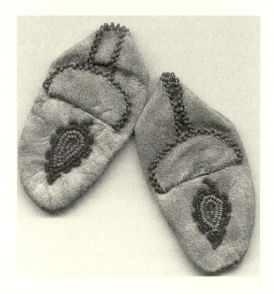

Beaded deerskin moccasins made in 1911 by Mary Eastman Faribault for her newborn great-niece, Lillian Moore.

Mary Faribault, whose Dakota name was Tipiwakanwin, Sacred Lodge Woman, would have learned to work with hides and decorate the moccasins from her mother, Wakantankawin, Great Spirit Woman, Nancy Eastman, her grandmother Wakaninajinwin, Stands Sacred Woman, and her great-grandmother, Canpadutawin, Red Cherry Woman, who married Mahpiya Wicasta, Cloud Man, in 1810. In making these moccasins, Mary honored the new baby. She also honored the baby's mother, Grace Eastman Moore, and the baby's grandmother, Mary Jane Faribault Eastman, wife of Mary's brother John.[1]

When Mary created these moccasins, she fulfilled the historical role of Dakota women: making footwear, garments, equipment, and shelter for their families as well as bearing and caring for young children. Dakota women also taught older girls the skills they would need as adults in their communities and the obligations they would have within their families. Among those obligations were honoring relatives and celebrating life cycle events and accomplishments with gifts of functional items—clothing or pouches, for instance—that were delicately ornamented with the woman's best efforts and sincerest prayers. For in proffering these gifts, women honored not only their relatives but the spirits of ancestors and all creation around them. When Mary Faribault made these moccasins, she was following in the footsteps of her grandmothers, doing much as they had in their Minnesota homelands.

The moccasins made for Lillian by a woman who had lived through devastating changes inflicted on Dakota people during the nineteenth century bear witness to the endurance and survival of Dakota traditions in exile. They also testify vividly about the role of women in that survival. This book addresses many different strands of Dakota history that are woven into each delicate stitch. Through the story of the family who created them, we can begin to understand the lives of Dakota women in the times surrounding the U.S.–Dakota War of 1862, the most devastating moment in the history of the Eastern Dakota.

Mary's ancestors had come from different parts of the Minnesota homelands. Her mother, Wakantankawin, was the daughter of Seth Eastman, an officer in the U.S. Army posted at Fort Snelling; her mother's mother, Wakaninajinwin, had grown up among the Mdewakantunwan Dakota, the Spirit Lake Dwellers, who lived along the lower Minnesota River and the Mississippi. Wankantankawin married a skilled hunter named Tawakanhdiota, Many Lightnings, who had ancestors among the Mdewakantunwan but also among the Wahpetunwan, the Dwellers among the Leaves. The latter, along with the Sisitunwan, the Dwellers of the Fish Ground, lived upstream along the Minnesota River and on the shores of Lake Traverse and Big Stone Lake, which divide Minnesota from South Dakota.

Between the Mdewakantunwan in the East and the Sisitunwan and Wahpetunwan in the West lived the Wahpekute, the Leaf Shooters, along the upper Cannon River and west along the Blue Earth and Des Moines rivers. These Dakota peoples constituted four of the Oceti Sakowin of the Dakota Oyate, the Seven Council Fires of the Dakota Nation. The other three groups were the Ihanktunwan, Dwellers at the End, and the Inhanktunwanna, Little Dwellers at the End, who lived between the Minnesota and Missouri rivers, and the Titunwan, Dwellers of the Prairies, who lived west of the Missouri. The Titunwan, the largest of the seven groups then and now, were themselves divided into another seven council fires.[2]

One of the primary distinctions between the Dakota in Minnesota and other Dakota peoples was language. The peoples of the Oceti Sakowin spoke three mutually intelligible dialects of one language: the "D" dialect spoken among the four eastern bands, or Dakota; the "N" dialect spoken by the Ihantunwan and Ihanktunwanna, or Nakota; and the "L" dialect spoken by the Titunwan, or Lakota. In addition, different Titunwan groups speak slightly different dialects of Lakota, but the four Council Fires of Minnesota Dakota spoke, and continue to speak, different dialects. These groups have also developed some different practices and traditions, but, overall, they share structures of social organization and views of the relationship between the spirit and material worlds.[3]

The bands' geographical locations meant they had different experiences with westward-encroaching European Americans. The aftermath

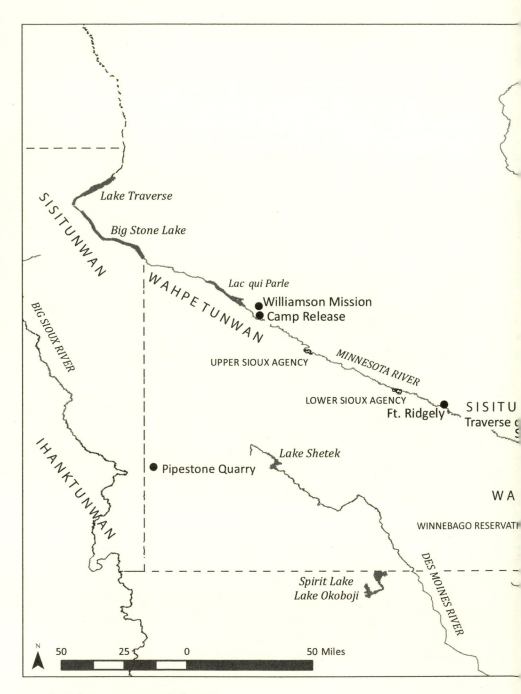

The Dakota in Minnesota before 1862.

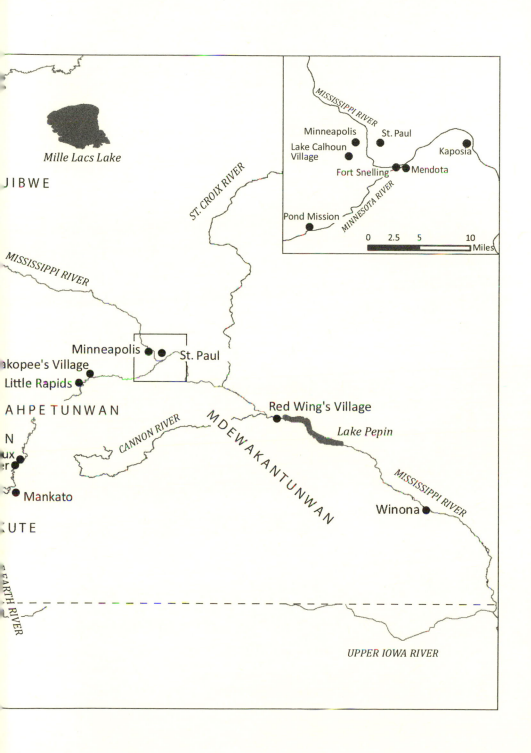

Mille Lacs Lake

JIBWE

ST. CROIX RIVER

MISSISSIPPI RIVER

Minneapolis   St. Paul
kopee's Village
Little Rapids

AHPETUNWAN

N

ux
r

Mankato

UTE

CANNON RIVER

MDEWAKANTUNWAN

Red Wing's Village

Lake Pepin

MISSISSIPPI RIVER

Winona

EARTH RIVER

UPPER IOWA RIVER

MISSISSIPPI RIVER

Minneapolis   St. Paul
Lake Calhoun
Village   Kaposia
Fort Snelling   Mendota

Pond Mission

MINNESOTA RIVER

0   2.5   5   10
Miles

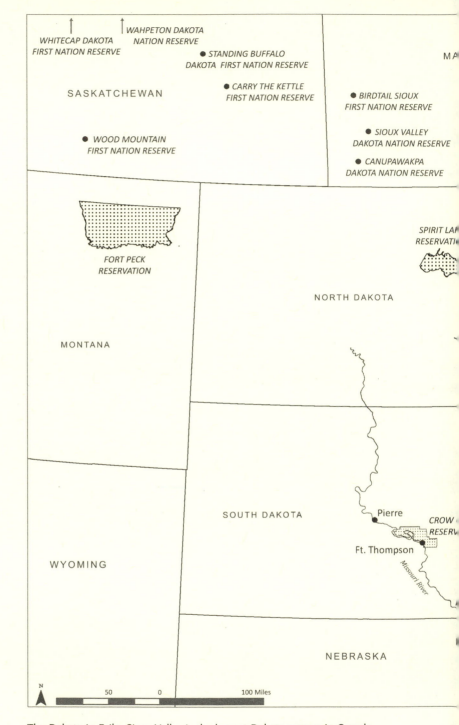

The Dakota in Exile. Sioux Valley is the largest Dakota reserve in Canada.
A full listing of Dakota reserves and communities in Canada is available at
www.aboriginalcanada.gc.ca/

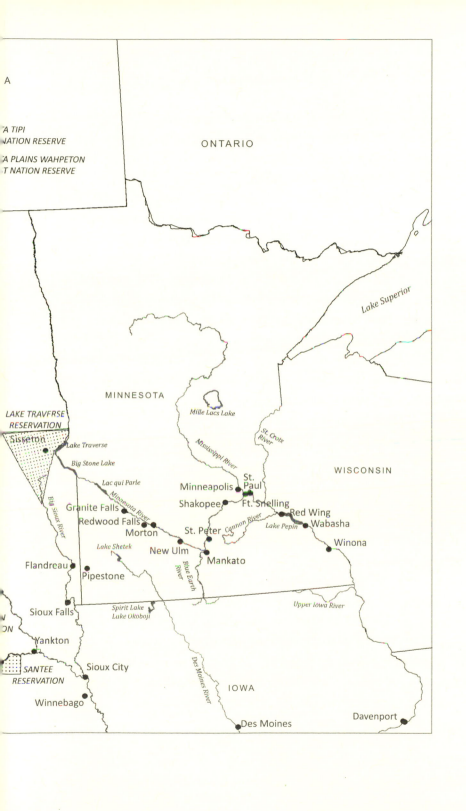

A

A TIPI
NATION RESERVE

A PLAINS WAHPETON
T NATION RESERVE

ONTARIO

Lake Superior

MINNESOTA

Mille Lacs Lake

St. Croix River

Mississippi River

WISCONSIN

LAKE TRAVERSE RESERVATION
Sisseton
Lake Traverse
Big Stone Lake
Lac qui Parle
Minnesota River
Granite Falls
Redwood Falls
Morton
Blue Sioux River
Lake Shetek
New Ulm
Mankato
Blue Earth River
Minneapolis
St. Paul
Shakopee
Ft. Snelling
St. Peter
Cannon River
Lake Pepin
Red Wing
Wabasha
Winona

Flandreau
Pipestone
Spirit Lake
Lake Okoboji
Upper Iowa River

Sioux Falls

Yankton

SANTEE RESERVATION

Sioux City

Des Moines River

IOWA

Winnebago

Des Moines

Davenport

of the U.S.–Dakota War of 1862 created distinct trajectories among Dakota families. Fewer than a thousand warriors, out of a population of more than seven thousand, fought in the war, but President Abraham Lincoln would sign an order nullifying all treaties with the Dakota in Minnesota and removing them from the state. A few hundred Dakota remained there overtly, under the protection of powerful white men, or clandestinely, in communities protected by geography or as individuals trying to blend in with their European American neighbors. Many Dakota, perhaps half the population in Minnesota, fled westward or northward, where they eventually settled in Canada and North Dakota. Approximately two thousand men, women, and children, whether they were involved or not, were imprisoned and forcibly removed from the state. Consequently, by the early twentieth century, the Eastern Dakota lived on reservations at Santee, Nebraska; Flandreau and Lake Traverse, South Dakota; Spirit Lake, North Dakota; Fort Peck, Montana; and several reserves in Manitoba and Saskatchewan, as well as in the Lower Sioux, Upper Sioux, Prior Lake, and Shakopee communities in Minnesota.[4]

This book focuses on the Dakota, mostly Mdewakantunwan and Wahpekute, who were imprisoned following the war and then taken far from their Minnesota homelands. After the war, the federal government removed them, first to prison camps and then to new lands in Santee, Nebraska. A few years later some, including Mary Faribault's family, established a community in Flandreau, South Dakota, that embraced Christianity, and the majority of people still in Santee converted as well. No longer able to live from hunting, harvesting wild plants, and cultivating small crops, they turned to farming and other occupations. A significant number of men from these two communities began working for the church, including Mary Faribault's husband, David Faribault, Jr., and her brother, John Eastman, a grandfather of the baby Mary honored with the moccasins she made.

The lives and experiences of Dakota peoples on other reservations bear some resemblance to those of the Dakota peoples at Santee and Flandreau, but each community followed its own historical path, shaped by internal dynamics as well as by geography and federal policy. Their distinct stories intersect with those of the Dakota at Santee and Flandreau through enduring bonds of kinship and culture. Indeed, Mary Faribault, whose father Tawakanhdiota, Jacob Eastman, helped found the community at Flandreau, lived most of her long life at the Lake Traverse reservation among Sisitunwan and Wahpetunwan Dakota.

Mary's mother, Wakaninajinwin, died in 1858. Although she did not experience the devastation of war and exile in her brief twenty-seven years, she lived through profound changes: with the decline of the fur trade, Dakota women experienced transformations in their work, including the new practice of making beautiful moccasins and other goods specifically for sale to the increasing numbers of white people living around them. They also witnessed the arrival of Protestant missionaries dedicated to erasing Dakota ways, making Dakota men into farmers and converting Dakota women and men to Christianity.

For the Dakota peoples of Minnesota and all Indigenous peoples, objects carry spiritual meaning and embody family and community relationships. This is especially true for objects created for an individual, for a special accomplishment, or for a life cycle event. Richard W. Hill, Sr., a Tuscarora museum curator, maintains that for many Native peoples, it is impossible to separate "spirituality from aesthetic principles, or from community ethics." As Dakota women's lives were cataclysmically transformed over the course of the nineteenth and early twentieth centuries, the nature of their work changed as well, but, in many ways, the meanings embodied in the beaded, quilled, and other ornamented items they created remained much the same as before the dislocation of their nation. They demonstrate cultural continuity, even in the face of war, exile, conversion to Christianity, and the many other dimensions of colonization.[5]

The history of Dakota women in this period broadly parallels the history of Native peoples across the continent. Other Indigenous women exercised similar complex and essential roles in their communities that entailed both material and spiritual obligations and that were defined with more or less flexibility by a clear gender division of labor. The functional art that women created was central to the physical subsistence and spiritual well-being of their people. Like Dakota women, Native women in the northern tier of the United States participated in the fur trade alongside the men in their communities and lived in communities that missionaries and the U.S. government sought to eradicate and reconstitute in their own image. Finally, Indigenous women faced war, violence, and loss of their homelands as the U.S. Army and European American settlers took over Native lands and destroyed Native peoples' ability to support themselves as their ancestors had for innumerable generations.

For the Dakota, the path to war and its brutal aftermath began in the late eighteenth century with their first contact with European Americans, who began competing with their British and French predecessors in the lucrative fur trade. Contact with the white men—whether French, British, or American—brought changes to the lives of the Dakota, including new materials with which women made their art. Yet, for many decades, stability in the trade allowed the Dakota to sustain relatively intact their subsistence patterns and the culture that grew out of them.

When the United States acquired territories that included the Eastern Dakota's homelands and increasing numbers of white American farmers moved in, changes came rapidly. Missionaries and civil authorities sought to sever the Dakota from their subsistence economy based on seasonal migrations and to turn them into sedentary farmers. In 1862, the growing presence of white settlers, the increasing strength of the U.S. military in the region, and ongoing efforts by missionaries to Christianize the Dakota erupted into war and genocide. The Dakota who survived were forced to leave their homelands and rebuild communities, having lost nearly one half of their population as well as all of the lands that had sustained their people since their origins at Bdote (Mendota), where the Minnesota River runs into the Mississippi. These events necessarily altered the work of Dakota women: bearing and caring for the next generation; feeding, clothing, and sheltering the older generations; and working not only for physical survival but for cultural and spiritual survival as well.

Women's work intertwined these realms of existence. Women honored the spirits of ancestors by passing on their traditions to younger generations and as they cared for their children, called *wakanyeza,* sacred beings. Women brought together these traditions most immediately in special gifts such as moccasins made for children but also in functional art created for ceremonial and everyday use. The Dakota language has no word that translates into "art," but the task of making aesthetically rich utilitarian objects expressed the relationships between different realms of experience. According to Mi'kmaq artist and art curator Viviane Gray, Native art "is a way of life—a holistic experience that incorporated not only their cultural experiences (Indian and non-Indian) but also their personal and tribal beliefs, historical events, stories, dreams, and personal visions." When Dakota women made moccasins and leggings, for instance, they incorporated all these elements of their lives. In the process of creation, they embellished and adorned them with quills, feathers, bones, and dyes, and, later, with materials acquired from traders, including ribbons, artificial dyes, metal, and beads. Women composed patterns and combined colors and textures in designs that they shared with one another. The objects they created, in their production as well as their use, were central to the identity of the Dakota and other Native peoples.[6]

Only in the last two decades have the creations of Native women—and the "craftwork" of other women—been recognized as "art." Reflecting the influence of feminist and Native artists and art critics, scholars have begun acknowledging that quillworkers, potters, weavers, beadworkers, and others produce artwork of the same technical and aesthetic sophistication as the paintings and sculptures by European and European American men traditionally recognized as "art." In response, some museums are attempting to identify the Native creators of objects, not just their tribal origin. Even the phrase "unknown artist" on a museum label reminds viewers that an individual created the object.[7]

This reevaluation of Native material culture has, in turn, necessitated a reassessment of what is known as "tourist art," items made by Indigenous peoples explicitly for sale. While long belittled as "inauthentic" or "too commercial," this genre of creative production has become central to discussions regarding Indigenous people's strategies for coping with their changing lives. Production of items for sale is now recognized as both a strategy for material survival and a way of resisting an economy that would otherwise force people into low-wage work outside of their own communities. At the same time, production of moccasins, dolls, and other objects explicitly for sale is an essential part of the history of "collecting Native America."[8]

Europeans and European Americans began gathering mementos of "exotic" cultures at the time of first contact. By the nineteenth century, this habit had emerged into a full-blown obsession. Collectors of Native American "artifacts" scoured the continent for physical vestiges of cultures they believed were on the path to extinction. As colonization of Native lands and genocidal attacks on peoples and cultures advanced, the perpetrators stepped up their efforts to collect evidence of the soon-to-be-gone nations. The powerful myth of the "vanishing Indian" led to the ransacking of Native communities in order to build collections that eventually stocked "natural history" museums in cities across North America and Europe in the late nineteenth and early twentieth centuries.[9]

The arrival of collectors, however, opened new ways for Native women to make economic contributions to their families. Women became increasingly attuned to the tastes of white consumers and began catering to them, even as women continued to produce items for use within their own community. Far from abandoning their own values and traditions, these women created new opportunities for themselves, expanding their creative repertoire as well as their incomes.

The production of this art took place against the backdrop of colonization and genocide. The market for Indian artifacts emerged just as their subsistence economy collapsed under the assaults of land cessions and white settlement. Women responded by accelerating their production for sale. Among the Dakota, this work was arrested by the 1862 war and subsequent incarceration, but it resumed when they were removed to new lands. The story of Dakota women's art is therefore intertwined with their efforts at survival, and it highlights the relationship between art and survival. Women's art opens the door to understanding the experiences of women facing multiple layers of assaults on their persons and way of life.

Dakota Women's Work seeks to sort out interrelated strands in the history of Dakota women and Native women more generally. Chapter 1 establishes the relationship between Dakota women's art and Dakota society in the early nineteenth century, when Dakota peoples still controlled their homelands. This ethnographic discussion centers on gender roles and subsistence and defines the cultural context of women's artistic production. Chapter 2 examines the impact of the declining fur trade and increasing white population on subsistence patterns, focusing on women's changing relationship to the fur trade and the emergence of artistic production for sale. As the fur trade declined and white farmers arrived in Minnesota, the Dakota faced an onslaught of people dedicated to "saving" them through a new religion. Missionary efforts and resistance to those efforts, culminating in the 1862 war, constitute the focus of Chapter 3. The full force of genocide is explored in Chapter 4, which details the incarceration and internment of the Dakota in the three and one-half years following the war. Chapters 5 and 6 explore the ways in which the Dakota rebuilt their families, communities, and culture within the new realities of reservation life. Several generations of Mary Faribault's family experienced these traumas and transformations, and they continued to create beautiful tools for everyday life and for special celebrations. Their stories lie at the heart of this book.

Historians trying to reconstruct the lives of Native peoples face special challenges that multiply when focusing on the lives of women. As a consequence, *Dakota Women's Work* draws on a wide range of resources and methodologies. It begins with the voices and actions of Dakota women as they exist in the stories they tell and have told and in the objects they have created; oral tradition, oral history, and material culture together can shape a historical narrative that starts with Dakota women. Yet this narrative must also draw on more conventional historical sources, including official documents, traders' records, and missionaries' correspondence and organizational papers. "Using problematic sources is always a matter of reading critically," write Rebecca Kugel and Lucy

Eldersveld Murphy regarding the use of European and European American men's documents to study the history of Native women. Such texts must be read with care to sift out the useful evidence from the values and judgments about the lives of the Indigenous people they discuss.[10]

In the end, however, the historical record remains thin in many places. Sometimes this makes drawing solid conclusions impossible. In these cases, it is reasonable to speculate carefully, weave together the evidence that does exist, and hypothesize about what additional sources might reveal. This account of the lives of Dakota women at times ventures into this uncertain terrain, but it always makes clear where the gaps in evidence appear.

One certainty that emerges from this study is the common goal of subsistence and survival that united Dakota women and men. Their culture assigned them different roles and tasks, but, in the end, they shared the goal of ensuring the material and spiritual well-being of their family, their village, and their nation. As a result, while *Dakota Women's Work* begins with the experiences of women, it necessarily encompasses the lives and experiences of the men with whom women shared responsibilities, burdens, and the work of survival.

CHAPTER 1

Work, Art, and Dakota Subsistence

I<small>N 1813, A D</small>AKOTA<small> WOMAN GAVE BIRTH</small> to a daughter who would later be known as Wicacaka, Like a Man, because of her physical strength and ability to perform much of men's work. Wicacaka was also a talented creator of quilled and beaded garments and equipment. As a young woman growing up in the Dakota homelands, she learned the skills necessary for this work. Upon reaching womanhood, she was expected to participate in creating special gifts for relatives as well as the necessities of everyday life. No doubt she fulfilled her role as "auntie"

Cradleboard collected by George Catlin from an unidentified Dakota woman during his visit to Fort Snelling and environs in 1835. National Museum of Natural History, Smithsonian Institution.

and worked on a cradleboard cover for a new baby in her extended family, or *tiospaye*. Like other women, she would have made numerous items for everyday use as well as specially ornamented moccasins, shirts, and cradleboard covers for honoring new babies.[1]

In 1835, when Wicacaka was twenty-three, one of these cradleboards attracted the attention of a visitor sojourning among the Dakota. It was a particularly ornate baby carrier, both solid and delicately ornamented. Its wooden backboard carried a wooden bow toward the top and two wide strips of deerskin completely covered with quillwork. From these decorated strips hung various feathers and shells as well as musical jingle cones for the baby's amusement and stimulation. The baby's feet rested on a piece of wood at the bottom of the board, where she would spend much of the next few months until she began to crawl. As the mother went about her work, the baby slept comfortably, lulled by the tinkling of the decorative cones. The beauty of this cradle embodies the care and nurturing showered on children, but it also tells many stories about the work of Wicacaka and other Dakota women. The cradleboard reflects the hours spent on creating and decorating implements of daily life in the midst of many other responsibilities and the hours of work that women spent together creating and beautifying these items for each other and for each other's families. The *Wakinyan*, Thunder Being, design that the woman created with black-dyed quills invoked the *wakan*—the sacred and mysterious—nature of women's artwork. Dakota peoples shared their world with Wakinyan and other spirit beings who inhabited skies, rivers, lakes, and forests and protected and sometimes threatened them as they went about their lives. Adorning their artwork with images of these *wakan* spirit beings highlighted the association of artistic creation with the *wakan*.[2]

This particular cradle tells another story as well. The visitor eyeing the carrier in 1835 as the woman carried out her chores was George A. Catlin, an aggressive nineteenth-century collector of Indian objects. Eventually, through a somewhat tortuous path, artifacts amassed by Catlin, including the cradle, found their way into what would become the Smithsonian Institution. Collectors like Catlin removed innumerable objects that women made for their families to use and celebrate new life and special accomplishments. Almost two hundred years later, these collections provide important sources for reconstructing the history of the women and the communities where they were created.[3]

By themselves, such objects can give only a few clues about their creators. Used in conjunction with accounts of everyday life and the rich oral tradition of the Dakota, however, cradleboards and other objects evoke two elements that remain marginal to most discussions of Dakota culture and history: the prominence of creative work in Dakota peoples' lives and the centrality of that work to women's roles and, ultimately, to the material and spiritual existence of their families. The various strands of women's obligations and responsibilities were interwoven with their artwork. Thus cradleboard covers, parfleche bags, awl cases, garments, and moccasins help explain Dakota culture and women's role within that culture. This complex and multilayered role has frequently been minimized or distorted in the accounts of Europeans and European Americans who documented Dakota patterns of subsistence.[4]

Women's roles and responsibilities centered largely on sheltering, feeding, clothing, and equipping members of the *tiospaye,* the extended family to which each Dakota person belonged, and members of the larger village band. Tasks related to shelter changed because the Dakota inhabited different sites during each season to make use of particular resources. During the winter, bands dispersed into tiospaye groupings of just a few tipis. Later, some families traveled to the band's "sugar bush," stands of maples where they gathered for a few weeks to harvest syrup, while other families went on spring hunts. Smaller village groups came together during the summer at larger, more permanent encampments. There, Mdewakantunwan women built lodges made of poles covered with elm-bark mats, while the Sisitunwan, Wahpetunwan, and Wahpekute lived in buffalo-hide tipis throughout the year. In the fall, smaller family groups once again went on their own hunts before settling in for another winter.[5]

Bands occupied permanent summer villages usually known by the name of their leader. Little Crow's band, for instance, inhabited Kaposia, meaning "Not Encumbered with Much Baggage," on the west bank of

the Mississippi, eight miles downstream from the mouth of the Minnesota River. Little Rapids, forty-five miles upriver from the Mississippi
on the Minnesota, was the site of the village of Mazomani, Walking Iron.
The town of Winona, Minnesota, was founded in 1851 on the summer
village site of the Dakota leaders of Wabasha's lineage.[6]

Seasonal migrations and hunting expeditions were particularly significant for women because dwellings and everything they contained were
considered to be women's possessions, which they were responsible for
arranging, maintaining, and then transporting. Seasonal moves were, in
effect, women's work. Once women set up their family's tipi or bark
lodge, they turned to the work of acquiring and preparing food. They
harvested wild foods, tended small fields, and, as participants in hunting expeditions, set up tipis, prepared meals, and began preparing skin,
organs, flesh, bones, sinew, horns, and hoofs for eventual use.[7]

While producing beautiful garments or pouches was its own responsibility for women, the numerous associated steps involved in gathering and preparing materials were also part of gathering and preparing
food and other necessities. Hunting tasks, for instance, provided the
skins and some of the bone tools that women used to produce functional
and ceremonial items.

The annual cycle of migration and food-gathering that began in early
spring at the sugar bush required women to collect sap, boil and strain
it, and shape the sap into loaves. After the sugar set, the loaves were
transferred to covered baskets while the molds, made of birch bark
bent, stitched into shape, and sometimes decorated, were disassembled,
flattened, and buried in the earth to be used again the following year.
A few women skipped sugar-making in order to accompany men on
the muskrat hunt. When the men speared the animals in rivers as the
ice was breaking up, women butchered the "rats," cooked the meat, and
processed the pelts.[8]

Once sugar-making and muskrat-hunting were complete, the Dakota
moved to their summer encampment. Many planted small gardens,
although horticulture remained secondary to gathering wild plants and
hunting and not all bands planted gardens. Corn was the largest crop,

interspersed with squash and beans. Some corn was eaten green, while ripe corn was dried and buried in the ground in bark containers for retrieval after the last deer hunt in January.[9]

Growing corn required careful preparation of the soil and labor-intensive preparation of the seeds. Marie McLaughlin, the daughter of a mixed-blood mother and a white father who grew up in the Dakota community of Wabasha in the 1840s and 1850s, recalled that "after the best seed has been selected, the planter measures the corn, lays down a layer of hay, then a layer of corn. Over this corn they sprinkle warm water and cover it with another layer of hay, then bind hay about the bundle and hang it up in a spot where the warm rays of the sun can strike it."[10]

Once the corn was ready to plant, women and girls prepared small mounds in their fields and carefully set four kernels in each one, offering prayers for their growth. This painstaking process, which had spiritual as well as material dimensions, was only possible for a small crop. Corn constituted a relatively small share of the Dakota's nonmeat diet, most of which came from wild plants.[11]

The cultivation of corn was intertwined with these wild harvests. When preparing the ground for corn, women looked for a growth of wild artichokes that would indicate rich and moist soil. Once the seeds began to germinate, the women looked for ripe strawberries to tell them it was time to plant. The painstaking preparation that Dakota women undertook in cultivating corn ensured that their crops could ripen largely unattended while the women turned their attention to the now-ripe strawberries and other plants that matured in the summer months.[12]

The Dakota homelands along the Mississippi and Minnesota rivers offered a bounty of edible foods, a fact that frequently drew the attention of white visitors and settlers. Writing about the area in which he had established his mission, Stephen Return Riggs extolled the riches of the landscape: "Crab apples grow in the neighborhood of Traverse des Sioux [where Riggs established a mission], back some distance from the river, and probably in other parts also. Cranberries are gathered in quantities on the Lower Saint Peters [Minnesota River] . . . Strawberries are abundant in some parts. Plums, choke cherries, gooseberries, raspberries, black currants, black haws and grapes are found, more or less, all over the country."[13]

Working in small groups, women gathered these fruits and then dried much of their harvest. Some of the dried fruits and berries would be worked with tallow to produce *wasna,* rich pemmican that could be easily transported and provided dense nutrition over the winter. Most would be added to soups with dried or fresh meat, and some, like grapes, would be used to make dyes for decorative work.[14]

The Minnesota River valley and surrounding streams and lakes also provided the Dakota with nutritious edible tubers, among them *psinca,* about an inch in diameter, and *psincinca* (child of *psin,* wild rice), the size of a hen's egg, which grows in shallow lakes and "is raised from its muddy bed by females, who use their feet for this purpose." *Mdo,* often referred to as Indian potato, grows on dry land, with a vine that coils around nearby plants. According to Riggs, who, with his wife Mary, depended on the Dakota for survival in their first years in Minnesota, it tasted somewhat like the sweet potato. These and other roots, like the *tipsinna,* or wild turnip, were also dried and stored for later use as well as consumed fresh. While mdo and tipsinna provided no materials for women's artwork, they were preserved in a way that, like women's art, had aesthetic as well as functional value. The stems of the bulb to be eaten were braided and hung in a decorative way, allowing the food to dry while ornamenting the dwelling.[15]

Toward the end of the summer, Dakota women and men worked together to harvest *psin,* the grass that grew abundantly in the lakes and rivers of Minnesota and Wisconsin. It provided a grain that became known as wild rice. A few weeks before the rice ripened, family members paddled canoes though the plants and tied them in bunches to protect the grain from wind and birds. When the rice was fully ripe, two women or a woman and a man returned, and while one paddled, the other bent the seed heads into the canoe and beat them so that the seed fell inside. The harvested grain was then dried, sifted, and parched. For storage, women dug holes in the ground and lined them with deerskin before pouring in the rice.[16]

A contemporary interpretation of tipsinna braid by Ben McGuire, Yankton Nakota.

Whether accomplishing the seasonal tasks of gathering, preparing, and storing foods or the daily tasks of preparing meals, caring for young children, and tending the family's shelter, Dakota women and their *tiospaye* were surrounded by the fruits of women's productive and creative work—clothing, baby carriers, and much more. Because their livelihood took them away from their dwellings to gather and prepare foods, the Dakota needed to be able to carry tools and equipment. Because both women and men periodically left their communities for spiritual reasons—men for their *hambdeciya,* vision quest, and women for their menses—they needed to be able to transport their own personal necessities. As a result, Dakota women produced not only large parfleche bags but also knife sheaths, tool cases, medicine pouches, and pouches for flints, tobacco, and a pipe. All were designed with straps and strap slits to enable convenient wearing on the body. Each carrier also became a canvas for a woman to practice her art.

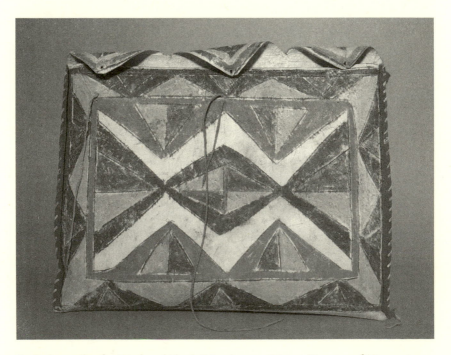

Parfleche made of painted rawhide. Artist unknown; Science Museum of Minnesota.

Food, tools, and other belongings were transported and stored in raw-hide containers called *parfleches,* a term given by French fur traders to these bags, which were strong enough to turn away (*par*) arrows (*fleches*). Buffalo skin was scraped, cleaned, and dried but otherwise untanned. It was then cut into a rectangle, which would be folded over the items to be packed and tied with leather strips or sewn up to make boxlike or flat containers. Parfleches were easily carried on the *travois,* the two poles used to carry the tipi, equipment, and family members who were too old, infirm, or young to undertake the journey on foot. They also kept belongings organized in the intimate confines of the tipi. Each family member had his or her own space, and "everyone kept his personal things in skin containers, which were always ornamented, sometimes handsomely," wrote Ella Deloria, a Dakota ethnologist who conducted research among the Dakota between the 1920s and 1940s.[17]

The parfleches' large flat surfaces lent themselves to decoration, although the thickness and roughness of the rawhide made delicate quill-work and other ornamentation difficult. Women painted the containers in colorful, often geometric designs suited to the full and to the empty, flattened parfleche. According to Dakota artist Ramona Kitto Stately, these linear, symmetrical designs represented the organization of Dakota families and the order necessary for families and communities to survive. Many parfleches, like other objects created by women, were designed with red borders representing women's powers, both physical and spiritual. Ubiquitous in Dakota life, these containers embodied tribal values and the connections between the material and spiritual realms.[18]

The work required to create this functional art was extensive. The beauty of the cradleboard that Catlin took when he left the Dakota gives few clues to the magnitude of the work involved in producing it and even less to the work necessary before women decorated the cradleboard covers and made the ornaments that completed the carrier. These labors made up a significant portion of women's work, which was performed while they did other tasks, for women's creative work pervaded their lives and the lives of those around them. No tasks or activities connected with the creation of functional pieces were performed in isolation from many other tasks that women performed in their daily round of activity.

Some of these tasks demanded great physical effort. After the hide was taken from the animal and brought back to the village, for instance, women removed any remaining flesh and hair. They then lashed the skin to tipi poles in order to dry it by the fire. Dressing the hide required boiling in a solution of water and deer brains and then stretching it and scraping it before a fire as it dried. The process of boiling, scraping, and drying, which required maintaining a constant fire and bringing adequate supplies of water, was repeated until the skin obtained the desired texture. The final step in the process required hanging the skin in a bag over a fire to give it more color.[19]

Seth Eastman's painting *The Tanner* vividly portrays the effort to prepare a hide. Eastman, a captain in the U.S. Army posted at Fort Snelling in the 1830s, took a Dakota wife, Wakaninajinwin, Stands Sacred Woman (Mary Eastman Faribault's grandmother) and spent much of his time in her family's village as well as in other Dakota villages. He returned to Fort Snelling in 1841 with his white wife, Mary Eastman, and remained there until 1848, spending much of his time studying, drawing, and painting. His portrayal of the Dakota woman tanning, executed in 1848, demonstrates the physically demanding nature of the work. The tanner appears both weary and worried, as she perhaps thinks about other tasks awaiting her. At the same time, her moccasins and leggings and the cradleboard in which her baby sleeps remind the viewer of the fruits of her exertions.[20]

When Wicacaka set out to create a special gift for an elder, perhaps a pouch decorated with quilled designs, she needed to prepare the hide and construct the pouch itself and also acquire the quills. For this, she or a man in the family hunted the porcupine or caught live ones and removed some quills from each, but this was only the beginning of her work. In a memoir about growing up on South Dakota's Pine Ridge reservation, Delphine Red Shirt, a Lakota beadwork artist born in 1957, muses about how she would have used quills had she lived one hundred years earlier: "I would have sorted the quills by size, knowing that the

The Tanner, oil on canvas, painted by Seth Eastman, 1848. Rockwell Museum of Western Art. In the background stands a bark lodge, the Mdewakantunwan summer dwelling.

largest and coarsest quills come from the back and tail of the porcupine; these I would save and use for larger pieces I wanted to decorate, such as a cradleboard for my daughter. The slender and delicate quills come from the neck of the porcupine, and the finest quills from the belly of the animal . . . I would have taken the quills and worked them carefully between my teeth, thereby flattening them, and dyed them in order to use them the way I use beads today."[21]

Wicacaka and other women in the period Red Shirt imagines followed those same steps, but before dyeing the quills, they would have had to prepare the dyes themselves. This required special processes, some of which were already being performed for other purposes. Women gathered wild sunflowers and yellow coneflowers to make yellow dyes, and they made black dyes from wild grapes, hickory nuts, and walnuts, which women also harvested for food. Consequently, when sorting through their harvest, women set aside those items to be used for coloring quills and painting parfleches and those to be dried and processed for food.[22]

Food preparing was also woven into relations with whites. Fur traders active among the Dakota stocked equipment that men used in hunting and trapping and equipment that women used in preparing and cooking foods such as kettles, ladles, and knives. Traders also brought their Native customers stock supplies such as ribbon, beads, and vermilion, a red dye used both in decorating hides and in personal ornamentation. When men traded furs for goods, they acquired what they needed to fulfill their own roles in their families, but they also exchanged for things the women in their household needed, including goods for ornamenting the equipment of daily life. When women began making these purchases themselves in the 1840s, they also would acquire things men needed to fulfill their obligations.[23]

Among the items purchased from traders were tools for making and decorating articles of everyday life, including knives and needles. Before this merchandise was available through trade, women had made these tools, and even after they could acquire metal components, women continued to make some of their own equipment, for instance, handles out of wood or bone or antler for iron awls. Used to pierce holes in hide pieces before stitching them together with deer or buffalo sinew and decorating them with quills or beads, the awl and its handle were carried in a special handmade case.[24]

Such an awl handle appeared among the objects excavated in 1980 in what had been the garbage dump in the village of a Wahpetunwan leader at Little Rapids in the early nineteenth century. As described by archaeologist Janet Spector, it was "a small antler awl handle, with a series of dots and lines." Despite its age and condition, the awl handle still showed traces of red pigment coloring the dots. The carvings most likely represented the owner's accomplishments, but the coloring suggests that the markings on the handle were not simply of functional value. They also had aesthetic value. Before creating and decorating functional and ceremonial items, Dakota women made and beautified the necessary tools. In the novel *Waterlily,* which Ella Deloria wrote using ethnographic evidence she had gathered in the 1930s and 1940s, a young Dakota woman named Leaping Fawn takes on the responsibility

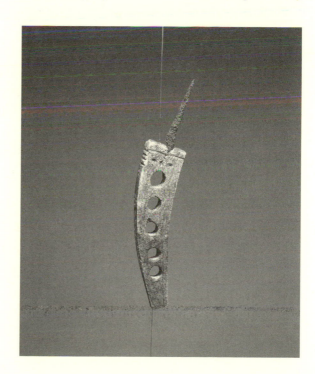

Awl handle, 1830s, excavated at the Wahpetunwan Dakota village at Little Rapids led by Mazomani. Artist unknown; Minnesota Historical Society.

of honoring her recently deceased grandmother by preparing items for a giveaway in her memory. With "her two mothers, her aunt Blue Bird, and the other women relatives, she worked in all her spare time, turning out many pieces of fancywork for the redistribution feast to come." While this work and other preparations were taking place, however, "time did not stand still in the *tiospaye;* the daily life did not differ from the normal." When Leaping Fawn made pouches, moccasins, and shirts to decorate for the giving away at the feast, she also made some that would remain unadorned and be put to immediate use.[25]

Ella Deloria's writing about Dakota women is highly detailed and evocative because of both her training and her personal identity. As an ethnologist, she worked with Franz Boas, Ruth Benedict, and Margaret Mead, who set the discipline's standards for research and writing. As a Dakota woman, she sought to preserve the culture in which she had grown up in the face of increasing assaults and challenges. Consequently, Deloria could write both authoritatively and empathetically about such topics as menstruation, courtship, marriage, and other life cycle events as well as everyday life.

While Deloria does not explicitly focus on women's "fancywork," this topic arises frequently throughout her writing. In the chapter "Wedded Life" in her posthumously published monograph *The Dakota Way of Life,* Deloria describes the newly married couple's responsibilities vis-à-vis relatives and the new husband's activities, which frequently took him away from his bride. In these times, "she busied herself with the socially important gifts that a bride made with her own hands for her husband's parents; handsome moccasins for both and sometimes, in addition, an elaborate tobacco pouch that her father-in-law would be sure to carry pridefully." In the chapter "The Home," Deloria describes the "back yard" area of the circle of tipis that was "the real area of activity . . . especially for the women." This was where they worked hides, preserved meat and fruits, and prepared food together for feasts. "Occasionally," writes Deloria, the women "could sit in a group in the back yard to chat and do fancy work with a modicum of privacy." Not only was the production of "fancy work" interspersed among other responsibilities; the creation of highly ornamented objects intended for special ceremonial uses was interspersed with the production of items for everyday use.[26]

Moreover, just as women's creative work was a thread that wound through all women's work, so a thread of spirituality wound throughout women's creative work. Significantly, when Deloria describes Leaping Fawn's "fancy work," she tells her readers that the young woman is preparing gifts in honor of her deceased grandmother. Readers uninformed about Dakota rites and spiritual beliefs thus learn that the work of creating special objects belongs as much to spiritual practice as to physical action. Indeed, the intermediary between the physical act of the giveaway and the spiritual practice of honoring the departed was women's creative work.

For the Dakota, the tiospaye constituted an essential element of physical survival because members relied upon one another during hunts, at the sugar bush, in cultivating fields, in raising children, and in seeing each other through long, hard winters when food supplies ran low. Indeed, the tiospaye held far more significance among the Dakota than one's immediate family of husband, wife, and children, which is evident in the fluidity of such arrangements. Women could freely choose to leave mates they found unsuitable, and men frequently took multiple wives. In addition, a woman could remain with her parents instead of marrying if the parents could provide for her. Conversely, raising children was a collective responsibility within the tiospaye and even the village, rather than the exclusive responsibility of parents.[27]

The responsibility for members of the tiospaye was expressed in the Dakota's spiritual practice as well as in practical matters. Dakota women and men honored members of their extended family, those who had died as well as the living, and when individuals gave gifts for their relatives, they affirmed the sacredness of those relationships. The tiospaye, a unit of physical survival, was also a community of spirits. Consequently, when a woman made a tobacco pouch to honor a member of her tiospaye, she was performing a spiritual act as well as creating a tangible object.

Two-eared pouch made of buckskin, decorated with quills, metal jingle cones, and mallard skin, probably Dakota, donated by a Miss Purinton to the Peabody Essex Museum in 1835. Artist unknown.

The spiritual and sacred nature of women's artistic work comes across most vividly in the items that women made for newborn babies, who, like other children, were considered *wakanyeza,* sacred beings. In making cradleboard covers for babies, women were performing work to honor the *wakan* in that young being. They also made items that would be a part of this young being's spiritual life as an adult. When the remainder of an infant's umbilical cord, the *cekpa,* dried and fell off, it was wrapped in soft fibers which were encased in a beautifully decorated piece of hide cut in the shape of a turtle. These turtles—representing longevity for the child—became his or her toys, along with others made of bone, wood, or stuffed deerskin. When the child reached puberty and began participating in community ceremonies, the cekpa pouch was no longer a toy but part of Dakota community observances: the turtle containing the cekpa was worn as an element of the young person's ceremonial outfit.[28]

Cekpa pouch made of hide decorated with quills. From the collection of the Swiss count Albert-Alexandre de Pourtalès, who traveled across the United States in 1835 and 1836. The objects were found in the Pourtalès family castle in the Bern Canton and donated to the Bern Historical Museum. Artist unknown.

Women's artwork partook of the spiritual in other ways as well. Many items made by Dakota women, like the cradle that Catlin took away and a two-eared pouch that is in the collections of the Peabody Essex Museum, were decorated with images of the *Wakinyan,* the Thunder Beings who controlled the skies and thunder. The Wakinyan governed the weather, the clouds, and the rain. They were at times fearsome and threatening, but they were ultimately forces of benevolence (see photo page 32). The floral patterns that women created with dyed quills and beads represented Dakota medicines, plants that were themselves wakan because of their powers to heal physical, emotional, or spiritual afflictions. Through these designs, women wove into their creations elements of the wakan that were all around them, associating the objects with the sacred dimension of life.[29]

The wakan nature of these objects also came from the belief that the women creating them were inspired by a spirit being: the Double Woman, or the Two-Women. In the 1940s, Ella Deloria visited the reservation at Santee, Nebraska, for her research on the Eastern Dakota. By that time, the Dakota who could remember life in Minnesota before exile had passed away. The elders she knew, however, had been raised by parents and grandparents who had come to adulthood in the Dakota's ancestral homelands and followed the traditions and teachings of generations before them. Therefore, when they talked to Deloria about their spiritual practices and beliefs, they were relating some of their Minnesota ancestors' traditions. One elder told her that "the Two-Women are the artists of the Earth. It is they who give or withhold artistic skill to Santee women . . . Sometimes when a Santee woman is very gifted with her hands, she will say as in a joke, 'I have dreamed of the Two-Women, doubtless!'" Double Woman, *Winyan Numpapi,* appears in numerous Dakota stories as a spirit being who holds both promise and threat. The promise lies in women's creative capacity, and this figure is widely associated with women's artistic talents. Because the Double Woman belongs to the realm of spirits and appears to individuals in dreams, the talents that she bestows belong to the realm of the wakan. The Two-Women were a distinct wakan power in Dakota women's lives and especially in the lives of women who excelled in quillwork and other arts.[30]

The term *wakan*, which is conventionally translated as "sacred," holds many meanings for the Dakota, reflecting both its etymology and its use to describe many different beings and phenomena. George Sword, a Lakota elder, explained in the late nineteenth century that *wakan* derived from the word *kan*, meaning "anything that is old or that has existed for a long time." He also noted that *kan* "may mean a strange or wonderful thing or that which cannot be comprehended." Little Wound, another Lakota elder, added to this definition the notion of power. Food is wakan, he explained, "because it makes life," and medicine is wakan because "it keeps life in the body." Quillwork and other "fancy work" partook of all these attributes of wakan: it was an ancient knowledge handed down from one generation of women to another; the talent to do this work came from a mysterious being who appeared in a dream; and it possessed the power to make beautiful the tools and equipment of everyday life.[31]

Some Dakota believe that the work itself is wakan. For Ramona Kitto Stately, a gifted beadworker and teacher who has studied Native women's arts and spirituality, the act of decorating moccasins is itself sacred. Creating and beautifying an object in order to honor the spirit of a relative requires special attention and focus that, for her, make the work a sacred spiritual practice. Ella Deloria did not pay particular attention to the spiritual experience of the women she wrote about, nor did the white men who gathered the testimony of George Sword and Little Wound in the late nineteenth century inquire about the spiritual practices and beliefs of women in their communities. Still, existing evidence about the Dakota people's spiritual lives suggests that for women in Minnesota in the first half of the nineteenth century, quillwork and other forms of "fancy work" were indeed sacred acts.

Young women were expected to begin this work at a spiritually powerful moment in their lives: the time of their first menses. Starting when they were six or seven years old, girls learned from their mothers and other women, as boys did from their fathers and other men, the roles they would fulfill as adults in their communities. Girls sat with their mothers and other women, imitating them to learn the skills they would need as adults, including the skills of various forms of creative work. In the chapter "Adolescence" in *The Dakota Way of Life*, Deloria discusses

Knife sheath made of rawhide decorated with quillwork, tin cones, and red cloth. The knife is made of bone and steel, with etching on the side of the handle. Artist unknown; Brooklyn Museum of Art.

Detail of knife sheath.

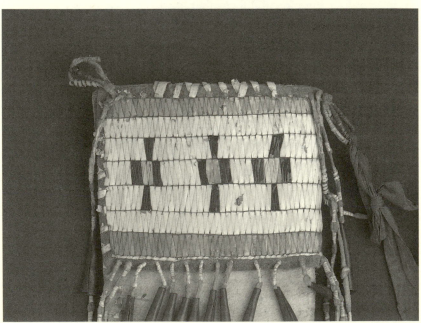

what Dakota boys learned from their fathers about male adulthood. When she turns to adolescent girls, she begins with observances and practices related to *catamenia,* the onset of menses. These revolved around the seclusion of the young woman in a tipi erected for this purpose somewhat apart from the others in the village. There, older women kept her company and taught her what she would need to know as a woman. During this time, the young woman "was instructed to keep busy at fancy work; porcupine quillwork, traditionally, and bead work in more recent times." From that point on, young women were expected to work along-side adult women, fulfilling their responsibilities as Dakota women. Thus, the adolescent Leaping Fawn in *Waterlily* already understood her familial and communal obligations, and working on her fancy work among the women of her community furthered her education as a woman.[32]

The Dakota also taught the norms and values of their people through the stories that elders told in the long winter nights. "Stone Boy," for instance, tells of a pebble that turned into a powerful hunter and over-came numerous challenges and threats from humans, animals, and spirit beings. Listening to these stories, young boys and men learned lessons they would need in order to fulfill their roles as adult men, growing from something as small and unremarkable as a stone into important protectors and guarantors of their family's well-being.[33]

Other stories provided girls and young women with lessons on their roles. In the story "Cantektewin—The Ill-Fated Woman," a young woman leaves her family and encounters one set of dangers after another. Each time, she survives and escapes, and in the end she is able to return home, where she takes "care of and comforts her father and mother all the days of their lives." The young woman alone is resourceful and resilient, but in the end, her highest responsibility is to her parents. Not only does this story reinforce the importance of family ties and duty toward elders; it offered a model of a woman remaining with her parents rather than mar-rying and bearing children.[34]

This story and others also suggest that Dakota cultural roles were far from rigid. A society that moved frequently, relied on wild foods, and engaged in warfare in a climate of widely varying conditions could not afford to be rigid in the social formations or responsibilities that it assigned to its members. In "Wechah the Provider," all the men in Wasula's community are killed in a raid by the Ojibwe. Young Wasula is skilled in her gender's tasks, but she proves herself a talented hunter as well. With the help of Wechah, her pet raccoon, she tracks and shoots a doe and expertly prepares her to drag back to the village. Yet she is not the only woman out hunting. Other women might not be as successful as she, but they too bring back meat for their families.[35]

Conversely, other stories taught about men surviving quite well on their own. In "Tasinta Yukikipi," a young woman comes to live as a sister with five young men on their own in the forest. The narrator notes that "she was very skillful in needle and quill work. She embroidered quivers, moccasins, knife sheaths, and carrying straps for them, so they greatly rejoiced." The young men, who had been living together on their own before the young woman's mysterious arrival, presumably performed tasks habitually assigned to women such as making clothing and preparing meals, so they do not really need her for their survival. What she brings to their lives, however, is the delicate decoration for their footgear and hunting equipment.[36]

While Dakota women and men thus had clearly defined tasks, responsibilities, and obligations, they were each flexible enough to perform the others' tasks when survival demanded it. Yet women brought special gifts and talents that beautified and embellished the lives of all Dakota. Because ornately quilled and beaded garments were not worn every day, their appearance during community celebrations enhanced those gatherings. The beading and quillwork itself, however, enhanced daily life for women creating it.

In addition to providing much of the basic equipment of everyday life, Dakota women had the additional responsibility of bringing art and beauty to what they created. They also made tangible the presence of the wakan in the daily lives of their nation. As the wakan permeated the environment in which they lived, the functional art made by women brought the wakan into the tools and equipment of everyday life.

CHAPTER 2

The Fur Trade
and the Treaty of 1837

O N FEBRUARY II, 1845, CANKUDUTAWIN, Red Road Woman,
left the trading post at Mendota with a large tin kettle, a scarlet
blanket, and some lace, as well as gun powder, hunting equipment, and other supplies. Between that time and November 6, 1846, she
came back seven more times, acquiring, among other things, a calico shirt,
another blanket, needles, thread, and vermilion. She also bought traps,
knives, flints, and more powder. Twice she stopped in just to make a payment on her purchases, and on three visits she made payments as well
as purchases. On September 25, 1845, she made a payment of thirty-one
dollars "by Cash," and the next year, on January 29, 1846, she paid "by
11 does [deer] $5.50, 3 bucks $3.00, 20 rats $2.00, 3 otters $15.00."[1]

Cankudutawin was related by marriage to Henry H. Sibley, the American Fur Company's agent in charge of trade with the Dakota. Her cousin
Tasinasawin, Red Blanket Woman, the daughter of Bad Hail, a Mdewakantunwan Dakota leader, had married Sibley "in the style of the country," as they said at the time, meaning that the relationship was without
either civil or church sanction. Cankudutawin's presence at the post,
however, cannot be explained by the prominence of her relations, since
she was just one of approximately two dozen women who, since the late
1830s, had begun visiting the trading posts to make purchases. These
new customers at the post heralded many changes taking place among
the Dakota in the second quarter of the nineteenth century.[2]

Throughout much of the fur trade, Dakota women acquired the trade goods they needed for artwork and other work through the men in their family. Men brought to the posts skins and pelts prepared in collaboration with their wives and exchanged them for the trader's goods: kettles, yard goods, ready-made clothing, and other items that women used in their work, as well as traps, ammunition, weapons, and tools that the men used in theirs. By the mid-nineteenth century, however, the division of labor that gave men the role of bartering with white traders began to change. Transformations in gender patterns appear in fur trade records starting in the 1840s, revealing that women did business at trading posts with greater regularity and frequency.[3]

In the same period, women selling moccasins for cash also become more visible. Not only did they take advantage of commercial opportunities offered by whites entering their lands, but they also traveled to growing military installations and urban centers to do so. A brief note in the January 1851 issue of *The Dakota Friend,* a monthly newspaper published by missionaries, observed, "There are a few lodges of women spending the winter at Mendota. These make moccasins which they will sell in St. Paul and thus supply themselves with the various articles necessary for their comfort." The establishment of the Minnesota Territory in 1848 had accelerated the growth of St. Paul, and each year it welcomed new arrivals, all of whom were eager to explore this exciting "frontier." While some of the travelers would sink roots in the region, many were just passing through. Either way, these men and women would be looking for mementos of their initial experience in Minnesota, and the growing fashion of collecting moccasins and other Indian-made items meant white travelers were good customers for footwear and other goods Dakota women brought to sell. Some of the travelers and collectors frequently purchased Indian-made clothing and moccasins to wear when dressing "as Indians," a phenomenon that dates to the late seventeenth century, but whites living among the Dakota also acquired moccasins as working footwear.[4]

What links these two developments—women selling moccasins and women going to trading posts—is the appearance of money. The demand for furs and the subsequent decline of fur-bearing animals, as well as increasing white settlement, had brought dramatic changes, especially for the Mdewakantunwan who lived on the easternmost Dakota lands. The arrival of cash, however, can be attributed most immediately to the treaty that they signed with the United States in 1837. The treaty ceded five million acres east of the Mississippi River to the United States and gave Dakota people in return significant annuity payments from the government. This put cash into Dakota men and women's hands for the first time, an event that would have a transformative impact on subsistence patterns and gender roles.

In the face of the accelerating colonization of southern Minnesota lands in the mid-nineteenth century, Dakota people experienced significant transformation in gender dynamics. The payment of cash annuities at the same time villages lost access to the lands that had supported them for generations meant that families and communities needed to develop new strategies for survival. The creative work of women would be a part of these strategies, as it had been in earlier times, but under the new economic and political realities, the nature of this work would also be transformed.

The changes coming to Minnesota in the second quarter of the nineteenth century have their roots in the fur trade and in U.S. relations with Britain. Since the arrival of the first French traders in the 1660s, the Dakota had incorporated traders into their social and economic networks and foreign goods into their cycles of subsistence. The first century and a half of the fur trade created kinship ties between Europeans and Dakota families with the expectation among Dakota that they would be equal partners in transactions with the French, French Canadians, British, and Americans who entered their lands. With the U.S. victory over the British at the close of the War of 1812, however, relations between Dakota families and white traders became less familial and more exclusively commercial.

As the United States gained control of the Upper Mississippi and Great Lakes region of North America, the government sent out exploratory expeditions and military missions that resulted in the signing of several treaties. The first of these treaties, in 1805, acquired from the Dakota nine square miles at the confluence of the Mississippi and St. Peter's (later renamed Minnesota) rivers "for the purpose of the establishment of military posts." When Fort Snelling was completed on that site in the 1820s, it became the garrison of military units charged with maintaining a U.S.–dominated peace in the Upper Mississippi valley. The fort also became headquarters of a U.S. Indian agent charged with maintaining peaceful relations with and among the Native peoples in the region.[5]

The limited presence of civilian and military white populations in the Upper Mississippi River valley until the establishment of Fort Snelling and the first major Dakota land cession in 1837 allowed the Dakota to continue their customary cycles of subsistence with relatively little disruption. The abundance of fur-bearing animals made it possible for them to process some furs for exchange while keeping what they needed for their own use. Access to other resources in their homelands allowed the Dakota to continue subsisting from their seasonal migrations. The rifles, traps, scissors, awls, ribbon, fabric, and beads they received in exchange for furs added to the resources at their disposal without radically transforming Dakota political or cultural systems.

Since entering the trade, the Dakota had incorporated hunting and trapping for trade within their own seasonal cycle of subsistence. Between October and January, hunting parties set out in search of deer, which became increasingly valuable for their meat and skins when the buffalo disappeared from the Mississippi River valley. Deerskins were used by women to make garments, pouches, and other functional items, but they were also traded along with the pelts of bear and raccoon brought back by hunters. Spring hunts yielded ducks and geese that supplemented depleted food supplies and added feathers and skin to women's art materials, but hunters also caught muskrats, or "rats," whose furs were most valuable for trade at that time of year. Large hunting parties traditionally set out on buffalo hunts in both summer and winter, but by the early nineteenth century the Mdewakantunwan and the Wahpekute living on the eastern edges of Dakota lands hunted buffalo only in summer. By the 1830s, only the Sisitunwan and Wahpetunwan, who lived closer to the remaining buffalo herds in the Dakota Territory and owned more horses, regularly engaged in buffalo hunts.[6]

Westward expeditions were undertaken not only for the purpose of hunting, however. Each year, Sisitunwan Dakota brought goods supplied by traders to the trade fair on the James River. They exchanged the supplies with Titunwan Dakota for buffalo hides and other goods that they then traded with more easterly Dakota in Minnesota. Trade with whites became incorporated into existing networks with other Native groups that extended from the Mississippi to the Missouri River.[7]

The white fur trader's year, to a large extent, mirrored that of the Dakota. It ran from June through May, beginning with the signing of contracts between the fur company and its agents, the men who exchanged goods for furs with the Dakota. The agents, sometimes referred to as *engages* even after French traders departed, purchased trade goods usually on credit from the fur company in Montreal, Mackinac, or, later, Prairie du Chien. The agents then transported the goods and their own supplies for the long winter to their posts among the Dakota. There the agents distributed hunting equipment such as rifles, ammunition, and traps that the Dakota needed in order to supply furs, as well as the manufactured goods that drew them into the trade: tools, cooking equipment, clothing, fabric, ribbon, beads, jewelry, tobacco, and other goods that rapidly became necessities. In the late spring of the following year, when the Dakota brought in their furs to pay off their debts, the trader shipped the pelts to the fur company to settle his own debts. The fur company then shipped the furs for sale in New York or London.[8]

The fur trade, then, operated entirely on credit. Fur traders bought trade goods on credit from merchants or from large fur trade companies. The Dakota acquired those goods on credit as well. Ultimately, the system depended upon the Dakota's ability and willingness to provide furs to pay for goods. As anthropologist Mary Whelan has demonstrated, the Dakota were able to maintain control of the fur trade for a time by limiting the amount of furs that they brought to the trader. Faced with a

strong demand for furs, a business built exclusively on furs, and the relatively autonomous population of Dakota producers, traders continued
to provide goods in the hopes that they would receive enough furs to
pay off their own debts by the next spring. Declining fur populations,
increasing white populations, and the resulting new economic opportunities for whites involved in the fur trade beginning in the 1820s and
1830s eroded the control the Dakota had been able to maintain over the
trade since its inception.[9]

Throughout the history of the fur trade, Dakota women, like other
Native women, had been essential actors in this economy. They played
many different roles, although the one that has received the most historical attention is their marriage to white traders. As scholars have demonstrated in their studies of the trade in the United States and Canada,
Native women who married traders played a pivotal role in cementing
economic relations between Native men and white traders. For white
men, these marriages solidified trade relations and offered entry into
extended family networks that assured a steady flow of furs. For Native
men, family marriages with fur traders established ties that they believed
maintained trusting and peaceful relations and, consequently, access to
valuable trade goods. Native women became economic, political, and cultural brokers between different cultures, facilitating for both sides relatively advantageous exchanges.[10]

Cankudutawin's cousin Tasinasawin was one of these women; she
was the daughter of Wasusica, Bad Hail, who would eventually act as a
spokesman for the Dakota in negotiations with the United States. In
the winter of 1840–41, Wasusica and his family left the Mississippi River
valley to join a large hunting expedition to the Cedar River, about sixty
miles to the west. Joining the Dakota on this expedition was Henry
Sibley. In August 1841, Tasinasawin bore a daughter fathered by Sibley.
The young woman remained in her family's village, but Sibley took
sufficient interest in the child to ensure that she was baptized. When
Tasinasawin died just a few years later, Sibley placed his daughter,
Helen, with a white farmer's family and continued to support her and
remain in contact. In those same years, he used this family connection

when negotiating with Wasusica and other Dakota leaders, and so, it would seem, did Wasusica.[11]

Tasinasawin's life was cut short by illness, but it is unlikely that she would have left any record of her own views on her relationship with Sibley had she lived longer. In fact, none of the Dakota women who married white traders appear to have left any traces of their understanding or preferences regarding such marriages. We can, therefore, only speculate about their motives and experiences. At the same time, however, the complementary nature of men's and women's roles in the *tiospaye* and the authority of women over dwellings and their contents suggest that these women would also have exercised some decision-making power in their marriages.[12]

Nevertheless, kinship ties and relations of mutual obligation were so central to the communities in which women lived that they may have agreed to marrying white traders in deference to the needs of family and village. These women could also have acceded to the wishes of male relatives with the expectation that their marriage would incur reciprocal obligations toward them. Moreover, the abundance of goods that Dakota men purchased from traders for women's purposes might have persuaded women to marry in order to ensure that kettles, ribbon, and cloth would be available. One historian writing about marriages in Canada speculates that Native women might have found life in the fur trade post less physically demanding and therefore preferable to life in their own community.[13]

Regardless of expectations or motivations, it is clear that a number of the Dakota women who married white traders ended up as wives of wealthy and influential men. Susan Frenier was the granddaughter of Red Wing, a prominent Mdewakantunwan leader, and the stepdaughter of Akipa, Arrow, a Sisitunwan man. Family ties with two different groups of Dakota no doubt contributed to her husband Joseph R. Brown's success as a fur trader, which, in turn, led him to an appointment as Indian agent and later into land speculation and politics, where he became a member of the territorial legislature and the Minnesota constitutional convention in 1857. Angelique Wapa married Joseph Rocque, one of the founders of the Mississippi River town of Wabasha, the anglicized name of her brother, Wapahasa, Red Hat. Madeline Robinson, the daughter of the leader Little Crow, married Angelique's son Augustin Rocque, founder of Wisconsin's Buffalo County, across the river from Wabasha. Mahpiyahotawin, Grey Cloud Woman, married Hazen Mooers, whose farm eventually became Grey Cloud Island Township.[14]

Women born in Dakota communities who married white traders had grown up seeing women as partners with men in fur trade–related activities and many other facets of life. When they married, they undoubtedly brought with them this conception of their role as women and wives. Their husbands' status and power can therefore be attributed not only to their Dakota wives' family relations but also to their wives' personal contributions. Women taught their husbands the Dakota language and served as interpreters; they educated men about Dakota customs and practices; and they served as intermediaries between their husbands and Dakota communities. These women also hosted white business associates and visiting dignitaries, and they had a hand in managing the affairs of the trading post. Just as Dakota women were integral to the fur trade within their Dakota families, women who married white traders participated fully in the activities of the trading post. Many of these women also came to enjoy the material comforts and opportunities open to the wives of men prospering from the influx of whites and the business possibilities available to them.[15]

For some women, marriage to a white trader had far more basic perquisites. Rosalie Marpiya Masa, Iron Cloud, born in 1830, married Louis LaCroix, a trader whose post on the Minnesota River was twelve miles from Fort Ridgely. When the U.S.–Dakota War broke out in August 1862, LaCroix, Rosalie, and six of their seven children headed in their cart toward the fort, where white women and their children had taken refuge. However frightened and vulnerable she must have felt among these women, Rosalie was nevertheless able to survive the war because her husband's whiteness had afforded her and her children protection otherwise reserved for white families. After the war, when the U.S. government established a reservation at Lake Traverse for the Sisitunwan and Wahpetunwan Dakota, Rosalie and Louis settled there with their children for the rest of their lives. At that point, Louis benefitted from his wife's Dakota identity, which entitled her to land on the new reservation.[16]

The lives of the vast majority of these women remain unknowable. The Dakota woman who married the trader Joseph LaFramboise is known only as the daughter of Istaba, Sleepy Eye, the leader of the Sisitunwan Dakota community at Swan Lake, and Rosalie LaCroix's life story has come to light only through the arduous research of her descendants. Still, a very small number of exceptions exist, most prominently the life story of Pelagie Faribault, the wife of Jean-Baptiste Faribault, a French-Canadian fur trader who had established a post near Pike Island in the early years of the nineteenth century.

Pelagie Faribault is known because her name appears in a clause at the end of a treaty signed in 1820 by representatives of the U.S. government and the Dakota nation. The treaty gave Jean-Baptiste Faribault ownership of Pike Island, opposite the site of the newly erected Fort Snelling at the confluence of the Mississippi and St. Peter's rivers. Although the treaty was never ratified by the U.S. Senate, this clause remained a point of discussion in later treaty negotiations. These discussions and the information they provide about Pelagie Faribault's life open a window into the role of women in the fur trade and in the early history of Minnesota.[17]

Pelagie was born in 1783 to French Canadian trader Joseph Ainse and a Dakota woman whose name has been lost. This anonymous woman, however, ensured her husband's financial success. Her kinship ties smoothed the way for profitable trade relations and helped him acquire her language, facilitating his business among the Dakota. Joseph Ainse was eventually appointed Indian agent under the British, and in the 1780s he negotiated peace between Dakota and Ojibwe communities, another professional assignment that was surely aided by his family ties to the Dakota.[18]

Pelagie in turn facilitated her husband Jean-Baptiste Faribault's business ventures by making him a member of her Dakota family and solidifying his trade connections. She bore eight children, including several sons who would join their father's business. She maintained permanent residences for the family at Prairie du Chien, then at Pike Island, and finally at Mendota while her husband traveled on business. She offered hospitality to other traders and to current and potential business partners. Pelagie's graciousness as a hostess was mentioned by several white men who benefited from it.

Pelagie no doubt learned from her mother how to run a fur trader's household, but she also picked up Native values and assumptions from her Dakota family. Like Dakota women, Pelagie learned that the dwelling and everything in it belonged to the woman. Like other Native wives, she brought into her new homes—however different from tipis and bark lodges—conceptions of her role in the family's dwelling and the values of generosity and hospitality that were central to Dakota culture.

It was Pelagie's control over her family's dwelling that assured her an unusual place in the historical record. In the 1820 treaty signed by U.S. civilian and military officials and Dakota leaders, the Dakota ceded to the government fifteen acres of land on the bluffs overlooking the confluence of the Mississippi and Minnesota rivers for a military installation. The treaty also included two individual land grants: one tract of land to Duncan Campbell, a mixed-blood interpreter related to Dakota families in the area of the ceded land, and the tract that was Pike Island to Pelagie Faribault, relative of one of the Dakota signatories and wife of trader Jean-Baptiste Faribault. A complicated web of relations between the trader and local Dakota leaders resulted in this grant of land to Pelagie, which many have viewed as a gift to her husband. Nevertheless, this assignment of land to a woman in a treaty negotiated between the government and Dakota leaders testifies both to women's prominent place in the fur trade and to a wider recognition of Dakota norms.[19]

The recognition of Dakota women's control over living quarters might very well have been a shield for other transactions—both symbolic and material—between men, but it also suggests that Dakota women who married white traders were able to continue living by some of the norms and values of Dakota culture and perhaps even to convince their white husbands and others to adopt some of them.

Pelagie's own Dakota identity persisted through several generations. Her son David Faribault married a Dakota woman, Winona, Nancy McClure. Their daughter, Mary Jane, married a Dakota named John Eastman, who would become a pillar of the Dakota community at Flandreau in the last decades of the century. Mary Jane and John's daughter Grace played a leading role in the Flandreau Dakota community for many decades of her long life. Clearly, marriage to a white trader did not inevitably require abandoning the values and identity with which a woman had grown up.[20]

Women who married traders, however, represent only a small fraction of Native women and only one contribution that women made to the fur-trade economy. In fact, every woman whose husband sold furs contributed to the trade because of her roles in hunting expeditions, setting up shelter, cooking meals, and preparing meat and skins. Whether on a hunt for bison, elk, or deer or on an expedition for beaver, marten, fisher, or other fur-bearing animals, women took charge of the animals shot or trapped for trade, just as they did with those caught for daily subsistence. They cleaned, dried, and prepared skins and furs, processing them to be presented to the trader. In addition, some women themselves hunted and trapped.[21]

Throughout the Great Lakes and Upper Mississippi regions, women also played direct roles in the trade. They frequently added to the stores of food that traders brought with them for wintering, selling them dried meat, wild rice, and other foods. They also served as guides and translators, and they paddled their canoes and carried their goods. Like Ojibwe and other Native women in the region, Dakota women frequently provided company engages far from major posts the food and equipment that sustained them through the winter until they were able to sell the Indians' furs.[22]

Whether processing pelts, preparing food for sale, or even marrying traders, Dakota women participated in the supply side of the fur-trade economy as producers, contributing to traders' access to marketable furs and ensuring that the goods got to far-off markets. Yet women played an equally important role in the demand side of this economy. As consumers, they constituted a market for a significant proportion of trade goods: kettles and cooking implements, yard goods, ribbons, beads, and other supplies used in making and decorating clothing, footwear, and other items.

Collectively, women's goods made up an impressive share of the trade goods brought into the Great Lakes region beginning in the early years of the fur trade. Between 1715 and 1760, clothing and the materials to make and ornament clothing accounted for more than 60 percent of the value of all goods shipped from Montreal merchants to trading posts. Food-related items accounted for another 15 percent of the value of shipped goods. Of items that went to the trading post near Lake Pepin where Mdewakantunwan hunters came to trade in those years, clothing and clothing-related goods made up the largest category, some 44 percent of traders' expenditures. These included finished clothing as well as materials and implements with which to make and decorate clothing. Materials related to decorating clothing and other items also included vermilion, beads, and bells. Some 12 percent of the value of goods fell into the category of "cooking and eating," including forks, kettles, knives, spoons, and fire steels. In large part the goods shipped to posts in the western Great Lakes region, including the Lake Pepin post, thus went into the hands of women, most prominently for preparing food and producing functional items for daily and ritual life.[23]

Throughout most of the fur trade, Native men brought traders the furs that they and women in their families had prepared, returning home with bundles of manufactured goods. Given the high proportion of goods going to women, however, it is clear that, in the words of one historian, "women made considerable input into decisions about the types of goods" that men obtained in trade. No records exist to document conversations between Dakota women and men, but men's responsibility included maintaining relations with outsiders in order to protect their communities. Historically, these relations had focused on warfare and negotiations with other Native peoples, but after the arrival of whites, men's roles had expanded to include relations with traders, government officials, and other white men entering their lands. However, the relative balance of power that characterized gender relations among the Dakota ensured that women participated in decisions regarding relations and exchanges with traders.[24]

Moreover, gender roles remained flexible. Therefore, some men stayed with the women during expeditions for hunting and warfare. Women hunted small animals, and, in the late eighteenth and early nineteenth centuries, some traded furs and provisions at posts. In his first year as a trader among the Ojibwe in the St. Croix River valley, John Sayer, for instance, noted in his journal on March 7, 1805, that a woman "Called the Chiene came & traded 4 Rats for Oats." No other woman appears in Sayer's journal in this role, although the appearance of this woman does not seem out of the ordinary to him. When, in the 1840s, Dakota women became regular customers at trading posts, they built on the precedent set by earlier generations of Native women consumers who interacted directly with white traders.[25]

The entire system of exchanging furs for manufactured goods was predicated upon the continued existence of an adequate supply of furs. As the history of the fur trade in the eastern regions of the United States and Canada had already shown, however, the supply of fur-bearing animals was not sustainable, given the intensity with which animals were killed for their fur. Signs of such demographic brakes on the trade in Minnesota became apparent as early as the 1820s and 1830s, when muskrat pelts replaced beaver as the primary focus of the fur trade. In addition, this economic activity could not profitably coexist with agriculture, and the increasing population of European American farmers hungry for cleared land and timber for houses, barns, and fences decimated the forest habitat of fur-bearing animals. As savvy businessmen, fur traders looked ahead to a time when buying and selling furs would no longer remain as profitable as enterprises meeting the demands of the growing European American population. As a result, traders joined would-be European American settlers in calling on the U.S. government to "open up" more land for settlement and development.[26]

These calls fell on highly receptive ears. Just a few years earlier, in the resolution of conflicts that had resulted in the War of 1812, the United

States had wrested control of the Upper Mississippi region from the British and in 1819 had begun to establish the first permanent military installation in the region. Fort Snelling allowed the United States to assert its presence in these territories and to provide military protection of American businessmen's monopoly over the fur trade. Seeking to advance its own imperial goals of extended control over the lands of the western Great Lakes, the U.S. government eagerly acceded to growing demands for greater access to the timber- and farmlands under the control of the Dakota. As a result, in 1837 the federal government pressed upon the Mdewakantunwan Dakota, who had lived until then on both sides of the Mississippi, a treaty that gave the U.S. authority over Dakota lands between the Mississippi and St. Croix rivers. The Dakota would no longer have access to their homelands east of the Mississippi. Compensation for these lands would come in three major forms: annuity payments, annual allocations for food supplies, and annual allocations for agricultural implements, cattle, medicine, and "other beneficial objects" as well as for the services of a physician, farmers, and blacksmiths. These terms gave the appearance of an equitable exchange of land for cash while serving the interests of people intent on "civilizing" Native peoples. Annuities forced the Dakota to enter the cash economy, and the distribution of tools and other provisions of the treaty would prepare them to participate in this economy.[27]

The Dakota had signed two earlier treaties ceding land, in 1805 and 1830, but neither had resulted in comparable payments. In the 1805 treaty, the Dakota gave up land at the confluence of the Mississippi and Minnesota rivers that would be used to establish a fort. The miniscule payment to the Dakota—even by the ruthless standards of U.S. treaties with Indigenous peoples—came in the form of gifts and liquor to Dakota men who had signed the treaty. When the U.S. Senate ratified the treaty in 1808, it added a provision to pay two thousand dollars to the Dakota, but the treaty was never proclaimed by the president and the meager payments in goods and cash were never made. The 1830 treaty signed by the Mdewakantunwan Dakota and several other nations, intended by the United States to put an end to warfare and raids between them, included annuity payments for the cession of lands in southern Minnesota that came to two thousand dollars per year for ten years. The 1837 treaty, in contrast, provided for fifteen thousand dollars to be distributed annually and "forever." Much of this money would go first to traders to pay off the supposed debts incurred by individual Dakota, but the 1837 treaty still put far more cash in the hands of the Dakota than ever before.[28]

Food rations and annuities led to a rapid, if short-lived, improvement in the physical well-being of the Dakota. With farmers encroaching on their homelands, the Dakota had found it increasingly difficult to subsist on what they could hunt and harvest, and the declining fur population made it harder for them to acquire supplementary provisions from traders. Seeking better conditions in the early 1830s, many Mdewakantunwan and Wahpekute had relocated farther west, where they competed with their Sisitunwan and Wahpetunwan relations for resources along the upper Minnesota River and in eastern Dakota Territory. The Dakota remaining along the Mississippi and its tributaries had faced frequent starvation and numerically diminished communities. The treaty's food rations seem to have reduced child mortality rates, elevating the proportion of children in Mdewakantunwan villages from 33 percent in 1844 to 45 percent in 1849. The overall population of the villages also grew dramatically, from 1,400 in 1836 to 2,250 in 1849. Not only did Mdewakantunwans return to their villages along the Mississippi, but they frequently brought with them Sisitunwan, Wahpetunwan, and Wahpekute relations with whom they had sought refuge.[29]

Any improvements in physical well-being, however, were accompanied by severe cultural dispossession, a development disproportionately affecting men. Distribution of food supplies by U.S. personnel and declining rewards of the hunt robbed Dakota men of essential roles they had played in their communities. No longer needed as hunters and prohibited by U.S. officials from engaging in warfare with other nations, Dakota men had little materially rewarding or culturally relevant work to perform for their families or their villages. Under these circumstances, the attraction of alcohol, which white traders had liberally proffered since their arrival and which had become even more abundantly available on newly ceded lands, became increasingly difficult to ignore. A few Dakota men tried to take up the sedentary agricultural life preached by missionaries and government officials, but far more commonly men succumbed to alcohol, using their annuity money to purchase spirits from white traders eager to profit from the men's dispossession and addiction.[30]

Rum and whiskey had been integral to exchanges between Indigenous peoples and colonizers since their earliest encounters. Not only was alcohol among the goods that traders brought to exchange for pelts and skins; it was also widely used in diplomatic relations and treaty negotiations. By the time the Mdewakantunwan signed the 1837 treaty, heavy consumption of alcohol had become commonplace, and traders used rum and whiskey to their benefit in economic transactions, despite efforts by Indian agent Lawrence Taliaferro to curb such practices. After the Mdewakantunwan ceded lands east of the Mississippi, the river bank across from their villages became lined with grog shops. With declining game populations and fewer food and cash annuities coming from the government, Mdewakantunwan hunters unable to fulfill family responsibilities turned their time and cash to the consumption of alcohol. For some, trade in alcohol supplemented annuities and rations.[31]

White men who traded with the Dakota in the 1830s were poised to make the most of the new commercial possibilities offered by the 1837 treaty. They approached these business endeavors with a conception of their relations with local Indigenous peoples that differed significantly from those of their French, British, and American predecessors. Whites were no longer entering Dakota communities as relatives and no longer seeking furs in exchange for cloth and needles. Men like Hercules Dousman and Franklin Steele would make great fortunes in Minnesota and achieve exalted political status, but they felt no need to learn the Dakota language or to establish close ties, marital or otherwise, with the Dakota. Henry Sibley, who arrived in Minnesota in the early 1830s, never tried to hide the daughter that he fathered with Tasinasawin, and long after Tasinasawin died, Sibley paid for her education and support. Still, he never established the kind of bonds with them or their Mdewakantunwan family that Joseph Brown had maintained with Susan Frenier, their eight children, or her Sisitunwan family.[32]

At the same time, new access to lands between the St. Croix and the Mississippi made possible by the 1837 treaty provided many new opportunities for entrepreneurial traders in land speculation and the emerging timber industry. As their business interests diversified, many divested themselves of the fur trade entirely.[33]

These new circumstances reshaped relations between the Dakota and the traders. Gone was the "kinship of another kind" described by historian Gary Clayton Anderson, which had characterized Dakota-white relations until the 1830s. Rather, contact between the Dakota and the men who sold tools, cookware, clothing, and materials for clothing began resembling more closely the cash-based relations that existed between merchants and their customers in the growing city of St. Paul and across the United States.[34]

For Dakota women, the implications of these transformations were complex and numerous, but two in particular stand out: women themselves became direct customers of these new "Indian traders," and they began producing and selling moccasins and other items in their artistic repertoire. Records kept for six posts that agent Henry H. Sibley oversaw bring to light many of the changes in the years surrounding the signing of the treaty. They make clear, for instance, the arrival of women at the trading post, and they tell what each customer purchased. The Indian credit books also provide information about customers' payments and show how different groups of Dakota engaged with traders.[35]

These financial records were kept by Sibley's agents at various posts in Minnesota over a twenty-year period between 1831 and 1850. Some of these agents operated among the Sisitunwan in western Minnesota and others among the Mdewakantunwan and Wahpekute near Fort Snelling. Agents at each post kept track of the date of each transaction, the value and amount of goods purchased, and any payments made, in furs, cash, or, sometimes, traps, weapons, and ammunition.

The most inclusive comparison to be made from Sibley's records concerns the situations of different groups of Dakota. Starting in the 1820s,

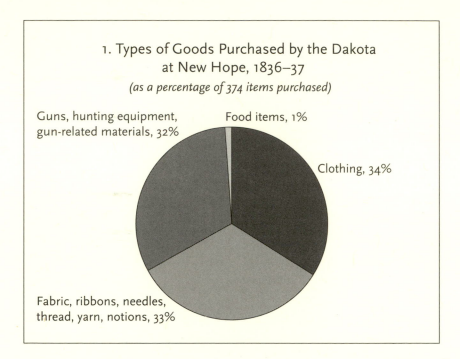

1. Types of Goods Purchased by the Dakota
at New Hope, 1836–37

(as a percentage of 374 items purchased)

Guns, hunting equipment, gun-related materials, 32%

Food items, 1%

Clothing, 34%

Fabric, ribbons, needles, thread, yarn, notions, 33%

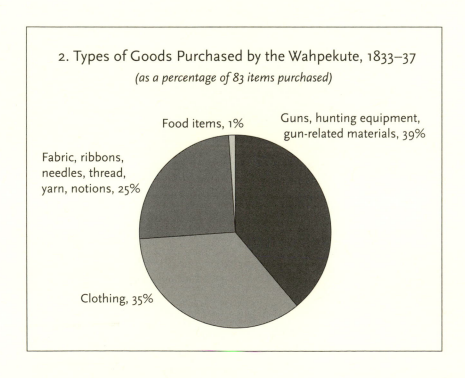

2. Types of Goods Purchased by the Wahpekute, 1833–37

(as a percentage of 83 items purchased)

Food items, 1%

Guns, hunting equipment, gun-related materials, 39%

Fabric, ribbons, needles, thread, yarn, notions, 25%

Clothing, 35%

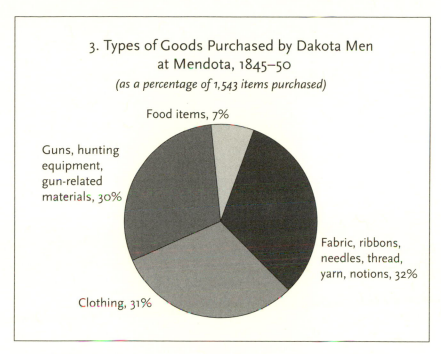

3. Types of Goods Purchased by Dakota Men at Mendota, 1845–50

(as a percentage of 1,543 items purchased)

Food items, 7%

Guns, hunting equipment, gun-related materials, 30%

Fabric, ribbons, needles, thread, yarn, notions, 32%

Clothing, 31%

This chart combines data from account books for 1845–46, 1846–48, and 1848–50, as do charts 5, 6, and 7.

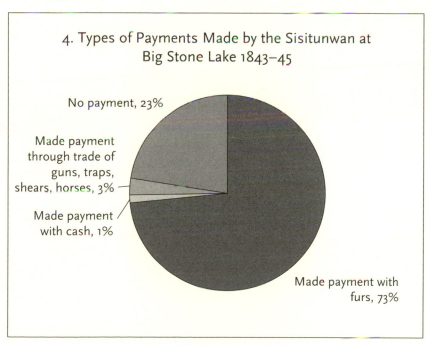

4. Types of Payments Made by the Sisitunwan at Big Stone Lake 1843–45

No payment, 23%

Made payment through trade of guns, traps, shears, horses, 3%

Made payment with cash, 1%

Made payment with furs, 73%

5. Types of Goods Purchased by Dakota Women at Mendota, 1845–50

(as a percentage of 172 items purchased)

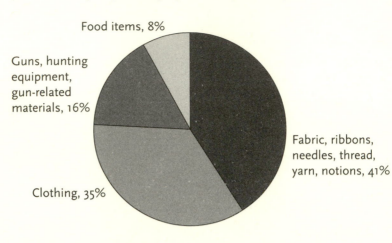

Food items, 8%

Guns, hunting equipment, gun-related materials, 16%

Fabric, ribbons, needles, thread, yarn, notions, 41%

Clothing, 35%

6. Types of Payments Made by Dakota Women at Mendota, 1845–50

(as a percentage of 103 transactions)

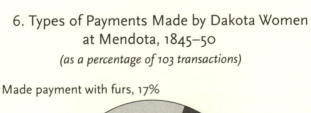

Made payment with furs, 17%

Made payment with cash, 45%

No payment, 17%

Made payment through trade of guns, traps, shears, horses, 21%

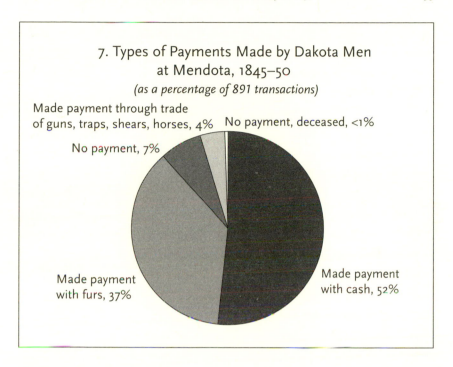

7. Types of Payments Made by Dakota Men
at Mendota, 1845–50
(as a percentage of 891 transactions)

Made payment through trade
of guns, traps, shears, horses, 4%   No payment, deceased, <1%

No payment, 7%

Made payment
with furs, 37%

Made payment
with cash, 52%

hunting became increasingly difficult in the eastern part of Dakota lands. The Sisitunwan and Wahpetunwan, in contrast, were closer to the buffalo ranges of what would become Dakota Territory and to other hunting grounds that remained more productive; they also had more horses for pursuing buffalo than the Wahpekute and Mdewakantunwan. Because the Mdewakantunwan lands were closest to whites coming from the East, they were the most depleted of game and the most attractive to settlers. The 1837 treaty was signed only with the Mdewakantunwan, who were the only Dakota to receive annuities and food rations from it. As a result, even before the Mdewakantunwan had access to cash annuities for buying necessities, they had already relied somewhat more on such purchases than even the Wahpekute, immediately to the west, whose lands were farther removed from new settlements. Records for the New Hope trading post across the Minnesota River from Fort Snelling show that during 1836 and 1837, some 32 percent of the purchases were for weapons and hunting-related articles, while 68 percent were clothing and sewing-related items (chart 1). The location of the New Hope post would suggest that the Mdewakantunwan made up the majority of its clientele. Among the Wahpekute, in contrast, in the years between 1833 and 1837, some 39 percent of the purchases went to hunting-related items and 60 percent to clothing and related items (chart 2).

Account books do not cover all years for all groups, but an examination of interactions with traders after 1837 suggests that the Mdewakantunwan continued to hunt although annuities reinforced their reliance on trade goods. Despite the declining rewards of the hunt, hunting-related purchases continued to account for 30 percent of purchases at Mendota in Mdewakantunwan lands during the 1840s, very close to what they had been a decade earlier (chart 3). This equipment for the Sisitunwan, who continued to rely far more heavily on the hunt for their subsistence, accounted for 44 percent of purchases at the Sheyenne River post in 1844 and 1845 and 49 percent of purchases at the post on Big Stone Lake from 1843 to 1845. At the same time, the Sisitunwan continued to rely less on traders for clothing: 50 percent of items purchased at Big Stone Lake and 54 percent at Sheyenne River were for clothing or sewing-related goods, while comparable purchases accounted for 63 percent of what men bought and 75 percent of what women bought at Mendota in the years between 1845 and 1850 (charts 3 and 5). Because they relied more on hunting, the Sisitunwan paid for almost all their purchases in furs, while less than 40 percent of payments made by customers at the Mendota post were in furs (chart 4). Apparently these men continued to acquire weapons and hunt even though they often returned empty-handed. The more western Sisitunwan were clearly able to remain closer to their subsistence food and clothing patterns for a longer time than the Mdewakantunwan.

The Sisitunwan hewed closer to traditional patterns in another way as well: no women appear in the account books for either the Sheyenne River or the Big Stone Lake posts in the early 1840s. No women appeared in the 1831 and 1836 account books for Mendota and New Hope, which served the Mdewakantunwan, but once they signed the treaty, the situation changed. It is not clear how quickly women took on this new role because no account books for any of the posts for the years between 1836 and 1843 survive. Books covering the years 1845 and 1846 at Mendota, however, indicate that some women at least took on the added responsibility of engaging with the trader. The numbers are significant, though not overwhelming: of the 175 individuals holding accounts in the book for 1845 and 1846, 20 are women. Of the 245 individuals with accounts between 1848 and 1850, 31 are women. Overall, between 10 percent and 13 percent of the customers were now women, although no women had been customers just a few years earlier. Some of these women were related to influential men, and several are identified as the wife, daughter, or niece of Wasusica, whose daughter bore a child with Henry Sibley, manager of the post at Mendota. Even if the opportunity to engage directly with the trader was not open to all Mdewakantunwan women, the small number of women who availed themselves of such opportunities nonetheless took on responsibilities that had not been known to their mothers or grandmothers.

Sibley's account books still leave many unanswered questions. They do show, however, what women purchased as a general pattern and how the purchases reflected the gender division of labor. Women tended to buy more of the supplies they would need for food preparation and for the production, maintenance, and decoration of clothing, while men tended to buy more hunting and trapping supplies. Most of the differences, however, are far from dramatic. In the three volumes from Mendota covering the years between 1845 and 1850, the proportion of goods purchased by women in the category of finished clothing—including shirts, leggings, socks, and "mantlets" (short cloaks)—ranged from 27 percent to 43 percent, while for men finished clothing ranged from 30 to 34 percent of purchases. The category of fabric, ribbon, needles, and thread accounted for 35 to 44 percent of women's purchases and 30 to 34 percent of men's purchases. Food-related purchases amounted to 3 to 12 percent of women's purchases and 3 to 10 percent of men's, almost the same. The only substantial difference occurs in purchases of hunting goods, which accounted for 28 to 33 percent of men's purchases and 8 to 19 percent of women's (charts 3 and 5).

The similarities in the contents of men's and women's "shopping carts" confirms the closeness of their working relationships: women knew what men needed and men continued to purchase the necessities of women's work, even when women could purchase those items on their own. One can speculate that more women continued to let their husbands interact with the trader because both husbands and traders knew what Dakota women needed. Hunting, nevertheless, remained an area clearly dominated by men. Not only did purchasing patterns differ more significantly in this category of goods, but payment patterns differed as well. Men continued to pay in furs, while women paid mostly in cash. Percentages of payments made in cash by women fluctuated between 60 and 82 percent, and by men, 45 to 57 percent. Conversely, the percentage of payments made by women in furs varied between 4 and 14 percent, while 35 to 76 percent of payments made by men were in furs.

Men continued to rely more on furs for payment than did women because hunting remained a significant part of their lives. Hunting constituted one of men's central responsibilities. Men's purchasing patterns reflected their strong identification with hunting but also reaffirmed their identity as hunters and the centrality of hunting to their identity. Data in Sibley's credit books thus provide one more means of understanding the losses that men experienced when they were no longer able to hunt. The data also reveal the depths of Dakota men's resistance to efforts of missionaries and U.S. government officials to transform them into farmers.

In contrast, women's experience with traders and with other agents of change suggests greater flexibility and greater ease in adapting to changing circumstances. Certainly the number of women who came to the trading post remained relatively small, yet some engaged in direct transactions with traders. They used cash because Dakota women were also beginning to enter the cash economy through another avenue: sale of their handicrafts to whites.

↢

Moccasins seem to have been the first and most common item produced for sale outside Dakota communities, perhaps because whites already living among the Dakota used them. By the late 1830s and early 1840s, even missionaries dedicated to bringing Christian "civilization" to the Dakota took to wearing moccasins, especially when other footwear was unavailable. In an 1839 letter to her parents, Mary Riggs, who had arrived in Minnesota with her missionary husband in 1837, bemoaned the absence of supplies coming from the organization supporting her husband's mission. She noted that she was still wearing the shoes and boots she had brought from Massachusetts, which were rapidly wearing out. While she remained optimistic about receiving boxes of necessities, she reassured her parents that she would not be going barefoot: "I can substitute moccasins, though they are not good in wet weather," words suggesting that she had already had experience with them.[36]

This concession must have pained Mary Riggs, whose mission work among the Dakota consisted largely of teaching them to live and dress like white Christians. On the other hand, she might have been persuaded of the appropriateness of moccasins for God-fearing Americans when she saw whites wearing this native footgear. Trader Martin McLeod, for one, had adopted moccasins, though he wrote that even two pairs of Indian moccasins were barely enough to keep from being frozen during one particularly harsh winter journey. More than a dozen years later, missionary Thomas Williamson was happy to obtain moccasins for his own use from another missionary, who probably also wore moccasins.[37]

If missionaries became customers for Dakota women's work, they also became promoters of women's handiwork as an income-generating enterprise. As Mary Riggs became accustomed to the idea of wearing moccasins herself, she began to see their commercial value and potential for assisting in the building of the mission among the Dakota. In 1842, she explained to her sister, "Some time in 1840 I wrote to a friend in Galena [Illinois, on the Mississippi River] inquiring whether we could dispose of moccasins advantageously there, provided our church members would forward them, and received an encouraging reply." At the time, she said, she had recently received a pair of moccasins from a

Dakota woman, which Riggs tallied as "her donation towards procuring a small bell for our mission chapel." Mary Riggs encouraged Christianized Dakota women to make moccasins in order to raise money for the mission, but this project confirmed the cash value of women's work with hides. For Dakota women, these transactions made clear that the goods they made for use in their community could also be sold outside their community in order to purchase necessities for their family.[38]

Women knew from long experience that white men prized lavishly decorated items, and they learned very quickly to respond to interest in the items they made from hides. Not only did one woman give painter and traveler George Catlin a baby's cradleboard off her back, but several women gave him their children's *cekpa* bag. In a gesture that revealed a clear understanding of the different value the object held for this outsider, each woman took the bag apart and removed the dried umbilicus before giving it to Catlin: "In every instance, they cut them open, and removed from within a bunch of cotton or moss, the little sacred *medicine,* which, to part with, would be to 'endanger the health of the child.'" These women were willing to give up gifts of art honoring their newborn *wakanyeza,* although they would not part with this very powerful piece of their being. Moreover, when Catlin visited the Dakota in 1835, they were barely surviving: widespread hunger and depopulation of Mdewakantunwan villages along the Mississippi no doubt made it easier to part with these objects if the recipient would reciprocate with gifts of food or other necessities. Through such exchanges, Dakota women learned that the objects they had always created to clothe and honor their families could now help feed them as well.[39]

As women began commercial production of moccasins and other items, they made certain kinds for sale and others for use by Dakota eople. This distinction was not lost on a very youthful observer of this work. In his memoir, Andrew Williamson, the son of missionary Thomas Williamson, took great pains to differentiate what some might call "authentic" Indian art from "tourist art." When Dakota women ornamented the moccasins of their husbands, he recalled, "The designs in general were neat, graceful, and beautiful, rather than showy. Such work was never produced for sale. A gaudy pair could be made in a day or less . . . The average traveler would pay more for a gaudy pair costing much less for labor than for one of these exquisitely beautiful pairs that could not be made in a week."[40]

Unfortunately, Williamson did not elaborate on either the gaudy moccasins or the beautiful ones. Differences in modern beadwork between "lazy stitch," in which beads strung on a thread are tacked down to the fabric or hide every ten to twenty beads, and the more demanding stitching of each individual bead to the backing might parallel the differing level of effort women put into work for sale and work for their family.

Since the eighteenth century, when the Huron on the east coast and other Native peoples had begun designing and producing objects specifically for sale to whites, a lively trade in Indian-made goods had spread across North America. For the Dakota this commercial demand began in the 1830s and 1840s upon the arrival of growing numbers of white missionaries, settlers, and soldiers. Because these developments were concurrent with the advent of annuities and women making purchases at trading posts, one can speculate that the experience of buying directly from the trader and paying in cash prepared Dakota women for the opposite transaction: collecting cash for goods they created for whites.[41]

At the same time as Dakota women took more control over the materials of their work, engaging directly with traders rather than through the intermediary of men, the nature of their work also shifted, as evidenced in the increased volume of yard goods and ready-made clothing that changed hands. The shift away from creating clothing out of skins, however, does not mean that women no longer made items using traditional materials. In fact, they continued to make them, although not exclusively for use by the Dakota. When the political economy changed, women were able to make changes in their work. They adapted to new conditions by producing some of their hide work for sale.

Wicacaka was seventeen when the leaders of her nation signed the treaty that ceded Dakota lands east of the Mississippi and brought annuities into Dakota villages. She had already learned how to prepare the materials necessary for making moccasins, pouches, parfleches, and other hide items, and she had already learned from her mother and other women the techniques and designs of quillwork and beadwork. Over the next few years, she would learn to make moccasins to the liking of the white people who would buy them. By the time she gave birth to her daughter Emma in 1845, she would be purchasing from a trader the supplies she needed. When Emma's daughter Mary began making dolls for sale several decades later, she would be following in the footsteps of her grandmother and other Dakota women who did what they needed to do in order to feed their families and raise the next generation of Dakota.

CHAPTER 3

Gender and Resistance

IN A MEMOIR WRITTEN LATE IN LIFE, Mary Huggins Kerlinger, the daughter of missionaries to the Dakota, described life at the Lac qui Parle mission in the 1840s and 1850s. The family home was always full, especially when her parents invited nearby Wahpetunwan families to visit with their children in order to learn the ways of white Christians. During the winter, Kerlinger wrote, "Indian girls came in . . . and pieced scraps furnished by the mission. They had pillow ticks of buckskin and covered them with their sewings."[1]

Kerlinger's casual observation about the young women's simple activities masks complex realities about Dakota women's relationships with missionaries. Dakota women came to the mission and learned from missionaries about the work and the materials preferred by the white Christian women who were to be their models, but they also brought into the mission house their own identity. When adults, these "Indian girls" would continue to move between their own customs, responsibilities, and work processes and the "scraps furnished by the mission," including the lessons, materials, and ways of white Christians.

Mary Kerlinger's parents, Alexander Gililand Huggins and Lydia Pettijohn Huggins, were among the first missionaries working among the Dakota. Alexander Huggins came to Minnesota in 1835 with Thomas Williamson, his sister Jane Williamson, his wife Margaret Williamson, and her sisters Sarah and Jane Poage. Together, they established the

Protestant mission at Lac qui Parle on the Minnesota River, two hundred miles west of Fort Snelling. These missionaries joined the brothers Samuel W. and Gideon H. Pond, who had arrived in the summer of 1834, and in 1837 missionary Stephen Return Riggs arrived with his wife, Mary Longley Riggs. Gideon Pond soon married Sarah Poage, and Samuel married Cordelia Eggleston, the sister-in-law of Jedediah Stevens, a missionary who settled a few miles from Fort Snelling. These families would raise their children and remain in the region for several decades, some for their whole lives. They became the nucleus of a community of missionaries whose history would be interwoven with the history of the Dakota in Minnesota and beyond.[2]

The timing of these missionaries' arrival could not have been more propitious for them. Not only did they have the support of a prominent missionary association, the American Board of Commissioners for Foreign Missions, but the missionaries could also secure resources and labor from the U.S. government through funds committed for the education and "civilization" of the Dakota in the treaty of 1837.

Throughout the nineteenth century, in the Dakota homelands and across Indian country, missionaries worked hand in hand with government employees to spread their intertwined messages of Christianity and civilization. This government support of religious organizations and their schools seemed entirely reasonable to white Protestant Americans at the time, and it characterized U.S. Indian policy throughout the century.

The particulars of the collaboration between missionaries and government officials were typical of encounters between Natives and whites. Whites believed they were fundamentally superior to Native peoples, whose culture should be destroyed and replaced with Christian, European American culture. Beginning in 1803, the federal government relied upon Protestant and Catholic institutions to implement its "civilizing" policies among the Indigenous populations whose lands the United States had appropriated. Relations between the Dakota and whites provide a case study in the partnership between missionaries and government to carry out this colonization.[3]

Missionaries and U.S. officials shared one assumption: the need to transform the Dakota into sedentary farmers. This undertaking required a major reconfiguration of Dakota gender roles; men had to be turned away from hunting and warfare toward European American–style farming, and women had to be taught to manage a household based in a permanent structure made of wood or brick. Because these activities violated the central tenets and patterns of Dakota life, however, each Indian-white interaction produced a new skirmish in an ongoing conflict not only between two value systems but between two gender systems as well. The results were disastrous.

On November 22, 1852, Mazasa, Red Iron, leader of the Sisitunwan community at Traverse des Sioux near Mankato, was imprisoned following a confrontation with Minnesota Territory Governor Alexander Ramsey and Indian agent Nathaniel McLean. In response, Lean Bear, an influential Sisitunwan warrior, appealed to fellow warriors to take up arms against the "Long Knives": "Dakotas! Must we starve like buffalos in the snow? Shall we let our blood freeze like the little streams? Or shall we make the snow red with the blood of the white braves?" This time Lean Bear was convinced to back down, and Mazasa was soon released. By the summer of 1862, however, the anger among some Dakota men had become all-consuming. They expressed their frustrations in numerous confrontations, overtly and sometimes aggressively rejecting the modes of existence and beliefs that whites sought to impose.[4]

Women, on the other hand, found ways of accommodating whites' demands within the context of their work. Their decorative and functional work with skins and other materials became a unique "weapon" in conflicts with European Americans, allowing them to meet both their families' needs and various restrictions that missionaries and other whites imposed upon them.

The U.S.–Dakota War of 1862 brought a violent and terrifying end to the lives that Dakota men and women had led in Minnesota for generations. Existing histories of this war have focused on relations between Dakota men and U.S. military and civilian officials. An exploration of the relations between missionaries and the Dakota, however, highlights

the breadth of European American assaults as the U.S. government col-
laborated with the church to expropriate the Dakota. These colonizing
efforts were highly gendered, and responses to those efforts were equally
gendered, reflecting the different relationships that emerged among
Dakota women and men and the Protestant missionaries who settled
among them.

From its beginning, U.S. policy toward Indigenous populations whose
lands were appropriated focused on "civilizing" and transforming them
into land-owning, self-supporting farmers. Farmers would not need the
large tracts of land necessary for hunting game, which would free the
government to open their homelands to white settlement. Native peoples
would become integrated into the nation's emerging commercial economy, learn to dress and eat in the style of white people, and live in homes
furnished like those of their white neighbors.

According to this development model, men needed lessons in growing crops and keeping livestock, and women needed lessons in cooking,
baking, cleaning, and sewing—in "making a house a home." For Thomas
Jefferson and government policymakers who followed, education was
the pathway to "civilizing" Indians in order to more easily acquire their
lands. Similarly, missionaries believed that instruction was the most
direct path to Christianity and a new, appropriate lifestyle.[5]

In the eyes of Protestant missionaries, farming had equally important
but somewhat different virtues. Missionaries believed agriculture would
build on Native peoples' ties to their land, but it would also teach them
the kind of work ethic that missionaries valued most. In addition, farming would provide Native peoples increasingly surrounded by white settlers a means of assimilating into that society and maintaining some
degree of financial independence within it. Most pragmatically, though,
farming would keep Indians in one place, making them easier to convert
and control.[6]

U.S. government officials and missionaries shared the belief that
Natives would most effectively be transformed into farmers through
educational efforts that taught Native men and women "the practice of

husbandry and of the household arts." These shared views led to a long-lasting partnership between church and state in the area of Indian policy. As early as 1819, Congress established a "civilization fund" to "instruct [tribes] in the mode of agriculture suited to their situation; and for teaching their children in reading, writing, and arithmetic." President James Monroe and Secretary of War John C. Calhoun believed the fund would be best used by churches and missionary societies that had already established schools for Native Americans or that could be encouraged to do so by the fund.[7]

In 1812, the American Board of Commissioners for Foreign Missions (ABCFM) began sending missionaries to work among Native peoples in the United States and its territories. Their missions, in particular the schools they operated, became significant beneficiaries of federal largesse. For most white Americans, in the words of one scholar, "public education and Protestantism went hand-in-hand," making the funding of missionaries an unexceptional allocation of federal dollars. This alliance endured through much of the nineteenth century, as the federal government made Catholic and Protestant churches responsible for overseeing individual reservations under the so-called "Grant Peace Policy" beginning in 1870. In sum, missionaries relied on federal monies to support their work, and the federal government relied on missionaries to carry out its policies.[8]

The most effective means toward their shared ends, missionaries and federal officials agreed, was "manual labor training." In his 1850 annual report to the U.S. secretary of the interior, Commissioner of Indian Affairs Luke Lea praised manual labor schools as "efficient auxiliaries in imparting a knowledge of letters, agriculture, and mechanical arts, and of advancing them in civilization." The ABCFM, which believed that converting heathens required the creation of independent small farmers, called the curriculum at these institutions an education for "head, heart, and hand," a phrase that also served as the mission society's motto. The ABCFM established its own manual labor boarding schools as part of its mission of converting Indians. Alumni of these schools would not only constitute the core of Christianized Native communities; they could also become missionaries trained to propagate Christianity and "civilization" across North America and even Asia.[9]

In some areas of the globe that would become U.S. possessions, missionaries preceded civilian officials by several decades. In Hawaii, for instance, the first mission was established in 1838, almost sixty years ahead of U.S. officials' arrival. By the time the United States overthrew the Hawaiian queen in 1898, Protestant missionaries had established a prominent position for themselves among the diverse populations of the Hawaiian archipelago. In contrast, the first missionaries arrived in Minnesota fifteen years after the establishment of the first U.S. Indian agency among the Dakota and the opening of the first permanent military installation in the region. These two institutions would provide material support for missionaries as well as opportunities for building on already existing contacts between the Dakota and the U.S. government.[10]

From a national perspective, the establishment of a fort on Dakota homelands beginning in 1819 represents the integration of the Dakota and their homelands into the expansionist agenda of the United States. From the perspective of whites in the area, the opening of Fort Snelling meant that the United States could exercise greater control over local Indigenous populations. Not only did Fort Snelling house soldiers who could subdue locals, but it also served as the headquarters of the first Indian agent to the Dakota, Lawrence Taliaferro. The goals of this man, who represented the U.S. government to the Dakota nation from 1820 to 1839, were those of his employer: to establish sovereignty in Minnesota, to protect the Dakota from what he saw as the nefarious influences of traders (chief among them the commerce in whiskey), to put an end to intertribal warfare, and to set the Dakota on the path toward civilization. While the first three were prerequisites for the fourth, it was the latter that was of greatest concern to Taliaferro and to which he devoted much of his energy in the second decade of his appointment.[11]

From the beginning of his tenure, Taliaferro had encouraged the Dakota to expand their farming. These efforts were unsuccessful until the deadly winter of 1828–29, when the absence of game convinced several Dakota leaders to follow Taliaferro's advice. The following spring,

Taliaferro selected Lake Calhoun as the site for an Indian farming community. He hired trader Philander Prescott to begin farming and "take as many Indians as would go and settle down." Taliaferro also hired several white men to build houses and establish fields at the site he named "Eatonville" after Secretary of War John Eaton. "No Indians would go at first except my old father-in-law and another old man," Prescott later wrote.[12]

Like many traders, Philander Prescott had married a Dakota woman, Naginowin, Spirit of the Moon Woman. Her father was Kinyan, Flying Man. The "old man" who accompanied him was Taliaferro's Dakota father-in-law. Taliaferro, who had worked hard to establish and maintain close relations with the Dakota, rapidly learned the political value of family ties with the Dakota. When he took a Dakota wife, he chose Anpetuinajinwin, The Day Sets Woman, daughter of village leader Mahpiya Wicasta, Cloud Man. It is therefore not surprising that Cloud Man was among the first Dakota to go to Eatonville, nor is it surprising that Taliaferro selected Prescott to lead his project: the two Dakota men could use their family relations to acquire food and other necessities for their village, while the two white men used their relations to advance the goal of converting the Dakota to an agricultural way of life.[13]

After Dakota families began arriving at Eatonville, Taliaferro brought in missionaries to implement his plan more completely. Using monies from the educational fund established by the 1830 treaty, he hired the Pond brothers and gave them a place to live at Eatonville. Taliaferro also used education funds to support the work of the Williamson, Riggs, and Huggins missionary families, and he hired Jedediah Stevens as the farmer for the village of Dakota leader Wabasha. Like many white men before him, including the Puritans in seventeenth-century America, Taliaferro strongly believed that Christianization of Native peoples could not proceed without prior civilization. As he wrote to the commissioner of Indian affairs in 1838, "An Indian must be taught all the *temporal* benefits of life first, before you ask him to seek eternal happiness hereafter." As the number of missionaries among the Dakota grew throughout the 1830s, Taliaferro made abundant use of their labor and their conviction that conversion to Christianity and to European American ways were inseparable processes.[14]

The white men Taliaferro hired and the missionaries the ABCFM sent to Minnesota worked primarily with Dakota men. If their shared goals of civilizing and converting the Dakota were to be met, however, they knew they would need to provide instruction to Dakota women as well. For this purpose, the missionaries turned to their wives and other young white women in Minnesota. The missionaries and their wives had sisters, friends, and other female relations eager for the adventure and fulfillment of missionary work and, most likely, for the marital prospects presented by unmarried missionary men. While the ABCFM never recognized women as missionaries in their own right, these women were regularly identified as members of the "Mission to the Sioux" and counted as "female assistant missionaries" in the reports that Stephen Riggs submitted to the ABCFM.[15]

White women who undertook missionary work among Native Americans and other peoples around the globe did so for their own reasons, impelled by prevailing ideas about middle-class womanhood and by the otherwise restricted opportunities available to the first generations of formally educated young women in the United States. The nationalist fervor of the American Revolution and the founding of the new republic had provided new arguments supporting education for women whose families could pay for it. In "female seminaries," these daughters of middle-class homes gained an education in literature and various arts, including "domestic arts." While they were encouraged to apply their education to their own homes, many young women sought a much broader stage. Missionary work became an avenue into new worlds of activism, self-expression, responsibility, and public recognition.[16]

Mary Lyon, an early and prominent advocate of women's education who founded Mount Holyoke Seminary (later Mount Holyoke College), saw her own school as preparing women for missionary work. This would, in turn, prepare them for the most important work of their lives: raising virtuous citizens for the young nation. While the majority of Lyon's pupils would make their missionary careers in Asia, her students also found their way to Minnesota. When Stephen Riggs arrived there in 1837, he was accompanied by his new bride, the former Mary Ann Longley of Hawley, Massachusetts. Miss Longley had been a student at Mary Lyon's Female Seminary in Buckland, Massachusetts, and had also attended the Ipswich Female Seminary, founded by Lyon's close associate, Zilphia Grant. Upon completing her studies in Ipswich, Longley traveled to Ohio to take up a position teaching. There she met the newly ordained missionary on his way to his first assignment.[17]

As a product of schools for women, Mary Riggs brought to Minnesota a clear vision of the "moral power of home" and the centrality of domesticity to civilization. Living in a civilized house, she and other women believed, had the power to transform Native women into civilized housewives by virtue of the labor required to maintain proper homes. Thus, in their own homes and in mission schools, Mary Riggs and her missionary sisters around the globe carried out their special female mission while they fulfilled their roles within their own families. The homes of missionary women served as models for the homes that Native women would eventually have themselves. When the ABCFM began its work in Hawaii in 1838, its Prudential Committee charged the missionaries with covering "those islands with fruitful fields and pleasant dwellings, and schools, and churches."[18]

Missionaries headed for other lands no doubt received similar instructions and took note of the special role that women played in this work. They believed in the division of labor that assigned the creation of "fruitful fields" to men and "pleasant dwellings" to women. When missionary men and women set out to spread the promise of eternal life in the hereafter, they made it contingent upon the adoption of their own customs and patterns of subsistence in this life.

Befitting the gendered ideology they brought to evangelical activities, missionaries divided their work along strict gender lines. Missionary men taught Dakota men and boys the basics of literacy and arithmetic. They also preached the virtues of plowing fields, although they left instruction in how to plow and the plowing itself to Indian agency employees. Missionary women divided their time between teaching women literacy, arithmetic, and Christian doctrine and instructing them in the skills deemed necessary for maintaining a proper home.[19]

The women's curriculum included "domestic manufactures" such as sewing, knitting, and embroidery. These activities began in earnest in the spring of 1839, when Fanny Huggins accompanied Thomas Williamson from Ohio to Minnesota, where she joined her brother, missionary-farmer Alexander Huggins. With an additional instructor available for teaching women and girls, the missionaries decided that "some manufacturing industries might profitably be introduced among Dakota women."[20]

The Lac qui Parle mission, where Thomas Williamson and Alexander Huggins were stationed, acquired several spinning wheels, and Huggins planted a field of flax. Wool was furnished by a flock of sheep inherited from a trader who had lived in the area. In the fall, under the guidance of Fanny Huggins, two Dakota women and two Dakota girls wove approximately ten yards of cloth. As Mary Riggs wrote in a letter to her family, fifteen-year-old Mahpiyaskanskanwin, Moving Cloud Woman, "claim[ed] the honor of completing the first short gown of Dakota manufacture." The experiment was considered sufficiently successful that by 1841 the missionaries were reporting to the ABCFM that "half the time of the females while at school is spent in learning to spin, weave, knit, and perform other domestic labors." Dakota women, they believed, were well on their way to living the lives of good Christian women.[21]

"Domestic labors" became a cornerstone of mission education, ensuring that female pupils mastered the skills necessary to clothe their families when they abandoned garments of skins and blankets and adopted European American attire. In his 1851 report to the Indian agent, missionary J. S. Hancock assured him that "the girls have been employed during a portion of their school hours in knitting and sewing, under the direction of Mrs. Aiton [wife of missionary John Aiton] with the following results. Garments completed for themselves: calico dresses, 12; short gowns . . . 4; shirts, 12; pairs of mittens, 3." While these did not meet all the clothing needs of the girls and their families, missionaries and U.S. officials could take satisfaction in the belief that the Dakota girls were on the road to providing for themselves in approved ways.[22]

In taking credit for the girls' abilities with needle and thread, however, these white men showed profound ignorance about their pupils. Much of what missionaries wanted them to learn they already knew. By the time the first missionaries arrived, traders had been selling needles, thread, yarn, and calico and other fabric to the Dakota for more than a hundred years. Finished garments such as leggings and shirts were also available from traders. Moreover, Dakota women had always made their family's clothing. Far from supplanting work that they customarily performed, the skills learned from missionaries could very well have given Dakota women new ways to perform and enhance that work, but they were sewing fabric with needle and thread long before the arrival of missionaries and Indian agents.[23]

Believing they were moving the Dakota along the path toward civilization, the religious and civil agents of the U.S. government continued their educational efforts. They also continued efforts to cut off the Dakota from traditional practices in other ways.

Soon after ratification of the 1837 treaty, traders and settlers began clamoring for more Dakota lands, and by the late 1840s, federal officials began pressing for a new land treaty. The Dakota finally conceded, negotiating and signing two treaties in the summer of 1851. In the treaty that the Sisitunwan and Wahpetunwan signed at Traverse des Sioux on July 21 and the treaty that the Mdewakanton and Wahpekute signed three weeks later at Mendota, the Dakota ceded more than 90 percent of their remaining lands in Minnesota and Iowa in exchange for annuities and a reservation along the Minnesota River. The missionaries who were present throughout the negotiations translated the treaties for the Dakota, no doubt influencing the outcome of these exchanges.[24]

The removal of the Dakota and the opening of ceded lands suited the missionaries' purposes. By confining the Dakota, the 1851 treaties facilitated the missionaries' work of converting them, and in the following years, Dakota families seemed to be adopting the life mapped out for them by missionaries and agency personnel. In 1857, the farmer for the Mdewakantunwan and the Wahpekute reported that thirteen log houses had been built in the previous year, and in the year ending September 30, 1858, fifty-five houses were completed and another seventeen begun. One hundred houses were built in the following year. In his 1859 report to the commissioner of Indian affairs, W. J. Cullen, the head of the Northern Superintendency, could barely contain his pride: "The improved condition of those who have betaken themselves to agriculture and assumed the dress and habits of civilized life has afforded me the liveliest satisfaction. Their houses are neat and comfortable, their clothing well preserved, and their deportment unexceptionable. The cultivation and fencing of their fields would do credit to a practiced farmer." The Dakota, it seemed to Cullen, were finally recognizing the superiority of white ways and embracing them enthusiastically.[25]

Cullen's optimistic report came on the heels of the signing of another treaty in June 1858. This treaty, initially proposed by Cullen himself, sold the Dakota reservation lands north of the Minnesota River and divided the lands south of the river into eighty-acre allotments. Over the next few years, Cullen and Indian agents surveyed the land to be allotted, ensuring that each allotment contained both land suitable for fields and land suitable for harvesting timber for building houses and fences for the farms. While Cullen took great pride in the "progress" he saw among those who turned to agriculture and "the dress and habits of civilized life," the teachings of missionaries and agency farmers no doubt did far less to create farmers than the repeated losses of their lands to treaties and allotment.[26]

The allotment of lands for individual farms, or severalty, is deeply rooted in ideas about Indians going back to the first British colonies. The leaders of the Massachusetts colony believed that settling Indians on family-sized plots of land would "civilize" them, and Thomas Jefferson, hoping to transform Indian men into property-owning farmers, pressed for a policy of severalty. The early years of Indian removal in the 1830s saw an increasing emphasis on this policy, and by the time the federal government ceased treaty-making with Indigenous nations in the 1870s, it had signed approximately seventy treaties that included provisions for assigning specific tracts of land to individuals who met certain requirements. The majority of treaties signed after 1853, including the 1858 treaty with the Dakota, contained these provisions as a central feature. In seeking allotment of the Dakota reservation, Cullen brought to Minnesota this new priority in U.S. Indian policy.[27]

Cullen also proposed the sale of reservation lands that would not be, in his eyes, needed by the Dakota after allotment was completed. According to Cullen's calculations, because the land south of the Minnesota River sufficed for the Dakota's needs for farmland and woodland, reservation land north of the river could be acquired, with the proceeds going back to the Dakota for education and roads. This land would then be available for sale to white homesteaders. As a result of the 1858 treaty, then, the Dakota would control even less of their own lands and compete with even larger numbers of whites for the resources of the lands surrounding their now halved reservation.

Under such circumstances, it is not surprising that increasing numbers of Dakota adopted the sedentary, agricultural ways promoted and rewarded by civil and religious authorities. In reality, however, the "progress" and accomplishments detailed by authorities remained limited. First, much of the acreage reported as having been plowed and prepared for planting was, in fact, worked by agency employees who left the work of planting and tending crops to the Dakota. The latter, though, left many of those plowed fields unplanted, and the numbers themselves say nothing about whether it was men or women who cultivated the planted acres. Finally, while the number of houses was growing, the few hundred constructed by 1860 could only house a small portion of the approximately sixty-four hundred Dakota living in the region in the 1850s and early 1860s.[28]

Similarly, the numbers of pupils at schools and the numbers attending church and converting to Christianity remained low. As responsible stewards of ABCFM resources, Williamson, Riggs, and the other missionaries among the Dakota made annual reports to the organization, accounting for funds expended and noting the number of students attending their schools. Between 1836 and 1862, missionaries operated eight schools at different mission sites along the Minnesota River; none

of them, however, stayed open for more than three years. The largest
number of students attending all schools was 112 in 1852, but even at
that high point, only 35 students, on average, attended on any given day.
In 1862, some 68 pupils attended schools, with a daily average of 17.
The number of church members was comparably unimpressive, with
41 converts reported for 1841, growing to 83 for 1862, after twenty-five
years of conversion efforts.

In order to keep open the purses of those who funded their work, missionaries reported these small numbers with great pride and predicted
even greater rewards to come for their efforts. Missionaries could also
point to the success of their work when, in 1856, approximately a dozen
families of Christianized Dakota joined forces with an equal number of
mixed-blood families to form the so-called Hazelwood Republic, which
then elected its own president. So convinced was missionary Stephen
Riggs that the men in this group—who had all begun farming on allotted
lands—were on the path to civilization that he petitioned the federal government to grant them citizenship. By 1860, however, ongoing harassment by other Dakota led to the community's dissolution. As the short
life of the Hazelwood Republic made clear, whatever successes missionaries could claim were extremely fragile and limited.[29]

The great majority of Dakota resisted the vigorous efforts made to
transform them into a sedentary farming population. Most immediately,
this resistance manifested itself in Dakota women and men carrying out
their traditional subsistence strategies and upholding customary spiritual practices. Dakota resistance took more active forms as well, through
assaults on various manifestations of conversion to farming and Christianity. Other forms of resistance were far less overt, especially those of
women, who adopted some of the practices imposed upon them while
pursuing their customary ways.

One of the most visible reminders of the failure of civilizing efforts
was the Dakota's continued reliance on the hunt. Missionaries and
Indian agents constantly complained that Dakota men persevered in
their hunting, and nothing was more irksome to them than the buffalo
hunt. These expeditions took families away from their villages for days

and weeks at a time, leaving missionaries to bemoan the resulting empty schools, church meetings, and fields. "The nearness of buffalo," wrote Stephen Riggs to Indian agent A. J. Bruce in 1845, "has been unfavorable to the enlargement of cornfields." Hunting took women and children out of the reach of missionary influence and undermined efforts to transform Dakota men into farmers who tended their fields.[30]

Hunting also allowed men to provide their families with meat, hides, and other necessities. These fruits of the hunt gave the Dakota a measure—however slim—of independence from missionaries, federal officials, and traders and their provisions. At the same time, the hunt itself and the communal work it embodied reinforced Dakota customs and practices. Finally, the migratory nature of the buffalo hunt reaffirmed an entire worldview and way of life that were directly antithetical to a settled agricultural life. When Riggs wrote that the presence of buffalo was "unfavorable to the enlargement of cornfields," he was no doubt speaking quite literally, but his words hold more metaphorical meaning as well: as long as the Dakota could continue to hunt the buffalo and other game, they would not abandon the patterns of physical and spiritual survival that the hunt encompassed.

Dakota men also directly resisted efforts to turn them into farmers, expressing their discontent through assaults on the implements of those efforts. Horses and cattle were frequent targets of Dakota hostility, as were fields, fences, and farm tools. Dakota responses to incursions into their lands and livelihood were anything but random. When, according to agent Joseph Brown, a group of Dakota men "immediately after the surveys [of their reservation along the Minnesota River] were made, pulled up most of the stakes and threw down the mounds," these men were responding very purposefully to dire threats. They were condemning the division of their homelands into farms and the use of plows by Dakota men. Their tradition assigned care of the earth to women, and they saw steel implements as violating the sacred relationship between the Dakota and *Ina Maka,* Mother Earth.[31]

Even when Dakota men did accept European American farming practices, they did not necessarily adopt the attitudes and values the practices supposedly embodied. Instead, men used the fruits of farming to strengthen their own cultural practices and community ties. Such was the case described by Thomas Williamson, who wrote to Samuel Pond that "our Indians made more corn last year than for many years before, but consumed so much of it in Wakan feasts last winter that many of them have none now." Instead of storing up surplus, in the manner of European American farmers, these Dakota farmers used the abundance of their crops in ways that Dakota had always used food and other material resources: to celebrate life cycle events, to honor family members, and to give thanks for the bounties of the land. This traditional use of foods demonstrates that the Dakota adeptly integrated observances, customs, and products brought by missionaries and other whites into their own community's practices. It also suggests that evidence of Dakota assimilation to white norms might very well have masked ongoing traditional activity and resistance to white influences.[32]

The Dakota, for instance, sometimes integrated objects given to them by whites into their ritual displays of generosity. After the failure of the Eatonville experiment, Philander Prescott, who had remained in the employ of the Indian agency and persevered in his efforts to "civilize" the Dakota, reported in 1851 to Indian agent Nathan McLean that stoves provided to the Dakota for their newly built log homes had been absorbed into the gift economy: "The stoves you furnished them, some of them have been used and some not; one chief gave his stove away, and the probability is, that some of the rest will do the same thing." As a white man who had married into a Dakota family, Prescott knew this act was not one of ignorance but rather one manifestation of the persistence of traditional culture. He noted in the same report that "the manners and customs of the Indians are yet unchanged . . . There has been more conjuring and witch craft going on this summer than I have known for many years."[33]

While Prescott's comment about increased reliance on conjuring and witchcraft might have been more polemical than truthful, it is clear that throughout the missionaries' years in Minnesota, from the mid-1830s through the early 1860s, the Dakota resisted efforts to sever them from their culture. While they accepted medicines from missionary doctors or sometimes turned to them to set broken bones, the Dakota still sought out traditional healers in their communities who addressed both physical and spiritual dimensions of illnesses. They engaged those same healers for proper burial of their dead, maintained reverence for elders, and respected their own leaders.[34]

At the local level, leadership had traditionally been invested in the village's *itancan*. Changing patterns in the fur trade in the 1830s had led to a loss of these leaders' power, as traders abandoned relations based on familial obligations incurred through marriage to the daughters of village leaders and instead worked directly with individual hunters. Through the advent of annuities, however, some Dakota village leaders regained influence when federal officials selected them to distribute these cash payments. In whatever ways possible, they retained authority in their villages and challenged the white men seeking to exert exclusive control over the Dakota. Leaders warned that those who learned to read and plow would lose their abilities as hunters, would never fully be accepted into white society, and would be condemned to live as outcasts. Dakota leaders also warned that if their people followed the instruction of the missionaries, they would suffer both material and spiritual losses because the spirit beings that watched over and protected them would depart.[35]

Some leaders demanded compensation for resources that whites appropriated from Dakota lands. In a letter to Stephen Riggs, missionary Amos Huggins (son of missionary Alexander Huggins) complained vehemently about one Kangi Ojinca: "He has the most assurance of any body I ever knew . . . He spoke to me several times about feeding the headmen some because I am here in their country and burning their wood, & c." As late as 1862, this particular leader remained secure in his relations with intruders, his people, and other headmen. He still saw himself as a spokesman for his people and as a protector of their resources and interests.[36]

Most telling of their commitment to perpetuating their own values and practices were the Dakota's efforts to raise their children in customary ways. In the 1902 autobiographical narrative *Indian Boyhood,* Charles

Eastman wrote about his childhood from his birth in 1858 until the 1862 war disrupted Dakota life. Eastman's accounts are filled with stories he was told and lessons he learned from elders in his Wahpetunwan village and from his family, especially his uncle, who was "a strict disciplinarian and a good teacher." Eastman's education included the "legends of his ancestors and his race," the skills necessary for becoming a good hunter, and the diet that would sustain him as he carried out his responsibilities as a Dakota man. "I remember that I was not allowed to have beef soup or any warm milk," he wrote, because "general rules for the young were never to take their food very hot, nor drink much water." Dakota adults raised their children fully expecting them to follow Dakota ways and eventually pass them to their own children.[37]

Because Eastman's mother died at his birth, he was raised by his father's mother, his *uncidan*. Part I of *Indian Boyhood* focuses on life with his grandmother until he reached the age when the training of boys for their adult responsibilities was turned over to a male relative. Eastman's paternal grandmother lived in many ways as her grandmothers and many earlier generations of Dakota women had. She gathered medicinal plants and wild foods, she made her grandson's clothes and moccasins, and she put him in a cradleboard while she carried out those tasks. Eastman writes with great affection of his grandmother and the traditional upbringing that she gave him, starting in his infancy: "Whether I was made to lean against a lodge pole or was suspended from a bough of a tree while my grandmother cut wood, or whether I was carried on her back or conveniently balanced by another child in a similar cradle hung on opposites of a pony, I was still in my oaken bed."[38]

When March arrived, his uncidan, like other Dakota women, turned her attention to sugar-making, an activity of particular delight to children, who helped stir the boiling sap and tasted it until they could tell their mothers and grandmothers that it had achieved the desired consistency. Eastman most vividly recalls his family's last sugar-making in Minnesota, when his grandmother had to reprimand a group of young boys for carelessly playing around the fire and allowing their knives to touch burning embers, which was strictly forbidden among the Dakota.

Even as she was occupied with her own tasks, this woman reinforced the cultural lessons of her community, preserving both the teachings and the livelihood of the generations that came before her and passing them along to the next generations.[39]

Eastman's accounts, written at a remove of four decades, provide more fully developed and Dakota-inflected descriptions of the activities that missionaries bemoaned in reports to supervisors. In southern Minnesota, Dakota men continued to hunt buffalo and other game, rather than take up the plow, and women continued to gather foods and medicines, to accompany hunting expeditions, and, most irritatingly, to hoe their cornfields, even when those fields had been plowed by agency personnel explicitly for Dakota men to tend. In one particularly aggrieved report, Prescott—whose official title was "Superintendent of Farming for the Sioux"—conceded that he "cannot perceive any more industry among [Dakota men] than formerly . . . I have seen several walking about with an umbrella or a lady's parasol over his head, while his wife was hoeing corn under the burning rays without any protection."[40]

While Prescott depicts the women as drudges, an image that pervaded European and European American descriptions of Native societies, the men themselves seem to have been flaunting behavior they knew white observers would see as lazy and irresponsible. Nevertheless, Prescott's portrayal reflects, in many ways, the gendered nature of Dakota responses and resistance to efforts to change their work roles. Men's responsibilities to their families—primarily hunting and warfare—allowed them to retain their autonomy from whites and to enact more overt and aggressive forms of resistance, including attacks on property and the kind of display put on, no doubt, for Prescott's benefit. Women's roles in their families, on the other hand, allowed them greater contact and a wider range of relations with whites. As a result, Dakota women responded to whites' incursions into their lives in a more diverse and complex manner than men. On one hand, like men, they mostly ignored the entreaties and rewards offered for changing their ways and changing their beliefs, and they continued to tend the crops. Yet they did so while engaging with whites: women were more likely to attend and join churches than men and to establish ongoing relationships with whites. Still, when they took these steps, they largely did so in order to continue to fulfill their responsibilities as Dakota women and to protect their families and their culture.

To the never-ending chagrin of missionaries, the majority of converts to Christianity were women, as were the majority of those attending church and church-related meetings. In 1840, after a dozen years of exertion, the missionaries' annual report to the ABCFM noted that "no full blood Dakota man has yet to come into the church." This was of particular concern to the missionaries for two reasons: first, believing that Dakota men made decisions for their families, missionaries hoped converted men would bring their wives and children into the church and, second, missionaries wanted male converts who could be trained to become preachers and missionaries. Without larger numbers of male converts, progress, the missionaries feared, would remain excruciatingly slow.[41]

To a certain extent, the missionaries' greater success in attracting female converts reflected the fact that they made conversion easier for women. Missionary men who, by law and custom, were the all-powerful heads of their own households assumed that Dakota husbands and fathers had the same control. Women, therefore, could not be held responsible for their actions. As a result, missionaries tolerated behaviors in women that they would not tolerate in men. Male converts, for instance, were disciplined or even suspended from church for traveling on the Sabbath, but women were not. Men in polygynous (multiple-wife) marriages were not accepted into the church, but women were. Finally, while men had to take up farming in order to be converted, women were not required to abandon their work in the fields or other heavy labor.[42]

Because of their dual responsibilities for children and the family's small cornfields, women remained in their villages for much longer periods than men and were therefore more likely to have contact with missionaries, who carefully sited mission stations close to Dakota villages. Women could therefore see missionaries as resources for their families' survival. In years of bad harvests or bad hunts, for instance, Dakota women responded positively to the lure of extra food that missionaries offered churchgoers, converts, and children who attended schools. In June 1845, the students at the Traverse des Sioux missionary school received a pint of corn daily, along with instruction in reading and gender-specific manual labor. The corn probably encouraged women to send their children to school and perhaps to attend church themselves, especially when annuities payments were delayed, as they frequently were.[43]

Native women also used food to establish relations with missionary women that could benefit them in other ways. Mary Riggs seems to have been especially partial to strawberries but only as long as her pleasure did not interfere with her religious convictions. In a letter to her sister, written just one year after her arrival in Minnesota, Riggs tells her about how "a poor Dakota woman" had brought to her family some strawberries that she had gathered "at a considerable distance from this place." As the Dakota woman brought her gifts on the Sabbath, however, Riggs turned them away because she did not condone this kind of work on Sunday. The Dakota woman drew her own conclusions from this refusal, and Riggs wrote, "Though I have inquired several times for strawberries since, no one has brought any, all saying they grew a great distance off."[44]

Within her Dakota frame of reference, the woman had brought strawberries as an expression of generosity and as a gesture toward a relationship of mutuality. Knowing that Sundays were special days for whites, she might even have chosen to come on a Sunday, calculating that she would receive a better response from the white woman on that day. Mary Riggs's negative response, however, signaled to her and other Dakota women a refusal to engage. They, in turn, responded with their own refusal to engage. Fortunately for Riggs, Dakota women living around the mission at Lac qui Parle tried again the following year. This time Riggs reveled in the strawberries. Because she received the gift of fruit warmly, she was well supplied for the whole season with a delicacy she greatly appreciated.[45]

In the eyes of the Dakota, the acceptance of gifts obligated individuals to similar acts of generosity, and Dakota women who came into the houses of missionary women bringing fruit, rice, meat, or moccasins felt entitled to receive gifts in return. Consequently, when they saw items they needed or desired, women took them. Mary Riggs experienced this repeatedly. "We were constantly annoyed by thefts," she wrote her mother. "An ax or a hoe could not be left out of doors, but it would be taken. And in our houses we were continually missing little things. A towel hanging on the wall would be tucked under the blanket of a woman, or a girl would sidle up to a stand and take a pair of scissors." Riggs used the Dakota word *wamanonsa,* thief, to describe these women, but for them, bringing food or supplies to white women entitled them to goods that white women had and that they needed. By bringing food and supplies to white women, Dakota women were able to acquire tools and supplies for themselves and their families.[46]

In Dakota women's engagements with missionaries and other whites seeking to eradicate their culture and beliefs, they were able to create opportunities for themselves and to utilize both the missionaries' skills and activities and those they had learned from their mothers and grandmothers. The image that Mary Huggins Kerlinger creates in her memoir of Dakota girls sewing both with fabric and with hide in the missionary's house makes an apt metaphor for the ability of women to retain their ancestral identity at the same time they demonstrated evidence of hard work, discipline, and other indicators of "civilization."

Dakota men had no such options because farming required rejection of other subsistence pursuits. At the same time, the dearth of wild game and the invasion of hunting grounds by white settlers made alternatives to farming fruitless. Finally, the changes in appearance required of men who converted forced them to abandon ritual practices and beliefs as well as subsistence practices. With few of the options for occupying a middle ground that women in their families had, Dakota men were forced into far starker, more public choices.

Since the first conversions of Dakota men, missionaries had made a great show of cutting off the converts' traditional long hair. This was important symbolically to both the missionaries and the new converts. In the summer of 1859, when several prominent Dakota leaders conceded to stepped-up assimilation efforts by the Indian agent, Superintendent

Cullen personally cut their hair. This symbolism was not lost on those who sought to retain the beliefs and practices of their ancestors. One prominent leader, Taoyateduta, His Red Nation, tried to navigate between the traditions of his ancestors and the ways of whites, although he stead-fastly rejected both farming and Christianity. When Cullen suggested to him that he could "have his hair cut and put on pantaloons" without giv-ing up his beliefs, Taoyateduta rejected this notion: a Dakota man could not take up the clothing and work of a white man without relinquishing his beliefs, he told Cullen.[47]

This confrontation between Taoyateduta and Cullen took place in 1859, before a backdrop of drastically deteriorating conditions for the Dakota. Annuities resulting from the 1851 treaties had brought some improve-ments, but these were short lived, especially when annuity payments arrived late, as they did most years. Moreover, with the 1858 treaty, the Dakota had lost access to their last hunting grounds. While Dakota men continued to hunt off the reservation, white settlers poured in around them. At the same time, a new Indian agent, acting with the full support of the superintendent, began imposing on the Dakota a program of acculturation that was far more coercive than previous efforts. These developments combined to invigorate opposition to farming and Chris-tianity and to revive trading networks with Dakota peoples farther west.[48]

In 1857, Joseph R. Brown, a white man who had lived among the Dakota for more than three decades and had raised a large family with his Dakota wife, Susan Frenier, was named Indian agent for the Dakota. Within weeks of his appointment, he began planning what one historian has called "an agricultural revolution." Subverting the treaties that had put in place the system of annuities, Brown sought to make annuities a reward for building houses and fences and plowing fields, rather than a right earned by the sale of homelands. He put his plan into effect very quickly, and his successor, Thomas Galbraith, pursued it even more energetically.[49]

These aggressive new assaults prompted many young Dakota men to reaffirm commitment to their traditions and to revive practices that had fallen into disuse. According to interpreter Thomas Robertson, the son of a white trader and a Dakota woman who grew up among the Dakota, young men reestablished several long-inactive secret societies a year or two before the outbreak of the 1862 war. The Bear-Dance Society, the Buffalo-Dance Society, the Elk Lodge, and others had their own songs, dances, and secret rules and rituals. The Soldiers' Lodge, which had never completely disappeared, also gained new prominence. Historically, members of the Soldiers' Lodge, or Soldiers' Society, had organized hunting expeditions, and most of the young men who joined the revitalized groups had remained hunters. While these societies promoted adherence to traditional practices by encouraging feasting and dancing, they also became vehicles of opposition to conversion to Christianity, land cession, and policies created to force Dakota men into farming.[50]

Young Dakota warriors also turned to ritualized depredations to express their anger at the loss of their lands and assimilation efforts. Traditionally, the Dakota took revenge for insults by destroying property or slashing the tipi of the offending party. From missionaries' and Indian agents' earliest efforts at changing Dakota people, men had made these culturally sanctioned attacks on property. In the late 1850s these attacks escalated and began targeting white settlers rather than just missionaries, agency personnel, or Christianized Dakota.

By the summer of 1862, starvation sharpened the young men's anger, as did the annuity payments' delay caused by the Civil War, which began in 1861. The refusal of traders to extend any more credit to the Dakota or to open up their warehouses full of grain increased Dakota resentment and frustration. Tensions mounted, and confrontations erupted. Young men drew strength from their Dakota traditions, venting their frustrations at Dakota neighbors and relations who had turned to farming as well as at white agency officials, traders, and settlers. The incident that finally set off the war drew on all of the challenges facing the Dakota that summer and underlined the particular assaults made on Dakota men.[51]

In the frequently recounted incident that ignited the fighting, four young men had set out on a hunt to bring home food for their starving village. The countryside, however, was void of game. Hungry and thirsty, they stopped at a white settler's farm. Accounts differ regarding the ensuing confrontation between the hunters and the farmer, but by its conclusion, seven white settlers, including a woman and a young girl, lay dead.

White farmers had come to embody the major threats to Dakota men's existence: whites took over their lands and then chased away game with their fields. They trapped the remaining animals and sold the furs to white traders, further encroaching on the Dakota livelihood. Finally, these intruders refused to share their resources. In one incident, a farmer caught an abundance of fish from a river in plain sight of hungry Dakota but refused to share his catch. Although Dakota families had lived in proximity to whites for several decades, the Dakota had never abandoned their ethic of generosity and never understood or accepted that these interlopers did not share their values.[52]

When the hunters returned to their village after killing the family, it was members of the Soldiers' Lodge who took control and asked their leader, Taoyateduta, to go to war. Taoyateduta had taken on the name of his father and grandfather, Little Crow, when he had been selected by his community to succeed his father as leader of the village at Kaposia, downriver from Fort Snelling. The younger Little Crow was also a traditional healer who had resisted both farming and Christianity. When the Soldiers' Lodge came to him, its members followed Dakota protocol. While Little Crow himself believed that going to war against the United States would prove disastrous, his loyalty to tradition led him to accede to the warriors' entreaties to go to war.

This war, then, in which the Soldiers' Lodges would continue to play a significant role, stands as the statement by Dakota men desperately seeking to maintain their autonomy and reassert their roles in their society. These men had rejected entreaties to adopt a new way of life that could have fended off starvation because they had not been willing to give up the beliefs and practices that made them Dakota. In their eyes, as well as in the eyes of most white religious and civil officials, there were no halfway possibilities.

Decades of colonization had taken their toll on the Dakota. The arrival of missionaries, the decline of the fur trade, the signing of treaties, the establishment of a reservation, and the inexorable growth of the white population around them had made it impossible for the Dakota to continue as they had just a few decades earlier. These transformed circumstances, however, held different consequences for women and for men. Dakota and white expectations, values, and assumptions about women allowed them to move with some ease between their own world and the world of whites. Dakota and white expectations, values, and assumptions about men made this same fluidity impossible for men. Those who wanted to retain their Dakota roles stood at an impasse. Devastating as the decision to go to war would prove, it was, in the eyes of some Dakota men, the only option. The responses that women and men would make after the ensuing genocide would, in many ways, reflect the different circumstances they faced as their nation went to war.

CHAPTER 4

Separate Survival

THERE IS NO FANCY WORK REMAINING from the years immediately following the U.S.–Dakota War—no beadwork, no quillwork, no moccasins, no cradleboards. The genocidal actions of the federal government severed the Dakota from cultural expressions and everything but their most basic physical necessities. Men did not hunt. Women did not make quilled or beaded gifts for family members. Separated and imprisoned Dakota were condemned to four years of physical abuse, spiritual deprivation, and isolation from family members who would have eased some of the horror of their circumstances.

In a special address to the Minnesota legislature on September 9, 1862, Governor Alexander Ramsey vowed to destroy the Dakota, adding that "if any escape extinction, the wretched remnant must be driven beyond our borders." To implement Ramsey's plan, Minnesota paid bounties to whites who killed Dakota people and brought in their scalps as proof. Yet the actions taken against the Dakota in the years after 1862 were also more sustained and far reaching. Many of these fall within the definition of genocide established by the United Nations in 1946: "the denial of the right of existence of entire human groups." U.S. policy called for the deliberate attempt to eradicate Dakota culture.[1]

The years between the war's end and the establishment of the new Dakota reservation at Santee, Nebraska, embody one particular aspect of genocide: "imposing measures intended to prevent births within the group." This purposeful effort to destroy the Dakota by removing adult men from the rest of the population is perhaps unique even in the history of atrocities perpetrated against Native peoples in the United States. With adult men imprisoned in Mankato and then at Camp McClellan in Davenport, Iowa, and women, children, and elders interned at Fort Snelling and then at Crow Creek in the Dakota Territory, the Dakota would be unable to bring life to a new generation. Survival of the current generation was itself in question. Two thousand Dakota were taken prisoners at the end of the U.S.–Dakota War; only twelve hundred survived three and a half years later. By the time the two groups were reunited in Nebraska in 1866, nearly one half of their population had perished.[2]

Losses of this magnitude are impossible to grasp fully, and for several generations the experience was too difficult even to talk about. Cora Jones's great-grandmother, Pazahiyayewin, She Shall Radiate in Her Path Like the Sun, Ellen Kitto, had been moved to Crow Creek, but for many decades her family knew little about what happened there. "So many people wouldn't even talk about it after they left there," said Jones in 2007. "They didn't want to remember any of it. They didn't want to pass it on to their children because it was such horrible, horrible conditions." Those who spoke of it did so "in low, mournful tones," as Hannah Frazier did when she told her granddaughter about what the young woman's great-great-grandmother had endured. One hundred years after the events she heard about from stories, Hannah Frazier almost wept as she recounted them for her granddaughter.[3]

Ending the silence on atrocities poses daunting challenges and risks, but the traumas suffered by the survivors and their descendants require that the silence be broken. In the final years of the twentieth century and the first years of the twenty-first, the descendants of the Dakota who lived through the genocide of the 1860s have begun breaking the silence about the unspeakable experiences through ceremonies, memorials, marches, and other gatherings. Like the annual Yom Ha-Shoah commemoration of the victims of the Holocaust perpetrated by the Nazis and their allies against the Jews of Europe, these events serve powerful spiritual and emotional purposes. They allow survivors to reclaim their history and to give the victims of genocide the recognition, acknowledgment, and honor that their brutal deaths prevented.[4]

Recounting, studying, and understanding the experience of genocide asserts the humanity and dignity of those whom genocide sought to dehumanize and eradicate. Recognizing their humanity requires scrutiny of the victimization and the people targeted for destruction—those who perished and those who survived but watched others die. Understanding the experience of genocide among the Dakota involves one additional step: reckoning with the separation of husbands and wives, parents and children, the members of the *tiospaye* whose culture existed on a foundation of mutuality and reciprocity.

Throughout the years of separate internment, Dakota women and men were forced to exist apart from the families and communities they considered essential to survival. They had to cope with military defeat, loss of homelands, death, disease, exile, and incarceration while struggling on a day-to-day basis for physical survival without the support of their communities. Despite these difficult conditions, the Dakota endeavored to overcome the distances separating them, remain in contact, and provide each other assistance in whatever small ways possible. In order to do this, they sought help from whatever resources were available.

These resources, for the most part, came from the missionaries, who maintained a forceful presence among the Dakota in each place of their imprisonment. The cost to the Dakota was heavy, though. In order to transform missionaries from religious oppressors into allies for survival, the Dakota acquiesced to demands they had resisted for a quarter of a century: conversion to Christianity and all the reorganizing of their individual and collective lives that this required. In exchange, the Dakota received some degree of material assistance, but they received far more as well. Desperate to endure from one day to the next, the Dakota also fiercely sought to overcome the distances that separated them. After missionaries taught them to read and write, women and men at Fort Snelling and Mankato, Crow Creek and Davenport could share information and provide solace to each other. Knowing how to read and write also opened up avenues to actions previously beyond their reach, such as petitioning, requesting, and urging authorities to alleviate their suffering nearby and far away.

In the years of internment at Crow Creek and Davenport, men, women, and children endured systematic assaults on their lives and human dignity. Exploring as fully as possible the ways in which they resisted unrelenting attacks honors their struggle. At the same time, it is crucial to acknowledge aid given by missionaries who brought literacy and thus a lifeline in circumstances where no other was available.

The separation of men from their families started soon after the war ended, and with it began the violence and abuse that would characterize internment for the years to come. Approximately two thousand Dakota surrendered to Colonel Henry H. Sibley at Camp Release in western Minnesota on September 26 and in the following weeks. The warriors were disarmed and tried before a military commission—the first time this procedure was used against Native peoples in the United States, and an action of dubious legitimacy. Of the 342 Dakota men tried, 303 were convicted and given the death sentence following "trials" that lasted little more than a few minutes. The army then removed the warriors from the camp and marched them one hundred miles to Mankato. The warriors, who walked shackled to one another, were brutally attacked in New Ulm, and on the night of December 4, soldiers had to restrain a lynch mob headed to the camp where the men were being held. Soldiers rapidly built a new stockade in downtown Mankato. During this time, President Abraham Lincoln, weighing competing political demands, ordered the hanging of thirty-eight warriors and commuted the sentences of the remaining condemned men. On December 26, U.S. officials, surrounded by a cheering crowd of white Minnesotans, hanged the warriors in the largest mass execution in the history of the United States.[5]

In the days leading up to the hanging, families and friends had come for their final visit with the condemned. Some men sent messages to relatives being held at Fort Snelling in one last effort to sustain the bonds of family. Hdaiyanka, Rattling Wind, in one oft-quoted missive, expressed anger at the fate of his nation, but in the end his thoughts were with his closest kin. "My wife and children are dear to me. Let them not grieve for me," he wrote to his father-in-law, the chief Wabasha. "Let them remember that the brave should be prepared to meet death." Aware of the pain that his death would bring them, Hdaiyanka sought consolation for the wife and children who would be left without the emotional and physical resources he had provided them.[6]

In the succeeding days and months, the remaining men imprisoned at Mankato faced the uncertainty of their own futures. Chained together in the inadequate shelter, they subsisted on insufficient rations in conditions that would characterize the existence of all Dakota for the next three years. When these men finally left the prison in April, their first stop on the way to their next site of imprisonment was Fort Snelling, where they could see for themselves the camp to which their families had been confined over the winter.

After the surrender at Camp Release, the U.S. Army had first moved the women, children, and elders to the Lower Sioux Agency near Morton, Minnesota. Then, in November 1862, soldiers forcibly marched these prisoners in wind and cold, under the taunts and violence of white men and women in towns along the way, some 150 miles to Fort Snelling. The distressed group remained imprisoned there in an illness-infested enclosure throughout the winter, surviving on rations of crackers, flour, and salt pork. Grief compounded the physical distress that pervaded the crowded, cold, and dank camp that descendants of internees now call a concentration camp.

"The crying hardly ever stops," wrote missionary Stephen R. Riggs. "Five to ten die daily." There was no escaping despair or disease. According to Riggs, "About three acres of ground is enclosed with a board fence twelve to fourteen feet high having one gate where the guard is kept. In side of this there are more than two hundred *teepees* standing close together. It is a low flat place in parts of which the water stands . . . then the measles have swept over Minnesota . . . The great number of deaths occurring in the Indian camp now result from these things." Many did not survive this imprisonment. A census on December 2 counted 1,601

Dakota prisoners at Fort Snelling, but only 1,318 survived until May 1863, when the U.S. government removed the women, children, and elders from Minnesota entirely.[7]

Meanwhile, in Washington, DC, lawmakers were deciding the fate of Indians remaining in southern Minnesota. On February 16, 1863, Congress enacted harsh legislation that abrogated all treaties with the Mdewakantunwan, Wahpekute, Sisitunwan, and Wahpetunwan Dakota, dissolved their reservation, and terminated all other treaty rights. On March 3, Congress passed a law that, among other things, called on the president of the United States to establish a reservation for the Dakota beyond the limits of white settlement. Responding to white settlers' fears of Indians living close to their towns and farms, Congress also voted to remove the nearby Ho-Chunk (Winnebago), whom federal officials had relocated to a reservation southwest of Mankato just a few years earlier.[8]

The Dakota removal began on April 22, when the prisoners at Mankato, still shackled to one another, were loaded onto the steamboat *Favorite*, which first made its way down the Minnesota River to Fort Snelling. There, approximately twenty women and forty-eight men from Mankato were allowed to join the prisoners at the fort, and Dakota men and women had a brief opportunity to see each other, many for the last time. The report in the Davenport, Iowa, *Daily Democrat* highlighted the numerous uncertainties and anxieties of the moment: "Prisoners knew not but that they were going to their execution and that they were for the last time beholding their wives and children." The steamboat then carried the Mankato prisoners down the Mississippi toward Davenport, Iowa, arriving under cover of darkness in order to avoid arousing the local white population. Accompanying the prisoners were sixteen Dakota women (with four children) who would become the cooks and laundresses for the prisoners and soldiers at Davenport's Camp McClellan. From this camp on the river bluff, the prisoners a few weeks later watched as steamboats below carried their wives, sons, daughters, and parents down the river on their journey to Crow Creek on the Missouri River in Dakota Territory, where they would remain until their removal to Nebraska in 1866.[9]

Ironically, two of the steamboats, the *Davenport* and the *Northerner,* had recently transported up the Mississippi to St. Paul several dozen African-descended men, women, and children who had risked death escaping from slavery. Minnesota state leaders welcomed these refugees, in part because they would help relieve the labor shortage caused by the ongoing war in the South. This crossing of paths by two abused and vilified populations raises two issues concerning the historical moment in which it occurred. First, it serves as a reminder that the U.S.–Dakota War and its aftermath took place against the backdrop of the American Civil War. In what ways, one might ask, were Minnesotans' fears and anxieties about that war expressed in violence and hatred toward the Dakota? At the same time, the welcoming of one group on boats that would then forcibly carry away the other confirms the existence of two distinct racial ideologies. Popular thinking identified African Americans as labor to be exploited in the "free" North as well as in the slave South; it viewed Native Americans as obstacles to be removed so that whites could fulfill their "manifest destiny" and exploit Native lands. The arrival of freed slaves in Minnesota would facilitate this exploitation, while the forced removal of the Dakota from Minnesota finally accomplished what policymakers, businessmen, and settlers had been seeking for thirty years: unlimited access of whites to lands from which Indians drew their subsistence and their identity.[10]

When U.S. policymakers removed the Dakota as obstacles to white settlement in Minnesota, they placed them on lands where they would pose no such barrier to satisfying whites' hunger for land. After Congress revoked its treaties with the Dakota, federal officials charged the head of the Office of Indian Affairs' Northern Superintendency, which included Minnesota, with finding a new location for the Dakota along the Missouri River. This location was to be as far as possible from other Native peoples in order to avoid conflict among them, but it was also to be as far as possible from white settlers to avoid limiting white access to desired lands.[11]

The land that superintendent Clark Thompson selected for the Dakota lay two hundred miles upstream from Omaha, where the Crow Creek runs into the Missouri River. Under pressure from Minnesotans to expel the Dakota and take their lands, the federal government began shipping the Dakota out of the state before any accommodations could be made at the new location. Thompson was still staking out the boundaries of the new reservations when more than one thousand Dakota arrived on June 1, 1863. Three weeks later, close to two thousand Ho-Chunk also arrived. Little was in place to provide for the dispossessed Indians, who, after a winter of disease, hunger, and despair, had found themselves on a terrifying trip to an unknown destination.[12]

William Beane, the descendant of a survivor of the Crow Creek internment, has devoted many years to researching Dakota history. Among the most painful developments he has uncovered is that "hundreds of deaths . . . started soon after the journey [began]" and that the Dakota were prevented from giving their dead customary burials and were forced to leave them behind in makeshift burial grounds. As would be true for the next three and one-half years, the Dakota, who had already suffered extreme physical traumas, experienced additional suffering because they were prevented from taking part in practices that could help bring them some measure of spiritual reassurance.[13]

Accompanying the Dakota on this cruel journey to Crow Creek was John P. Williamson, son of missionary Thomas S. Williamson and a new Presbyterian minister and missionary among the Dakota. On May 9, Williamson wrote to his parents that a Dakota child had died the day before. The child "was buried last night at a wood yard." On May 25, he wrote in another letter that "there have been thirteen deaths, one man, three women, and nine children, and there are more very sick." The deaths continued well after the *Florence* reached its destination. When Williamson described the trip for a congressional commission in 1865, he testified that "for six weeks after they arrived at Crow Creek, they died at the average rate of three or four a day. In that time, one hundred and fifty died, and during the first six months two hundred of them died, and I think that at least one hundred of them died on account of the bad treatment they received after they left Fort Snelling." Disease and starvation at Fort Snelling, the horrors of the journey—which Williamson compared to the middle passage on slave ships—and the demands of life in the new internment camp took a devastating physical toll.[14]

Emotional and psychological suffering continued as well. "It must have been horrendous," remarked Beane, "to make a life in strange surroundings while daily mourning for the many that continued to die." Adding to the burden of grieving was the prohibition of traditional Dakota practices, including funeral rites. Forbidden from placing their dead on platforms or in trees, thereby allowing the spirit to depart the body in peace, the Dakota saw their departed loved ones buried underground, without the benefit of the prayers and ceremony that had soothed the spirits of the dead and consoled their survivors for generations.[15]

The surroundings in which the Dakota found themselves when they arrived at their destination could not have offered much comfort. In his report to the commissioner of Indian affairs, Thompson noted that the reservation site had "good soil, good timber and plenty of water," but he also noted that "on the hills the grass is already dried up." In any case, the departure of the boats from Minnesota left him little time to find a better site. As a result, the U.S. government relocated a people whose culture and way of life depended upon woodland lakes, rivers, and streams into a semiarid environment and climate ill suited to the subsistence skills and strategies that had sustained them along the Mississippi and its tributaries. Neither was the site suited for the agricultural subsistence that missionaries and Indian agents had attempted to force on the Dakota on the Minnesota River reservation.[16]

Nevertheless, a succession of Indian agents worked at Crow Creek to establish fields to be worked by the Dakota. Because they expected the Dakota to grow their own food, they made few plans for the internees' subsistence. What rations they provided were inadequate, and the meat and flour spoiled. The turmoil the Dakota endured was sharpened by the close presence of the Ho-Chunk, who blamed the Dakota for their removal from Minnesota and with whom the Dakota competed for extremely scarce resources.

Crow Creek was the third new place in as many decades to which the federal government had moved the Ho-Chunk. Following their removal

to Minnesota in 1846, they had established successful farms and rejected entreaties from the Dakota to join them in warfare in 1862. Nevertheless, after the war they were forced to leave behind crops, homes,
and livestock because, as Ho-Chunk leader Little Hill put it, "another
tribe of Indians committed depredations against whites." While they
did receive annuities at Crow Creek, conditions remained extremely
harsh, and not long after arriving, Ho-Chunk men began making canoes
out of cottonwood logs and paddling down the Missouri to take refuge
among the Omaha people. By the following summer, the majority of
Ho-Chunk had left Crow Creek, and a delegation of leaders initiated
negotiations with the Omaha, whom they considered to be their cousins.
The Omaha welcomed the Ho-Chunk, and in 1865 the federal government signed a treaty with the Omaha and established a new reservation
for the Ho-Chunk.[17]

The departure of the Ho-Chunk and administrative changes at the
agency overseeing the internment camp made modest improvements in
the Dakota's living conditions, but supplies remained inadequate. Fur-
thermore, whites profited from their misery. Wagons loaded with supplies at Mankato or Sioux City arrived half full, with rotting food, because
white men ruthlessly helped themselves to goods destined for the desperate Dakota. Peter Tapetatanka, Charging Bull, who was imprisoned
at Davenport, wrote of these conditions to Stephen Riggs, asking the
missionary for help: "When men in authority plan to distribute blankets among us, I want them to issue us some too . . . Our widows and
orphans are pitiful, so I would like for them to receive their fair share. As
it is, they give blankets only to themselves and do not handle the money
properly. This is why I need your assistance." However insufficient in
number the blankets were, they were even more so after "the men in
authority" helped themselves.[18]

White corruption only added to the unimaginable burden on Crow
Creek women, who struggled to meet the requirements of daily life for
themselves and their families. Inadequate nourishment, nonexistent
medical care, and insufficient supplies required them to expend inordi-
nate amounts of energy to keep themselves and their families alive.

Chores were made all the more burdensome by numerous deaths in the camp and by the near-absence of husbands and other male relations. Without the men, women who had grown up in a culture of complementary men's and women's work were forced to provide on their own for everyone.

The white population living close to the camp offered some opportunities to earn cash for buying food and supplies, but this work was physically demanding, especially for women suffering from inadequate food. Virginia Driving Hawk Sneve's great-great-grandmother, Maggie Frazier, was among those removed to Crow Creek. In *Completing the Circle,* a book about her family's history, Sneve writes that "Maggie and other young women labored so that their children and older relatives would survive. They cut and hauled wood to the saw mills, to the boatyard to feed the boilers of the steamships, and to the stoves of the white settlers in the area, for whom they also planted and harvested corn." Dakota women also found work at Fort Thompson, the military installation established at Crow Creek to monitor the Dakota. Maggie Frazier cooked there and did the soldiers' laundry. Elizabeth Columbus, Tawizicewa-kanwin, Sacred Incense Woman, also cooked for soldiers. She told her granddaughter Jeanette Weston that "there were twenty women working for them, you know. They cooked and everything."[19]

Dakota women also produced food themselves. They worked the fields established by the superintendent, and when drought, heat, grasshoppers, and unsuitable soil overwhelmed their efforts, they returned to more familiar ways of producing food: joining buffalo hunts and gathering edible plants. Although officials wanted to "civilize" the Natives by moving them away from their traditional subsistence, it was very quickly obvious that food supplies were insufficient to keep their wards alive.

Early in the first winter at Crow Creek, Mahpiyakahoton, one of the few able-bodied men at Crow Creek, escaped and found a herd of buffalo at the James River some 125 miles to the east. He asked John Williamson for help in convincing Thompson to provide a few rifles and allow the Dakota to go on a buffalo hunt. After several weeks, Thompson finally gave in to Williamson, and eight hundred Dakota, with limited supplies, ragged clothing, and threadbare tents, set out on the hunt. Women prepared the campsites and fed their families, and when the hunt proved successful, they prepared the meat and the hides as they had always done.[20]

Women also used their knowledge of plants to find food and medicines at Crow Creek. Although the pervasive drought made this more difficult, they were able to harvest fruits to dry for later use, as their mothers and grandmothers had in Minnesota for generations. According to Williamson, the women "had pretty plenty of berries for a little while," plus cherries and huckleberries to supplement meager rations and failed crops. In a letter to his fellow missionary Stephen R. Riggs, he noted that the Dakota could not live on the rations provided by the Indian agency if they didn't also pick "a few roots and every thing eatable." Because the Indian agent refused to engage the services of a physician despite repeated pleas by missionaries, women sought to combat pervasive disease by gathering medicinal plants. Ida Allen, whose grandmother survived the internment, told an interviewer in 1971 that "there were no doctors, and the Indians did the best they could with their Indian medicine."[21]

Desperate to keep their families alive, women endured horrific degradation. They scavenged what they could from the grain being fed to white people's animals, collecting "a little corn from the cavalry horses that passed through," Williamson wrote Riggs. Rod Steiner, a descendant of women imprisoned at Crow Creek, described even more desperate efforts that his grandmothers made: "Women would have to sift through horse manure to find enough grain to make soup."[22]

Despite women's heroic exertions, disease and death persisted. Of the thirteen hundred Dakota who arrived there in June 1863, just over one thousand had survived by the summer of 1865, when the new agent, James Stone, took a census of the internees. Historian Roy Meyer has speculated that "the death rate must have remained high even after the first six months, when casualties were heaviest," because they had no physician to ameliorate the worst of their health conditions until after the removal to Nebraska in 1866. Mae Eastman, another granddaughter of Crow Creek survivors, recalled learning that "almost every day, a

funeral procession left the camp for the cemetery on the hill outside."
Sixteen hundred Dakota were imprisoned at Fort Snelling in December,
1862; only thirteen hundred survived until the following May, when the
U.S. Army removed them to Crow Creek. Within two years, another
three hundred perished. The imprisoned Dakota were rapidly facing
extinction.[23]

Women at Crow Creek also faced the horror of sexual violence, the
one aspect of the internment that causes most anger and pain to their
descendants. Almost 150 years after the fact, Roy Steiner still seethed
about the sexual violation of his grandmothers and other women at
Crow Creek. "The soldiers raped [the women] and the women were
called filthy hags," he said in 2002 during a speech honoring the memory of those who died at Crow Creek.[24]

A journal kept by Colonel Robert W. Furnas from 1864 to 1866 provides evidence from a contemporary observer of the sexual abuse at
Crow Creek; it also explains the pervasiveness of the attitudes that
allowed rape and sexual assault to occur. Because Furnas was the commander of the Second Nebraska Volunteer Cavalry, his journal consti-
tutes an official account of the regiment's activity. In writing about his
unit's stop at Crow Creek, he noted that women "swarmed our Camp
from 'early morn to dewy eve,' their dusky forms frequently seen flit-
ting in the pale moonlight performing their 'rites' among the shrubbery
and stumps to a much later hour—filthy hags whose ugliness was only
equaled by their want of anything like modesty or virtue."[25]

Furnas's account reflects the pervasive European American assumption that Native women's bodies were, in the words of scholar Andrea
Smith, "sexually violable and 'rapable.'" Furnas, the leader of a military
unit, served as a model for the soldiers under his command. Because
he made no move to intervene in the abuse, he gave tacit permission to
rape Dakota women. The attitudes and behavior of these men, in turn,
signaled to other white men that violence was acceptable and even unremarkable. Furnas and his soldiers created a climate of sexual victimization that pervaded life at Crow Creek, as it did Indian-white relations
more generally.[26]

The climate of sexual victimization, coexisting with the lack of food and other necessities, forced women into impossible choices for themselves and for their daughters. David Faribault, Jr., Pelagie Faribault's grandson, worked as an interpreter for the U.S. Army in the years after the war. In 1865 he testified before a congressional commission investigating conditions: "I know of many such cases—women who were virtuous before they came here. Others, who had daughters, would sell them for something to eat . . . Numbers of women have left the agency and gone to Forts Sully, Randall, Wadsworth, the Yankton agency, and other points, to obtain their living." Faribault's statement starkly states the unbearable choices that those surviving the internment at Crow Creek faced: selling their own body or their daughter's body in order to keep their families alive.[27]

In *Maze of Injustice,* a 2007 report on the U.S. criminal justice system's responses to crimes of sexual violence against Native women, Amnesty International states that gender-based attacks on women "were an integral part of conquest and colonization." Across the United States, white men's sexually degrading views of women, combined with economic and military power over them, left Native women highly vulnerable to sexual exploitation. At Crow Creek, the vulnerability of women was heightened by the near-absence of able-bodied men. With only a small number of men available to help acquire supplies and protect them against sexual assaults, women were forced to take more risks to feed their families. Of the 1,043 Dakota that James Stone counted at Crow Creek in 1865, more than nine hundred were women and children.[28]

The challenges of survival at Crow Creek were heightened further by uncertainty about the future. Not knowing if or when they would be reunited with the men held at the Davenport prison camp or if they would be removed again made the women's existence at Crow Creek even more precarious. Similar uncertainties pervaded the prison camp at Davenport, adding to the suffering of the prisoners there. Not only did the Dakota not know what their fate would be, but those responsible for implementing it were equally ignorant. Nobody knew what would be done with this defeated and dispossessed population, neither the

soldiers guarding the prisoners at Crow Creek and Davenport nor the
commanders nor civilian personnel. With the United States still engaged
in civil war, the future of fifteen hundred Dakota was hardly a priority for
policymakers.[29]

While material conditions at Davenport were perhaps neither as physically harsh nor as degrading as at Crow Creek, they nevertheless caused
physical and psychological suffering. When Dakota prisoners first
arrived at Camp McClellan, two and one-half miles upriver from Davenport, they walked one hundred feet up the steep bank to a two-hundred-
square-foot enclosure surrounding the four buildings in which they
would live for the next three years. These had been built as barracks
for U.S. soldiers, but the bunks had been removed. Prisoners slept in
two buildings, 140 of them in structures built to house a hundred.
Women and children slept in a building that also served as a hospital for
the prisoners, and the fourth building became a guard house. "Outside
the fence and four feet from the top," wrote a reporter in the Davenport
Daily Democrat, "is a staging running clear around, on which the sen-
tries run."[30]

The degradation of the Dakota at Davenport began with the presence
and role of the small number of women among the male prisoners.
The women were there to cook, clean, and wash for the prisoners, who
were probably relatives, but they did so under the watch of soldiers.
These women were therefore exposed to the same sexual exploitation as
their sisters at Crow Creek. "They are treating the women terrible," prisoner Robert Hopkins wrote to Stephen Riggs. "They do not let them
sleep." Like the small number of men at Crow Creek, the incarcerated
men at Camp McClellan were unable to protect the women from soldiers' harassment and assaults.[31]

The prison camp commander deliberately created a dehumanizing
environment. He openly stated that "if it was in his power he would have
them all hung before sunset," and he tried to prevent missionaries from
visiting the prisoners. He oversaw the construction of a prison camp that
turned them into creatures to be gawked at and exploited. The fence
around the camp was built with holes so that local whites could peek and

observe these "wild savages." Whites could also obtain passes "to inspect the prison of the savage tribe," and some took the opportunity to "pet the animals." Even the work imposed on the prisoners was organized to rob them of their dignity and humanity. According to Levi Wagoner, a resident of Davenport who recollected the scene decades later, camp officials compelled the men, "under a strong guard, to perform all the drudgery that could be invented in and about Camp McClellan." The prisoners swept the camp with "whatever would make a clumsy broom, and the order of sweeping must be done in military style." They also supplied the camp with wood from a woodyard down a steep hill. The sight of the Dakota carrying the wood up the hill reminded the observer "of the pack trains that we read of in ancient Asia, the only difference is in the latter being carried by mules and camels while the former named carried the wood under the supposed name of men."[32]

Like slaves in the American South, Dakota prisoners worked with such inadequate food and clothing that they had to perform additional labor in order to earn cash for food and necessities. Camp McClellan was a place where Union soldiers prepared to fight against the slaveholding Confederacy, and the Rock Island prison across the river held Confederate soldiers taken prisoner. At the same time, white Union soldiers held the Dakota in conditions similar to those endured by slaves in states the soldiers were fighting. Conditions for Confederate soldiers across the river were reportedly harsh, but military officials accorded them proper burials and grave markers. No such dignity was granted to the dozens of Dakota prisoners who died over the three years of internment at Camp McClellan.[33]

Letters written by Davenport prisoners to missionaries convey some of the magnitude of the losses the prisoners experienced. Hewanke, Frost, lost a brother and a cousin in the mass hanging at Mankato, and one of his children died at Fort Snelling. "And then at this place where we came," he continued, "my brother, Walks in the Midst, he died here. And one of my uncles, he died too. He was my father's youngest brother. And one of my brothers-in-law died too. Thunder Killer is his name. Those three died here. Six of my relatives died. One of my relatives, we are the last ones to be alive together. So that is why I am now sad all the time."[34]

In the second year of internment, prisoners were allowed to leave the deadly enclosure to work on nearby farms and in town, which, in some cases at least, provided a measure of respite from the dehumanizing camp conditions. Some prisoners converted and even took the Christian names of their employers. David Weston, according to his great-granddaughter Ellen Weston, took the name of a farmer for whom he had worked, in gratitude for the good treatment he had received from him. More commonly, however, prisoners worked hard for Davenport citizens happy to have access to very cheap labor.[35]

The people of the city were also pleased to have local suppliers of Indian-made "trinkets." Prisoners collected clam shells along the river's edge and carved them into items that Dakota women sold in town. According to missionary Stephen Riggs, they "often drove a brisk trade in rings, birds, fishes, crosses and other ornaments they made from the muscle [sic] shells of the Mississippi." It would appear that the craze for collecting Indian-made goods extended even to items created by men believed to have committed heinous crimes. However cruel and morbid this interest, it nonetheless enabled prisoners to earn a few pennies to buy food or tobacco.[36]

At Crow Creek, on the other hand, women seem to have ceased making decorated hide items of all sorts. The demands of survival were such that they had little or no reserves of physical energy to carry out this work and none of the necessary materials and implements. They also lacked the critical social and cultural environment that had supported their creative work in Minnesota and that would later support it on new reservations. The creation and decoration of clothing and other items was a collective effort that required the labor of men as well as women. The women at Crow Creek no doubt tanned and used the hides of buffalo killed in the hunt, but the small number of men and strict regulation of their behavior made hunting expeditions infrequent and, consequently, hides rare. Moreover, work with beads and quills and other adornment grew out of the needs and practices of a living community:

women made their most beautiful work to celebrate and honor life, prowess, and individual and communal accomplishments. Life at Crow Creek allowed no such moments. Women who endured rape and dug through horse manure for grains of food could hardly celebrate the arrival of a new baby.

In the third year of internment, Wicacaka's daughter Emma gave birth to a daughter, whom she named Winona, as was Dakota custom for first-born daughters. The father, a white soldier named Wheeler Hoffman, called her Mary. He would soon leave the area and eventually become a successful businessman and politician in Montana. Unlike other soldiers who fathered children with Native women, however, Hoffman acknowledged his daughter and gave her his name. Seeing the dismal conditions under which his daughter would have to survive at Crow Creek, he wanted to take her with him when he left to return home.[37]

One can only imagine the wrenching dilemma that Emma, Wicacaka, and their relations faced. Should they let the baby have a more materially comfortable life among white people and never see her again, or keep her and possibly condemn her to death? Such cruel choices faced the Dakota on a daily basis throughout their internment. Even the arrival of new life could not evince individual rejoicing or the communal celebrations by which the Dakota had, in their homelands, marked births and other life cycle events. Still, Emma refused to part with her daughter, and with her mother and other Dakota women she raised her and preserved one Dakota tiospaye.

Emma's decision to keep her daughter provides moving testimony to the determination to survive that characterized the Dakota imprisoned at Crow Creek and Davenport. In the commitment they made every day to sustaining themselves and each other, they experienced unspeakable indignities. They also sought assistance from the only people showing any positive interest in them. Unlike other whites, who seemed only to want to exploit and exterminate them, missionaries offered incarcerated Dakota assistance, albeit with very long strings attached. The Dakota accepted those offers and even in their early internment at Fort Snelling and Mankato began to convert to Christianity in large numbers. The

missionaries who had followed them from their communities along the
Minnesota River were elated at the number of women and men finally
responding to their teachings and encouragement.

Soon after the 1862 incarceration of the warriors in Mankato, Thomas
Williamson and his sister, Jane S. Williamson, traveled regularly, sometimes on foot, the fourteen miles from their home in St. Peter to visit
the prison. The men seemed to welcome the missionaries, and many
attended their worship services. As the date of the mass execution approached, Stephen Riggs wrote a few years later, "There was manifested
more than usual religious interest." This interest intensified after the
mass hanging, and Williamson called upon his longtime fellow missionary, Gideon Pond, to assist him in conversions. In a single day, February 3, 1863, Pond and Williamson baptized 274 Dakota men. Even this
religious zeal, however, failed to lessen the physical burden of captivity.
According to Pond, "They came one by one," to be received into the
church, most wearing "chains on their ankles."[38]

Missionaries took great pride in the numbers of converts they made
among the 322 prisoners at Mankato. By April 10, Williamson reported,
"The number baptized by Messrs. Riggs, Pond and myself, in Mankato,
is 305 or 306; to whom we may add 8 baptized in infancy, and 3 received
to the communion of the church on profession of their faith." These
men, each with close to three decades of Dakota missionary work, knew
that some of these men converted in efforts to gain release from captivity. Still, they firmly believed that the men would "never go back to
where they were before. Their old superstition is dashed to pieces, like a
potter's vessel." They were, no doubt, gratified to learn that the prisoners' religious enthusiasm was so vocal that one journalist said when the
steamboat carrying the men to Davenport passed Fort Snelling and St.
Paul, he heard them singing Christian hymns.[39]

Missionaries including John Williamson and Episcopalian Samuel D.
Hinman, who had established a mission at the Lower Sioux Agency just
two years before the war, took equal pride in their accomplishments
at Fort Snelling. When Riggs visited the camp, he witnessed large prayer
meetings held in tents and warehouses, some with three to five hundred

Dakota in attendance. By the spring of 1863, Williamson had baptized 140 Dakota at Fort Snelling and Hinman 144. Father Augustin Ravoux, a Catholic priest who did not remain at the camp, baptized 184. The Catholic Church did not maintain a strong presence among the Dakota, so it is likely those baptized Catholic either subsequently joined one of the Protestant churches or did not remain in the church.[40]

When U.S. officials removed the Dakota from Fort Snelling to Crow Creek, Williamson and Hinman continued to minister to them during the journey. Once at their destination, they resumed prayer meetings and baptisms and set out to acquire the lumber necessary to erect buildings for their congregations. Both men reported significant successes in their efforts. In a letter to Bishop Henry Whipple in Minnesota, Hinman wrote after six months at Crow Creek, "About two thirds of the Indians are under our influence." In 1865, Williamson told the congressional commission investigating conditions at Crow Creek that the Presbyterian church there numbered "about two hundred communicants, who mostly joined the church about the time of removal and along at times since then." Responding to a question about "the religious condition of the Indians," he told the commission that "attendance at the religious services is quite good; the church is always full; it will seat about two hundred."[41]

Hinman and Williamson also set out very quickly at Crow Creek to establish schools to advance their conversion work. Williamson was joined by four assistants: Edward Pond, son of Gideon; Pond's new wife, Sarah Hopkins, daughter of Dakota missionary Robert Hopkins; and Hugh and Mary Cunningham, who also had done missionary work. Together they were able to open a school within just a few months, and in Williamson's report to the Indian agent the following August, he stated that more than one hundred had learned to read and approximately thirty had mastered the skills necessary for writing "legibly." Following in the footsteps of his father and his father's associate Stephen Riggs, he and his colleagues taught in the Dakota language.[42]

Williamson and his missionary cohorts marveled at the eagerness of the Dakota to learn to read and write, which had first manifested itself during internment in Minnesota. In the prison camp at Mankato, the few who were literate began instructing others, and the desire for this knowledge caught on rapidly. An ecstatic Riggs described the scene: "During the whole winter that followed, any one going into the prison in the daytime could see these groups scattered all over, around little fires, made on the earthen floor, and all diligently engaged in learning to read and write . . . And the desire to learn was so contagious, that almost every man in prison, except a few who were too old, and some who had very sore eyes, made the attempt. Their progress was very rapid."[43]

This enthusiasm for learning was also on display at Fort Snelling, which, in the words of Stephen Riggs, "turned into a great school, and almost every tent is a classroom." In this great educational rapture, every individual, adult and child, who already knew the alphabet was "almost by force turned into a teacher." For Riggs, this was truly "a revolution in letters."[44]

Williamson reveled in these accomplishments. As he expatiated on the advancing literacy of his flock, however, he revealed the real motivation for the Dakota learning their ABCs: "In less than three months, the majority of [the men at Mankato] had learned enough to be able to write letters down to their families at Fort Snelling." Seemingly unaware that the prisoners' agenda for learning to read and write might not entirely coincide with his own, he boasted that the men's letters to their families "exhort[ed] them to learn also." Learning to read, both for missionaries and for federal officials, indicated that the Dakota were on the path toward civilization. For the Dakota, however, learning to read and write had a far more immediate reward: they could now remain in contact with one another through the mail and across the distance that separated them.

By all accounts, the Dakota made voluminous use of this means of communication. The Mankato *Weekly Record* reported in the spring of 1863 that the prisoners "are great letter writers, and from one to two hundred are weekly written to their friends at Fort Snelling and elsewhere." This epistolary outpouring continued when the men were removed to Davenport and the women, children, and elders to Crow Creek. Williamson reported sending one hundred letters each week to Davenport in the early months of the internment at Crow Creek, and when Hinman, the Episcopalian missionary, traveled between the two camps, he also carried letters for the Dakota.[45]

The mere occurrence of this letter writing is of immense significance. Acquiring paper, pens, and stamps, like acquiring other life necessities, required effort, and finding the time and energy to do so, when merely surviving from day to day was a victory, demanded still more from the Dakota at Crow Creek and Davenport. Clearly, the need to communicate with each other outweighed all these obstacles.

Literacy allowed the imprisoned Dakota to overcome, in a very small measure, the distance between them. Letters could not compensate for the physical, emotional, and spiritual burdens of separation, and letter writing could in no way re-create a living community among the Dakota. It did, however, give them knowledge about relatives several hundred miles away. With the centrality of tiospaye among the Dakota, communication through letters allowed for some fragmentary nurturing of familial bonds. Yet letters between prisoners also contained news of the horrific conditions endured in each camp. None of the letters between Dakota men and women survive, but letters that Dakota men at Davenport sent to missionaries are held among their papers. These letters leave no doubt that prisoners at the different sites knew of each others' circumstances. "The women and children are very hungry," wrote Elias Ruban, Ohanwayakapi, They See His Actions, to Stephen Riggs in November 1864.[46]

For prisoners at Davenport, the suffering of the women and children at Crow Creek was also their own, as Wasteste, Good Good, wrote in a letter to Riggs around the same time: "Because someone said they were very hungry, we are starving to death this winter. For that reason, I am very sad." Joseph Napesniduta, He Does Not Flee Red, wrote from Davenport that "we who are at the Muddy Waters [Missouri River] are having a difficult time." The terseness of the Dakota language—and, perhaps, the awkwardness of expressing themselves for the first time in writing—highlights the starkness of conditions the men report and the feelings they express.[47]

While we do not know what these men wrote to their families at Crow
Creek, they must have unavoidably communicated the harsh conditions
of their imprisonment. Still, the women wanted desperately to hear from
their husbands. Just a few weeks after arrival there, Kaskawin gave John
P. Williamson a pair of moccasins so that his father, Thomas Williamson, would in turn give her husband at Davenport "some stamps so that
he write to there whenever he wanted." Communication with her husband was so precious that Kaskawin was willing to pay for it with what
must have been some of her last remaining possessions.[48]

One prisoner at Camp McClellan sent Williamson twenty dollars
from his meager earnings to give his wife at Crow Creek, and another
sent him ten dollars. Yet even with few material resources to share, the
Dakota frequently asked missionaries to intercede on behalf of family
members. In a letter written in the hand of Samuel Hinman, Sarah F.
Marpihdagawin asked Bishop Henry Whipple for his assistance in getting land for her son in Minnesota. Having lost everything in the war,
she wanted her son to have "some land he can call his own" and she
wanted to "once more look upon the faces of our relatives in Minnesota."
In an undated letter from the Davenport prison camp, Wambdi Tanka,
Big Eagle, asked Riggs to testify in behalf of his brother Wakanozanzan,
Medicine Bottle: "My relative, I now want you to help me with one thing.
When my brother is made to testify, and they seek a truthful man and
you are among them . . . I want you to speak fairly on his behalf. This
is what I am requesting of you."[49]

Other men implored missionaries for personal help. Zenas Maza-
wakinyanhiyaye, Iron Flying By, asked Riggs to "go to where my older
sister Stands on Cloud lives to get me the shoes and coat. I want you to
bring them to me." A prisoner who signed his letter Iyozanzan, Light,
asked the missionary to send a letter to the "head soldier who takes care
of us," telling him that "I need a medicine man [doctor]."[50]

Many of these letters addressed the missionaries as relatives, as
Wambdi Tanka did, and began or ended with a reaffirmation of the letter
writer's faith in the powerful missionary's god. Augustin Frenier asked
Riggs to give him one dollar while he waited for money coming from his

father, but before getting to this request, he assured Riggs that "the holy spirit has pity upon me and I am not hurting any place." He also informed Riggs that "I pray to god for you." When Marpihdagawin made her request to the Episcopalian bishop, she began the letter by expressing gratitude to Whipple for having visited Fort Snelling and baptized her family, and she assured him of her continuing Christian faith.[51]

Some have suggested that the Dakota's conversion to Christianity was a gesture made within a culture of reciprocal relations among extended family members. By acceding to missionaries' entreaties, the Dakota accepted the religious men into their network of family relations and then expected actions or gifts in exchange. If this was indeed the case, requests made by Marpihdagawin, Frenier, and others reflect their expectation that the men they were petitioning would meet their request because they were kin and because the letter writers had fulfilled their reciprocal part by adopting Christianity. Without questioning the sincerity of the Dakota who converted, it is still possible to see conversion as a means for them to achieve their own ends of maintaining contact with relatives and trying to alleviate their suffering. Under dehumanizing conditions, these men and women nevertheless acted upon Dakota conceptions of dignity and human decency. Rather than approaching missionaries as submissive petitioners, they addressed them as equals, making clear what they brought to the exchanges they were seeking.[52]

The men imprisoned at Camp McClellan engaged in their own actions to defy their dehumanization. In March 1865, prisoners submitted a petition to President Lincoln asking him to "unite us all and send us to our kindred." They expressed gratitude to Lincoln for sparing their lives, confessed that "we did wrong," and thanked him for giving them food and shelter "and to our kinfolks the women and children also." However, they continued, those relatives were now facing starvation: "Our kindred write letters to us and tell us they are suffering for want of food." Because many had already died, the Dakota desperately wanted to be reunited with those who remained alive. In petitioning Lincoln for their freedom, they sought the ability to alleviate their families' suffering and in this way abide by their responsibilities to them. Through this petition, however, the prisoners also asserted their own humanity, which, in turn, helped them to survive their ordeal at Camp McClellan.[53]

When Primo Levi wrote about surviving a year in the World War II concentration camp at Auschwitz, he emphasized the importance of maintaining his dignity as a human being amidst the degradation and assaults of life in the concentration camp. By petitioning President Lincoln, by making requests of Bishop Whipple, and by learning to write in order to remain in contact with one another, the Dakota similarly worked to preserve their humanity and dignity. By acting upon the values and the knowledge that made them Dakota, the women at Crow Creek and the men at Camp McClellan defied the genocidal efforts to eradicate them and their culture.[54]

CHAPTER 5

Dakota Tradition at Santee and Flandreau

AROUND 1900, JOHN AND MARY JANE EASTMAN posed for a family portrait with six of their eight children and their dog. Showing all attired in their Sunday best, the photo suggests a comfortable family well-versed in the conventions of middle-class American culture. One detail, however, suggests a more complicated relationship to American culture: the beadwork ornamentation on Mary Jane's dress. One can imagine an auntie or another woman in the Dakota community at Flandreau, South Dakota, creating this beautiful decoration to honor Mary Jane, just as generations of Dakota women who created beautifully ornamented garments had done. For this particular piece of work, the artist selected a pattern of leaves and vines characteristic of Eastern Dakota beadwork and quillwork. When Mary Jane, the granddaughter of Pelagie Faribault, wore this dress, she honored the woman who had decorated it and the women's traditions it represented.

Yet weighing against the joys of producing this beadwork for an honored relation was the horror-filled history that the women shared and the unimaginable pain of trying to reconstruct a community after nearly half of its members had perished. When the Dakota were reunited after three and a half long years of separation, they faced the task of reestablishing relationships, families, and a functioning community that could provide materially, emotionally, and spiritually for its members.

Wrenched from their homelands, denuded of their belongings, and grieving for their dead, the Dakota also faced an entire new set of challenges, both immediate and long term. When federal officials moved them from Crow Creek and Davenport to Santee in present-day Nebraska, issues of land tenure and subsistence remained. Their recent conversion to Christianity challenged past Dakota practices. People faced difficult choices about their lives, their identity, and their culture. How to rebuild them despite the grief of the years of war and internment? How to reconstruct communities and raise new generations under the new circumstances they faced?

The beadwork on Mary Jane's dress suggests some of the ways in which they answered these questions. Despite the pervasive presence of missionaries and U.S. officials who pressed the Dakota to abandon ancestral traditions, men and women found avenues for perpetuating the customs by which generations had ordered their lives before the cataclysm

The John and Mary Jane Faribault Eastman Family, Flandreau, South Dakota, c. 1900.

of war and displacement. Even those who pledged their faith in the church found ways, as Mary Jane Eastman did, to retain and proclaim Dakota identity.

The devastating experiences at Davenport and Crow Creek were immediately compounded by new uncertainties at Santee. In March 1865, the U.S. Congress had appointed a joint special committee to investigate conditions on new reservations. The committee that visited Crow Creek that fall subsequently issued a report urging the commissioner of Indian affairs to move the Dakota to a location better supplied with timber and more suitable for farming. Six months later, after another long and deadly winter, federal officials removed the surviving families to Santee, one hundred miles down the Missouri River from Crow Creek. Around the same time, the prisoners at Davenport were also transported there. Consequently, when Dakota families were finally reunited, it was in a place that was new to all.

The Santee location, moreover, was riddled with problems. Federal officials had selected sparsely timbered land that had already been opened up to white settlers. Although the government proposed to compensate them for their land and crops, the Dakota arrival raised a storm of protest from settlers who also complained that Indians were committing depredations on their property. The settlers' congressional representatives in Washington pushed hard to have the Dakota removed across the Missouri River into the Dakota Territory, an area which, on the positive side, also had more timber.

As a result, a few months later federal officials moved the Dakota once again, approximately four miles downriver, but debate over the extent and location of the reservation would continue until August 31, 1869, when President Ulysses S. Grant signed an executive order establishing the boundaries of the reservation. By then, the continuing effects of malnutrition and the Dakota's depleted health had reduced their population to about one thousand.[1]

Adding to these disorienting experiences was the new name the U.S. government now used to identify the Dakota in Nebraska. While the majority of survivors of the Crow Creek and Davenport incarcerations were Mdewakantunwan and Wahpekute Dakota, officials began referring to them exclusively as "Santee." While this name derives from the name Isanti or Isanyati used by Titunwan peoples east of the Missouri to refer to the Minnesota Dakota, it was not a name the Dakota had used to identify themselves.[2]

In a document submitted to the U.S. Senate committee on Indian affairs in 1896 supporting legislation providing assistance to the Dakota, Reverend James Garvie, a Dakota man born in Minnesota before the 1862 war, asserted that "the Indians themselves do not know how [the name change] came about." Given Garvie's continuing dismay thirty years later, one can only imagine how the Dakota felt hearing themselves referred to in this way, in the midst of all the other confusions in their lives.[3]

Among these dislocations were changes in marital relationships among the removed Dakota. While living under the guidance of missionary Thomas Williamson, the prisoners at Davenport had converted to Christianity, and when they rejoined their families at Santee, they remained committed to living by Christian doctrine and teachings. Among the practices they rejected was polygyny—one husband with several wives—which had previously enabled the Dakota to cope with gender imbalance in their communities.

Prior to conversion to Christianity and exile, single women had been a rare exception among the Dakota, as among other Indigenous peoples. They nevertheless had had a place in Dakota villages. Women who did not marry remained with their families and looked after parents. A married woman who had borne children faced more difficult times if her husband died, but she would customarily become the wife of her husband's brother. He would take her in and raise her offspring as his own, regardless of whether he already had one or more wives.[4]

This integration of widows and orphans into other family groups was no longer possible with Christian monogamy, which created a whole group of marginalized "put-away" wives. These women now had to rely on the generosity of relatives, who themselves faced desperate material conditions. At Santee, former Davenport internees dissolved their marital relationships with all but one of the wives they had taken before the war. As a result, women who had lived through the traumas at Crow Creek, sustained perhaps by the hope of being reunited with husband and family, now found themselves adrift, relying on a community that had no place in its structure for adult women with children but no husband.[5]

Maggie Frazier was one of those women. When her husband John Frazier was released from prison and went to Santee, he married his second wife, Jennie, and returned to Minnesota with her and their children. This left Maggie, his first wife, who was pregnant, and their three children, Star, Mary, and Charles, behind at Santee. Maggie was extremely fortunate: her brother, Artemus Ehnamani, took her and her children into his home and helped her find employment at the mission. Most other put-away wives were far less fortunate, and the difficulties of supporting themselves and their children added to the burdens they carried from exile and internment.[6]

At the same time, women at Crow Creek who might have expected never to see their husband again had, in the years since their separation, established relationships with other men for companionship, physical assistance, and respite from despair. Not committed to the Christian notion of marital fidelity, they perhaps expected to return to their husbands when possible. Upon learning of these other relationships, however, the recently Christianized and released Davenport internees turned to their new religious leaders to seek divorces and new marriages. "When the men came home from the prison the men generally went immediately to the tents of their old wives," John P. Williamson wrote to fellow missionary Alfred Riggs in 1872. "Afterwards many of them found that during their imprisonment the women had been unfaithful, and they left them and wished to be married to others." Dakota men were granted divorces by the missionaries, although the latter were loathe to encourage divorce among their flock. Conflicting and evolving views on marital relationships became a profound emotional and practical challenge the Dakota faced in rebuilding their community.[7]

In order to ensure that the newly reestablished and reconfigured families remained steadfast in their commitment to the church, missionaries rapidly established schools and churches on the reservation. In 1867, Samuel Hinman, the Episcopalian missionary who had worked among the Dakota in Minnesota and lived for a time with them at Crow Creek, reported to federal officials the establishment of a school which employed, in addition to himself, five "American" teachers and four Dakota teachers. Not to be outdone, Presbyterian minister John Williamson noted that his mission, which consisted of himself and three other missionaries supported by the American Board of Commissioners for Foreign Missions (ABCFM), had completed a "temporary log school-house" for their educational endeavors. By 1870 the ABCFM mission had new buildings in place and was poised to establish the Santee Normal Training School, "a normal academy for the training of native teachers." Meanwhile, the Episcopalians had set up a mission complex that included a school, a mission house, a stone church building, and a hospital.[8]

While these new institutions sought to guide Santee residents toward Christian lives, agency personnel went to work clearing land for fields, building houses, and importing tools and supplies necessary to create the agricultural community envisioned by Indian affairs officials and missionaries alike. Indeed, within a year of the removal of the Dakota to Santee, agency officials had already taken substantial steps in this direction. In his 1867 report to the commissioner of Indian affairs, the northern superintendent noted that he had purchased 140 horses for the Dakota and was requesting money for two hundred more. He had also arranged for the purchase of three hundred head of cattle. J. M. Stone, the government's Indian agent for the new reservation, reported in the same year that 195 acres of corn had been planted and that he had hired a farmer and a blacksmith for the agency. By 1870, there was a sawmill and a flour mill as well.[9]

In order to carry out the "civilizing" plans of the federal bureaucracy, agency personnel sought out former village leaders in Minnesota and relied on them for help in distributing rations and equipment. This circumvented the selection of new leaders by members of the community.

During the internment at Crow Creek, federal officials distributed rations through the leaders Husasa, Wapahasa (Wabasha), Mazasa, Wakute, and Passing Hail. The Indian agent at the newly established agency at Santee used the same system, which provided material rewards to these leaders for their cooperation.[10]

Reports from Indian agents for the early years at Santee suggest there was little overt resistance to the goals and methods of missionaries and the federal government, but this empowerment by federal officials of certain chiefs angered many of the men who had been at Davenport. Mae Eastman, whose grandmother Josephine Allen was among the first group of Dakota settlers in Flandreau, told an interviewer in 1971 that when the Dakota were reunited at Santee, "they found that the government was backing the old Indian system and that they would have to submit to the old chief, if they were to receive their food and clothing at the agency by the government." In order to escape this situation, Allen and approximately forty others left Santee with their families in the spring of 1869 to take advantage of the final clause of the treaty signed in 1868 between the United States and the Dakota Nations at Fort Laramie. The agreement granted a homestead and citizenship to any Dakota who renounced his tribal affiliation and farmed his land. This group established itself on the banks of the Big Sioux River, just ten miles away from Minnesota, at the place they called Wakpaipaksan, and went to work clearing fields and building houses. They also founded their own church, which they called Wakpaipaksan Okodakiciye, Bend in The River Church, which would remain central to the community's development.[11]

The Dakota settlers at Flandreau sought not only to escape from a reservation system they saw as corrupt but to leave behind the reservation itself, which experience had taught them could easily be terminated and moved by federal officials. Through the homestead clause of the Fort Laramie treaty, these families established themselves as a community of farmers along the Big Sioux River who could claim title to their lands like other homesteaders.[12]

Conditions at Flandreau, however, were not conducive to the success of this enterprise. Drought, flooding, and grasshoppers quickly sapped people's strength and made it difficult for the new farmers to survive on their own. Responding to these conditions, John P. Williamson lobbied the U.S. government to provide assistance, arguing that the failure of the Dakota's experiment at Flandreau would harm efforts to assimilate the Dakota into the culture of the white settlers around them. As a consequence, the Dakota at Flandreau began receiving the same assistance in food and farm supplies as the Santee reservation, and the U.S. government placed the Dakota within the agency structure through which it managed and controlled the reservations. In 1873, Williamson was appointed special agent for Flandreau; when he resigned this position a few years later in order to devote himself to missionary activities among the Ihanktunwan at the Greenwood mission, the head of the Dakota Superintendency appointed a subagent who was accountable to the Indian agent at Santee. In terms of its relationship to the U.S. government, the Flandreau community very quickly came to resemble the Dakota community on the reservation at Santee.[13]

Despite their different origins, the Flandreau and Santee Dakota communities developed along very similar lines. Not only did the two communities remain dependent upon and controlled by the U.S. government, but the people themselves developed similar patterns of subsistence and social interaction. Church life became equally significant for the Dakota in both communities, as did the balance that the Dakota struck between the traditions of their ancestors and the beliefs and values of the missionaries.

Indian officials and missionaries at Santee and Flandreau determined that these communities would sustain themselves through agriculture, just as they had wanted them to do in Minnesota. In both communities, Indian agents provided much of the raw materials necessary to establish productive fields and farms, including wagons, tools, and livestock. They also provided labor for cultivating fields and building houses. Yet environmental conditions conspired to push the Dakota back to traditional sources of subsistence. The river bottoms of the Big Sioux and the Missouri Rivers were quite fertile, but they were also highly prone to flooding. Lands outside the flood plains were arid and better suited to grazing cattle than to cultivating corn or wheat. Dakota men in both communities worked hard to grow crops, but their efforts were thwarted, and many abandoned their fields to pursue game that could yield meat as well as furs for sale and hides for women's handiwork.

In his first report as Flandreau special agent, Williamson wrote to the commissioner of Indian affairs in 1874 that the people had "shared in the calamity which the grasshoppers [had] brought to so many communities" that year. As a result, they tried to earn cash through a number of different means, including cutting and hauling wood. "But they have made the most," he continued, "catching small fur, because they knew the best how to do that." Despite his eagerness for his flock to become fully civilized farmers, Williamson was forced to recognize the value of the Dakota's traditional survival strategies, just as he had when he stayed with the Dakota at Crow Creek and succeeded in having a small number of guns and horses distributed to the internees so they could hunt buffalo to supplement the inadequate rations provided by the U.S. Army.[14]

The Dakota at Santee similarly fell back on their traditional patterns of subsistence, including hunting expeditions, and missionaries and agency personnel were forced to accept that reality. In a letter Samuel Hinman wrote in January 1868, he observed without further comment that "in another month, when the Indians return from their winter hunt, there will be 200 [students]." Federal agents also had to resign themselves to the fact that the Dakota would continue to hunt and that "the culture of the earth is considered secondary as a means of subsistence," as one superintendent put it in 1875.[15]

These hunting expeditions yielded valuable resources for Dakota survival. A short note in the *Niobrara Pioneer* indicates these expeditions produced far more than food. One man and two women passed through the town, the newspaper reported, with two ponies and ten dogs, "as they returned from a hunt up Running Water and had two bales of beaver skins." A similar note more than a dozen years later observed that on the Santee reservation, "two out of every three houses are vacant, the Indians being off on their regular hunting and trapping expedition."[16]

It may perhaps have been the emotional or psychological as well as the material rewards of the hunt that kept Dakota men from fully embracing farming. Even among the Christianized Dakota at Flandreau, agent Isaiah Lightner reported in 1880, "But a few of them cultivate land enough to live from. They do not take care of their live stock and do not accumulate any." The fact that as late as 1891, twenty-five years after the establishment of the reservation at Santee, the agency still employed two farmers to help prepare and plow the fields for the Dakota suggests that they continued to dislike farming, as they had before the war.[17]

When the Dakota did cultivate fields, they resisted white "civilization" by maintaining the traditional division of labor that assigned women responsibility for working the earth. Indian agents and missionaries alike noticed that women at Santee were the ones cultivating "small patches of ground," and even when these fields were larger, women still worked them. When a delegation of Quakers toured the Santee reservation in 1885, they saw seventeen hundred acres of corn that had been cultivated entirely by women "with hoes, their hands, and a rude spatula made of buffalo horn." They could barely contain their disbelief at the women's effectiveness and productivity: there was "scarcely a weed or spear of grass to be seen . . . They raise from eighty to one hundred bushels of the acre."[18]

Determined to combat the starvation and illness that had burdened their existence since the end of the war, Dakota women worked very hard to provide for their families. In addition to carefully tending their fields in the ways of their grandmothers, they harvested wild fruits and plants, as they had learned to do in their early lives in Minnesota, and taught this knowledge to younger generations. Agnes Ross, who was born in Flandreau in 1910, learned about harvesting *tipsinna* from her grandmother. As she told an interviewer, "We used to go up on the hillside and look for turnips. We used to run ahead of Grandma and identify them for her. She would always give thanks, bless the plant, and offer a short prayer thanking God for giving us this food. She would dig it up and, if it had gone to seed, she took the hole where she had dug up the plant, then she would cover the seeds all up again." Agnes's grandmother continued not only the harvest practices with which she had grown up in Minnesota but the spiritual practices that had accompanied them as well.[19]

Dakota women at Santee and at Flandreau retained many traditional food preferences, too. Like their grandmothers in Minnesota, they dried the turnips they did not eat fresh and braided the leaves to hang them in their houses until needed, as Floreine Johnson recalled her grandmother doing in the 1920s. Women on these Dakota reservations also continued the custom of gathering chokecherries and other fruit, which they pounded and dried to make into *wasna* or to use in flavoring stews.[20]

By the end of the nineteenth century, almost all families at Santee lived in what agent Lightner referred to as "quite comfortable dwellings," with shingles, ceilings, painted walls, and wood floors. Nevertheless, they continued to cook the foods that Dakota women had cooked over fires in their tipis until the middle of the century, much to the dismay of whites. The Santee Normal Training School taught girls to cook and sought to "educate" both students and their mothers. As a consequence, when a mother came to the school to visit an ailing son or daughter, the staff "will not hesitate to leave her alone with him, knowing that she has learned better than to feed him dried wild cherries, stones, and pulp pounded together, or dried wild turnips, things that would stagger the digestion of an ostrich." When the Santee community prepared to host the 1921 Niobrara Convocation, the biennial gathering of Dakota Episcopalian clergy and laypeople, the women went to work drying strips of meat and preparing wasna and *wojapi* (a fruit pudding) for the families traveling to Santee. At Flandreau, traditional Dakota foods remained part of Dakota diets and even became woven into community celebrations at First Presbyterian Church. Christmas feasts hosted by Reverend Eastman and his family included such items as wild rice along with the turkeys, oranges, puddings, pies, and much more that would have appeared on the holiday tables of white neighbors. In July 1888, Joseph Rogers, the Dakota minister of the Wakpaipaksan Okodakiciye, hosted a barbeque that was attended by both Dakota and white residents of the area. According to the *Moody*

County Enterprise, "Ox and stewed dog were served to those who desired. Not many, except the Indians, indulged in the latter luxury."[21]

In bringing traditional foods to sick children at boarding school and including them in communal celebrations, Dakota women did more than provide physical nourishment to their family and community. In the process of healing from the experiences of genocide, foods like wild rice, wojapi, and stewed dog meat carried strong associations with more settled and peaceful times, no doubt providing some measure of solace and reassurance. In moments of particular joy or physical ailment, which heightened the emotional dimensions of foods, Dakota women made sure to provide them. By serving certain foods at times of stress or celebration or at any other time, Dakota women also reclaimed their Dakota identity and celebrated their survival.[22]

Pazahiyayewin gathered and used medicines at Santee. According to her great-granddaughter Cora Jones, she used her knowledge to take care of her people at Crow Creek, and she continued when the Dakota were removed to Santee. In some cases, brewing sweet flag into tea or pounding blue flag root into poultices supplemented the hit-or-miss aid that physicians hired by the Indian agent provided. Families frequently had little or no access to medical care, and, in the absence of physicians, traditional healers like Pazahiyayewin attended to the ill.[23]

At Flandreau, Anna Wasu, Hail, continued to gather medicines as well as roots, berries, and plants for teas. She passed along this knowledge of plants to her granddaughter Iola Columbus, whom she raised. She also demonstrated proper attentiveness to the plants to be harvested. Columbus recalled her grandmother telling her, "If there's two of them, take one, leave the other one so it can seed. Or if there's eight of them, you might be able to take five or six. You don't want to get greedy because that isn't good."[24]

Women at Santee and Flandreau also preserved practices that were less immediately tied to physical survival and well-being. Women who had come to adulthood in Minnesota, for instance, dressed as they had during the first decades of their lives, combining finished articles of clothing available from traders with blankets they wore as earlier generations had

Anna Redwing Garvie with her daughter, mother, and grandmother, Santee, Nebraska, c. 1885.

worn buffalo robes. Photographs of Dakota women throughout the late nineteenth century and into the twentieth indicate that even women who wore European American–style dresses and aprons continued to complete their attire with blankets.[25]

One telling photograph, taken around 1885, shows four generations of Dakota women posing outside a house: Anna Redwing Garvie; her daughter, Cornelia; Garvie's mother, Mahpicadawin, Louise Redwing; and Garvie's grandmother Tuhmagawin, Bee Woman. Anna was born at Crow Creek in March 1866, and she attended the Santee Normal Training School, where she met and married James Garvie, one of the teachers there. Anna remained active in her church for many years. In this photograph, Garvie wears a dark, European American dress enlivened by lace at the neck and sleeves and a brooch at the neck. Her mother and grandmother wear blouses and skirts made of patterned fabric, which they either bought ready made or, more likely, made themselves. Over these European American garments, they have blankets worn as shawls. These were among the women Indian agent Isaiah Lightner had in mind when he noted in 1877 that "the men have adopted citizens' dress in full,

Mary Jane Faribault Eastman, Nancy McClure Faribault Huggan, and Mary Eastman Faribault, Sisseton, South Dakota, c. 1890.

the women partially. They still cling to their shawls, which they use for bonnet and shawl."[26]

Anna Garvie was born a few weeks before federal troops removed the Dakota from Crow Creek to Santee. Unlike older women in her family, she did not display her Dakota identity in her dress. Mary Jane Eastman, on the other hand, was twelve years older than Anna Garvie and had lived the first few years of her life in Minnesota. Like Garvie, she forswore the blanket, but she found other ways of expressing her Dakota identity. As in the family portrait (page 120), her best dress prominently exhibited Dakota beadwork. In another photograph, she stands with her mother, Nancy McClure Faribault Huggan, and her husband's sister Mary Eastman Faribault. Both Nancy and Mary, who were active church women (Mary Faribault was married to David Faribault, Jr., the U.S. interpreter who became a Presbyterian pastor after the war), wear blankets over their dresses; Mary Jane, on the other hand, is carrying and displaying a beaded purse. In marrying John Eastman, Mary Jane opted for a life in the church, and with her husband, she worked to establish a stable community for the Dakota battered by war and its aftermath. Yet, throughout these traumas and displacements, she retained an enduring attachment to the traditions of her Dakota grandmothers and to her own Dakota identity. Like the beading on her best dress, the purse she carried expressed those deep attachments.[27]

The community to which Eastman remained committed had been almost completely eradicated just a few years before these photos were taken. Even seemingly superficial or trivial gestures of community identity held significance, not only as symbols of remembrance of those who had perished but as testimony to the process of reconstituting that community as well. Such symbols and testimonies pervaded life at Santee and Flandreau, even among community members who had embraced Christianity. Through names, language, and ritual practices, the families demonstrated honor for earlier generations and nurtured new ones who would continue the process of restoring culture and communities.

For the Dakota and other Indigenous peoples, personal names reflected and reinforced core values and beliefs, cultural identity, and social organization. In naming their children, parents situated them within their families, giving newborns names that identified them by gender and order of their birth. The first-born daughter received the name Winona, for instance, and the first-born son, Caske. The conferring of special names later in life became celebratory occasions at which the new name, which identified a unique gift, personality trait, or accomplishment or memorialized an ancestor, was proclaimed before the community as a whole. These ceremonies confirmed the special place of the individual among his or her people.[28]

When Dakota people chose to keep and use those names instead of bowing to pressures from missionaries, teachers, and others to adopt American names, they made statements about their continued connection to their nation and Dakota identity, even when they converted to Christianity. Of the 315 names listed on the 1869 census, all but fourteen are Dakota names, even though many had converted during the years of imprisonment. Even more telling, among the converted men and women who left Santee to establish a Christian community at Wakpaipaksan, all still used their Dakota names. While names appearing on census rolls probably reflect, to some extent, the recorder's familiarity with the Dakota language, the fact remains that these men and women still had Dakota names to give.[29]

Families and communities continued bestowing Dakota names into the early twentieth century. In a 1902 census of a thousand families at Santee, enumerators listed "Indian Names" as well as "English Names." Approximately one-third gave Dakota names, including thirty who only gave Dakota names and a handful whose "English name" was the translation of the Dakota name they gave. One of them, Anpetutokeca, gave his English name as Otherday Zimmerman, using the translation of his Dakota name as his first name. Wicacaka had an English first name, Jane, but her daughter Anpetuomani, Walks in the Day, only gave Wicacaka's Dakota name to census takers asking for her mother's name. Anpetuomani herself gave both her Dakota name and her English name, Emma. Wicacaka's granddaughter gave both Winona and Mary as her names.[30]

The Dakota also continued to use traditional birth-order names. In earlier times, some adults were known by these names throughout their lives, and in censuses taken at Fort Snelling in December 1863 and at Crow Creek and Davenport, which counted adults born before the disruptions of war and removal, a small number of the names given were birth-order names. Two decades later, a larger proportion of adults were using birth-order names. On a list of families and their members compiled in the 1880s, which used only the individual's "Indian name" (although it also translates all the names), 84 of the 551 individuals have birth-order names. This much larger proportion of birth-order names compared with those on the prisoners' lists or with those on the 1869 census suggests that the dislocations of the 1860s, when many of the Dakota on the 1880s list came to adulthood, disrupted the practice of giving individuals their own particular name. While these women and men had not received such names, they nevertheless retained the name that identified them unmistakably as Dakota to themselves and to each other.[31]

The abiding use of Dakota names was predicated upon continued fluency in the Dakota language, since these names did not belong to a well-defined repertoire of names as European names do but rather described features of individuals' lives or characters. The use of these names at Santee and Flandreau therefore reflects continued use of the Dakota language. Indeed, well into the second half of the twentieth century, adults in both communities spoke Dakota among themselves. In the 1970s, some individuals interviewed for an oral history project spoke entirely or in part in the Dakota language, and in the first decade of the twenty-first century, elders Edith Bickerstaff and Floreine Johnson recalled hearing parents and grandparents speak the Dakota language and even speaking the language themselves as children. For the generation of Dakota who experienced the horrors of Fort Snelling, Mankato, Davenport, and Crow Creek, speaking the language of their parents and grandparents asserted a continuity with those generations that overrode the disruptions and traumas wrought by war and exile. Teaching the Dakota language to children and grandchildren also constituted a courageous step in reestablishing their community and perpetuating the beliefs, values, and worldview embedded in the language.[32]

Paradoxically, language preservation in both Santee and Flandreau was promoted by institutions fundamentally dedicated to the erasure of Dakota culture. In Santee, Alfred Riggs opened the Santee Normal Training School, continuing his father Stephen Riggs's missionary work, which had included publishing the first Dakota-English dictionary. Alfred promoted use of the Dakota language as a means of reaching potential converts and teaching them scriptures. He even engaged in fierce debates with his fellow missionaries and federal officials who saw this practice as detrimental to all missionary endeavors.[33]

At the Santee Normal School, which recruited students from Dakota and non-Dakota reservations in the region, students were allowed to speak Native languages. Instruction was in both English and Dakota, and the school's monthly publication appeared in both English and Dakota under the title *Word Carrier* and its Dakota-language equivalent, *Iapi Oaye*. The missionaries and teachers were the primary contributors to the paper, but students also wrote for it in both languages.[34]

Only a small proportion of children on the Santee reservation attended the normal school, but the institution's influence in the community was

strong. Many students remained at Santee and helped to build this
new community and its institutions. Edith Bickerstaff's grandmother,
Anna Garvie, learned music at the school and for decades served as the
organist for the Pilgrim Congregational Church she attended. Others
remained as teachers, and young men who attended the school later
served the Santee community as ministers and lay church leaders. Their
studies in Dakota at the school supported their use of the Dakota language with their families, which, in turn, supported its use in the community as a whole.[35]

In contrast to Santee, the Flandreau public school and the federally
operated Flandreau Indian School, like most public schools and boarding schools, punished students who used the Native language. Still, parents and grandparents spoke Dakota at home. In addition, many of these
families worshipped in Dakota. The First Presbyterian Church—Wakpaipaksan Okodakiciye—was a Dakota church, organized by and for Dakota
people, and for the first sixty years of its existence "First Church"—as it
is known in the community to this day—was led by Dakota pastors who
used the *Dakota Odowan,* a Presbyterian hymnal published in the Dakota
language.

The Episcopalian Church also promoted, through its practices, use
of the Dakota language. Samuel Hinman and other white priests and
missionaries learned the Dakota language, and, in 1865, the church published Hinman's Dakota-language translation of the *Book of Common
Prayer.* In 1877, the first edition of the *Wakan Cekiye Odowan* offered
reservation churches translations of Episcopalian hymns.[36]

Lakota anthropologist Beatrice Medicine has noted that on Lakota
reservations, men and women went to church and used Bibles, prayer
books, and hymnals in their own language "to continue language use
under the guise of being civilized and Christianized." While the Dakota
at Flandreau and Santee might not have been as intentional in linking
their participation in church activities with speaking their own language,
use of the Dakota language drew strength from the church itself and its
Native leaders. In constructing a Christian community, the Dakota chose
to build it on the foundation of their language.[37]

With this foundation, Dakota women and men could more easily reconstruct the ritual practices they had known in Minnesota. Because both religious and civil authorities were dedicated to the goal of eradicating observances they saw as standing in the way of the Dakota becoming civilized Christians, however, these observances were largely forced underground. Still, they persisted, as is confirmed by contemporary documents as well as by modern testimony from Dakota elders. The Dakota continued both collective ritual observances and individual practices, including dancing, visiting, healing, and smoking the ritual *canunpa*, or pipe. Often these activities involved women and men who had converted to Christianity and who were active in their church.[38]

Most disturbing to nineteenth-century religious and civil authorities were the continued practices of dancing and visiting, especially at Santee. The *Niobrara Pioneer* regularly noted in its "Jottings at Home" column the comings and goings of Dakota families. On June 14, 1877, for instance, the newspaper reported that "a party of Santee Indians passed through town on Monday last to visit friends at Hastings, Minn." While such movements might have meant commercial activity for local merchants, for missionaries and Indian agents such traveling only meant trouble. For agent Charles Hill, "The practice of large parties of Indians visiting other agencies is detrimental to civilization . . . Instructions to agents . . . touching Indian visiting, strictly enforced at all agencies, will be the death-blow to Indian customs." Not only did these visits reinforce what Hill saw as uncivilized behavior and customs, but their timing conflicted with the agricultural discipline that officials sought to enforce: "They like to visit to talk and feast," wrote Indian agent Joseph Clements in 1895. "They often select for these amusements the best time for sowing and caring for their crops, haying and harvesting."[39]

For the Dakota themselves, "these amusements" allowed for the rebuilding and nurturing of relations with family members and others. It is certainly possible, too, that they intentionally timed visits to evade culturally irrelevant and frequently fruitless agricultural labors, but these times of the year also coincided with historical times when the Dakota cycles of subsistence had led them to leave their camps to search for food and to renew ties with members of other communities. The breadth of lands inhabited by the Dakota before the war had created patterns of long-distance visiting, and the dispersal of Dakota communities after the war required travel in the process of reclaiming Dakota culture and reweaving bonds of family and community.

Elizabeth Wakeman Lawrence was born in Flandreau in 1877 to John C. Wakeman, White Spider, and Esther Wakeman, Blue Sky. During her childhood, she frequently moved with her parents from Flandreau to West St. Paul, back to Flandreau, and to Morton, Minnesota, where Dakota families who had remained in Minnesota were reestablishing a community near what had been the Lower Sioux Agency. In each of those places, the Wakemans hunted for meat and fur and gathered wild foods while they lived for a few months or more with different relatives.[40]

The Wakeman family's life confirms Ella Cara Deloria's observation that "kinship continued strong despite dispersal." The family had always been central to Dakota social organization, and the tiospaye had been the basic unit of community throughout the generations. In exile after the war, Dakota family ties remained central to Dakota life. According to Myrna Weston-Louis, whose grandmothers had been at Crow Creek and whose great-grandfather, Gus Standing Cloud (or St. Cloud), was imprisoned at Davenport, "Our tiospaye values were maintained through all those things that were happening." Not only did members of the tiospaye continue to look after one another when they were reunited at Santee, but they did so even after family members moved on to communities hundreds of miles away. Weston-Louis learned from her grandmothers and aunties that family members at Santee frequently traveled to visit relatives in the Dakota communities at Shakopee, Prairie Island, and Morton, Minnesota.[41]

Weston-Louis, herself the daughter of an Episcopalian priest, grew up in the 1950s through 1970s on the Lakota reservations at Pine Ridge and Eagle Butte. She spent every summer at Santee with her grandmother Lavara James, born at Santee in 1898. Lavara grew up surrounded by women like her grandmother Emma Red Owl, who still remembered times in Minnesota. During those summers, Myrna learned a great deal about Dakota practices and customs. Virginia Driving Hawk Sneve also spent summers with her grandmothers while she was growing up in the 1940s. During those months, she learned about the Dakota from her *kunsi,* her great-grandmother, Hannah Howe Frazier, whose husband, Charles Frazier, was born to his mother Maggie on the way to Crow Creek. These intergenerational visits, which grew out of parents' need for childcare during summer months, served to strengthen family ties and reinforce the bonds of tiospaye. At the same time, they perpetuated knowledge of Dakota practices and experiences.[42]

For the Christian Dakota at Flandreau, visiting family on other reservations allowed them to maintain contact with Dakota traditions that might have been frowned upon in their own community, and when members of one Dakota community did not preserve certain ancestors' practices themselves, contact with relations in other communities allowed those practices to survive for future generations. Judith Peterson grew up in Flandreau in the 1940s. As a child, she visited her great-grandfather, Albert Heminger, on the Lake Traverse reservation, just one hundred miles north of Flandreau. Her grandmother Ruth was from Sisseton on that reservation, and relatives from the two reservations gathered two or three times each year at Sisseton or Flandreau. During the visits to Sisseton, Peterson's Flandreau family joined their Heminger relations and others in traditional dances and feasts. Before he died, Heminger taught Peterson's brothers about dances and ceremonies and prepared them to participate themselves.[43]

Partaking in traditional practices may have been more indirect at Flandreau, although there remained a respect for those practices. Agnes Ross, who would herself become a leader of the Flandreau community in the 1970s and 1980s, was very proud of her great-grandmother Hupahu Sna Sna Win, Mary Standing Cloud (Gus's second wife), who was a medicine woman. Hupahu Sna Sna Win was also among the earliest settlers of the Flandreau community: she and her sisters took out homesteads when the Dakota first arrived in the area. Ross's mother, Ida Wakeman Allen, born in 1890, lost her mother, Judith Wakeman, when she was an infant. Because Judith's mother, Winona, had died shortly after the 1862 war, the duty to raise Ida and her siblings fell to Winona's sister, Hupahu Sna Sna Win, who also helped raise Agnes. Hupahu Sna Sna Win, Ida's grandmother's sister, kept her medicine bundle with her throughout her life, and before she died in 1930 at the age of 103, she gave it to Ida. According to Ross, her mother "never used the bundle because she was a Christian, but my mother had a lot of respect for this bundle. Where some people might have discarded it, she kept it in reverence, and passed it on to me." Ida Allen herself did not engage in traditional Dakota practices, but, in holding on to the medicine bundle, she honored her grandmother, a medicine woman, and the medicines that she used. For Dakota individuals who had converted to Christianity and identified as Christian, this might have been the only way to retain some association with the practices of earlier generations.[44]

At Santee, which did not make the same explicit and collective commitment to Christianity, traditional practices were more common. Giveaways, for instance, were an important element of community life, which Deloria noted when she visited for her research in the 1930s. Anna Wolfe was born in the Dakota community of Prairie Island, Minnesota, in 1891, but she married a Santee man and moved to his father's farm near Bazile Creek on the Santee reservation in 1909. Interviewed in 1973, she recalled large gatherings on the reservation at which many different items were given away. "Sometimes they gave horses away," she told the interviewer. When her first daughter was born, her father-in-law gave away at a ceremony a horse and buggy in honor of the new baby. For Dakota communities that had experienced genocide, every new birth was reason for celebrating, and following the ancestors' traditions reaffirmed the community's commitment to previous generations and to generations to come.[45]

Dakota families also turned to their ancestors' traditions in times of illness and anxiety. During the 1873 smallpox epidemic, which took a devastating toll on the Santee reservation, Oliver LaCroix left his home near the agency and took his family to stay with a cousin who lived on his farmland. There, they participated in the *inipi*, the sweat lodge ceremony, led by LaCroix's cousin, who was a medicine man. LaCroix's descendants credit the sweat baths for protecting the family from the epidemic that caused seventy deaths and the departure of many more from Santee. Sixty years later, families on the reservation still called upon medicine men for particularly grave situations. When Edith Bickerstaff's father disappeared while crossing the Missouri River on his way home from Springfield, South Dakota, his mother, Edith's grandmother, called in a *wahpiya,* a healer, to help look for him.[46]

Although this healer came from another reservation, traditional healers were very much part of the Dakota community at Santee. Nellie De Cory, who was born and raised in Santee, told an interviewer in 1973 that her grandfather was a medicine man, and Nancy Mackey learned from family stories that her great-grandmother Sarah Robinson Mackey was both a medicine woman and a midwife. Born in Minnesota in 1851, she endured the exile at Crow Creek as a young girl, then the removal to Santee. She raised a family there and delivered the babies for many other families until her death in 1924. She and her husband and sons were pillars of the Santee community, her own status no doubt secured both by her skills as a midwife and by her gifts as a healer.[47]

Many Dakota women and men who continued the spiritual practices of their ancestors also participated actively in church life. Well into her seventies, Bernice Blakney, for instance, retained very clear memories of her grandfather, who was an elder in the Episcopalian church. As a child, she too lived with her grandparents during the summer, and she remembered her grandfather rising with the sun and greeting the new day with chants in Dakota and his *canunpa,* his pipe. Star Frazier, who was born in Minnesota around 1848 and lived on the Santee reservation until his death in the late 1930s, was a medicine man and one of the principal informants working with Ella Deloria in her ethnographic research on Dakota spiritual practices. Frazier had also been one of the first Dakota to welcome Alfred Riggs and his family to Santee when they arrived to establish a mission school in 1870. These individuals fully embraced the church and its practices, but they did so without abandoning their Dakota ways.[48]

For the generation who experienced the war and internment and went on to become leaders of the new communities at Santee and Flandreau, every aspect of life posed stark choices: the clothes they wore, the language they spoke, the names they gave their children, the spiritual practices they used to give strength and courage. After the genocide of the 1860s, each choice presented possibilities for reclaiming their culture and adapting the knowledge of their grandmothers and grandfathers. Most families in Santee and Flandreau never returned to Minnesota. Instead, they built new homes founded on Dakota culture and, at the same time, took advantage of white institutions still intent on erasing their culture. The church and its auxiliaries would be central to their efforts.

CHAPTER 6

Work, Gender,
and the Dakota Church

A s the Dakota went about the daunting task of rebuilding their communities in Santee and Flandreau, women returned to one of the central activities that had shaped their lives in Minnesota: creating functional works of art. Now, however, they engaged in this work with multiple purposes. Women made some items for use by family members, as generations of women had always done, and they also made other items for sale, as women had begun to do in the 1840s. They made moccasins, pouches, and garments decorated with the quillwork and beadwork of their grandmothers in Minnesota, but they also created pieces of art that reflected their new circumstances. They adapted traditional beadwork and quillwork, for instance, to ornament book covers for their *Dakota Odowan* and *Wakan Cekiye Odowan*, the missionaries' Dakota-language hymnals. Women also took up quilting, transforming into the characteristically Dakota design the eight-pointed star pattern they learned from missionaries.

Protestant missionaries had worked hard to alleviate Dakota suffering and lobbied U.S. military and civilian powers to improve the conditions of internment in the three and a half years after the U.S.–Dakota War. Once the Dakota were reunited, missionaries went to work building churches and schools, first at Santee and then at Flandreau. This way the Dakota who had converted to Christianity at Fort Snelling, Mankato, Davenport, and Crow Creek could pursue their new beliefs and practices

Episcopalian hymnal, published in 1894, with deerskin cover decorated with quillwork. Donated to Nebraska State Historical Society by Lily B. Munroe, who worked as a teacher on the Rosebud reservation from 1900 to 1905. Artist unknown.

in their own churches. Church buildings themselves became prominent features on the landscape. By the turn of the twentieth century, the Flandreau Dakota community, with a population of four hundred, was served by one Presbyterian church and one Episcopalian church. The Santee reservation, with a population of approximately one thousand, was served by three Episcopalian churches and two Congregational churches.[1]

When the Dakota joined churches, they did not passively file into an alien and alienating institution. Instead, they transformed the Episcopalian, Congregational, and Presbyterian churches into resources for employment, leadership roles, and community activity that supplanted

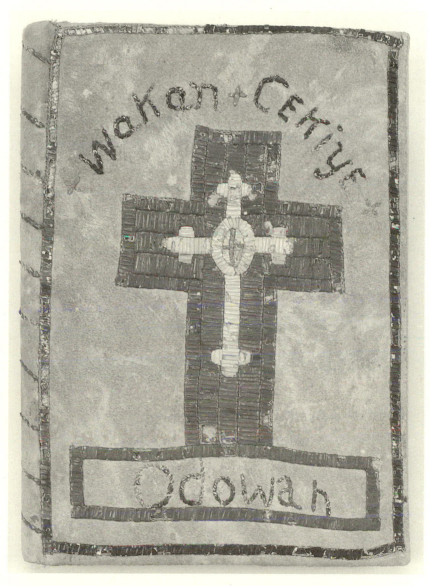

Wakan Cekiye Odowan (Holy Prayer Hymnal), Episcopalian hymnal published in 1894, with deerskin cover decorated with quillwork, owned by Edna Peninger Biller (1879–1952), whose husband, Reverend George Biller, served as an Episcopalian priest on the Rosebud reservation between 1908 and 1912 and as bishop of South Dakota from 1912 to 1915. Artist unknown; National Museum of the American Indian, Smithsonian Institution.

structures lost in removal. These churches also promoted the creation of art, both in its traditional forms and in the new forms that Dakota women were developing.

Recent discussions of relations between churches and Native peoples have frequently focused largely on Catholic and Protestant churches as forces of colonization and genocide. It is true that Christian teachings, church-sponsored boarding schools, and missionary work among Indigenous peoples frequently worked to eradicate Native practices and the entire cultural edifice within which they existed. The devastation wrought in the name of Christian beliefs continues to be felt by Native peoples to this day. Studying relations between churches and Native peoples only from the perspective of colonization, however, eliminates the possibility of understanding how Native peoples themselves experienced contact with missionaries, Christian clergy, and the church. While it is impossible to ignore religious institutions' assault on Indigenous cultures, it is equally impossible to ignore Native peoples' embracing of church life in many different ways.[2]

Men and women at Santee and Flandreau were fully engaged with the church. Even while working under the watchful eyes of missionaries, Dakota transformed traditional churches into their own institutions. Through churches, Dakota men found employment and roles in their communities not otherwise available. A small number of women also found limited employment, but far more found spaces in which to re-establish the bonds that had woven them together in Dakota communities in Minnesota. Missionaries created women's groups, especially the *winyan omniciye* or Ladies' Aid Societies, which brought women together to revive their creative work. Of course, the larger purpose of the winyan omniciye was to raise money for church work, and women's needlework was to be sold to help support those churches. Yet this revitalization of ornamented functional art also revitalized the production of beaded and quilled items for women's own purposes. Many women both sold their wares to help support their families and gave them away at family and community gatherings. For many living on the Santee and Flandreau reservations, church became the center of a strongly Dakota-identified social life. These women and men made use of the church to reestablish their own communities and aid their recovery from the ethnic cleansing of war, internment, and removal.

The survivors of these horrors took the churches set up by missionaries and transformed them into places where neighbors and relatives gathered on their own terms. These institutions helped inspire new energy in distinctly Dakota elements of community life. During incarceration after the war, missionaries and their institutions had made the Dakota language a vehicle of written communication. Later, their churches supported other dimensions of Dakota culture, including women's creative work with hide, beads, quills, fabric, needles, and thread.

Colonization and defeat stripped Dakota men of the roles they had played in their communities. Men were expected to abandon hunting in order to cultivate crops and raise farm animals. However, the difficulty of growing crops on the reservations in Nebraska and South Dakota rendered European American farming almost futile and made it nearly impossible for men to fulfill their role as family providers.

Reservation life erased men's traditional leadership and spiritual roles as well. Historically, warfare had occupied a central position in the lives of men in Dakota culture. According to Charles Eastman, the Dakota considered warfare "an organized trial of courage and skill, with elaborate rules . . . It was held to develop the quality of manliness, and its motive was chivalric and patriotic." Accomplished warriors were also considered to have spiritual powers, and success in war brought special honors and standing within the community. Many men waited for success in warfare before marrying. When the powerful role of warrior was taken away, Dakota men thus lacked opportunities to demonstrate their physical prowess, leadership, character, and devotion to their people.[3]

In 1883, Secretary of the Interior Henry Teller promulgated the Indian Religious Crimes Code that banned Native religious practices and eliminated the social roles of spiritual leader and healer. While women could also be gifted healers, leadership in spiritual affairs generally went to men, who organized and participated in medicine dances, sun dances, and other forms of collective public spiritual observance. By the 1880s, these men who had guided their communities in hunting and in warfare, as well as in ritual practices, found practically every form of Native religion criminalized. Even funeral ceremonies were outlawed, and drumming and dancing were officially banned as religious practices.[4]

The Religious Crimes Code established reservation-based Courts of Indian Offenses that gave Indian agents and superintendents the power to implement the bans and punish violations. As a result, the Dakota had to disguise their ceremonies as gatherings that would be acceptable to the Indian agent. This explains the popularity of reservation Fourth of July celebrations, which continue to this day. In his searing critique of Christianity and the massive efforts made to convert Native people, Vine DeLoria, Jr., noted that all ceremonies "had to be held for the most artificial of reasons," thus trivializing what had been core religious practices. Under such circumstances, possessing and exercising special spiritual or healing powers no longer gave men the stature or authority they had held in earlier generations and stripped away another functional role in their society.[5]

Finally, *itancan*, traditional leaders, no longer played a significant role in either community. At Flandreau, community founders abandoned tribal ties and structures as a condition of receiving homesteads. At Santee, federal officials decided—before the interned Dakota even arrived from Crow Creek—which chiefs they would recognize as representatives and leaders. This meant that Dakota men had to construct new roles for themselves.[6]

Of course, opportunities in the world of whites remained mostly closed to them. Employment was largely limited to low-wage, unskilled work, and education was restricted to mission schools, federally run boarding schools, and local public schools, all of which envisioned preparing Native boys for work in various menial jobs. College was an opportunity open to a very limited number. Moreover, while the Fort Laramie treaty of 1868 granted citizenship to Native men who renounced tribal affiliation and took homesteads, they did not gain voting rights. The path of electoral politics that gave white men opportunities to become influential in their communities was thus one more avenue closed to Dakota and Native men across the United States.[7]

What remained open to these men was the church. On reservations dominated by Protestant missions and churches, missionaries and ministers loomed large and wielded influence with civilian powers. In many cases, they advocated for the Dakota people. Episcopalian bishop Henry Whipple had lobbied President Lincoln on behalf of the warriors convicted in the fall of 1862, and during the internment at Crow Creek and the removal to Santee, John P. Williamson and Episcopalian missionary William Hare had written in support of more resources and a viable reservation. When the Dakota established the community at Flandreau, it was Williamson who appealed for assistance to the U.S. government.[8]

Dedicated to spreading the gospel, these white church leaders believed their evangelical goals could be most effectively furthered among Native peoples by community members themselves. From the mid-nineteenth century until the 1930s, church leaders actively sought to recruit and train Native men as lay and ordained clergy. From the earliest years of his mission in Minnesota, Stephen Riggs had encouraged his few male converts to share their faith with their kin, and when Riggs's son opened the Santee Normal Training School in 1873, one of his goals was training Native preachers and teachers.[9]

Under these circumstances, it is easy to see how Dakota men sought to regain stature and influence they once held through the ministry and lay service to their churches. Some men acquired education and ordination and then returned to serve and lead their own communities, while others moved to different reservations. John Eastman, the husband of Mary Jane Eastman, went to Flandreau with his father, a founder of the community. A few years later, he and six other young Flandreau men returned to Santee to attend the Santee Normal Training School. Three were eventually ordained, including Eastman, who served the Dakota Presbyterian church in Flandreau for three decades. The other two served Dakota communities at Lake Traverse as well as Titunwan communities in western South Dakota and Montana.[10]

Because the U.S. government gave churches a prominent role on reservations, gaining a foothold in these churches allowed Dakota men some access to resources they could distribute in their community. At the very least, men gained positions from which they could guide, advise, and listen, much as itancan had done. As ordained ministers like John Eastman or as missionaries, lay leaders, elders in the Presbyterian Church, and priests and catechists in the Episcopalian Church, Dakota men could find new identities that placed them at the center of their communities. They could become spokesmen for their people, and they could guide younger men into their own church careers.

The career of James Garvie, Tatanka Kinina, Buffalo Comes to Life, reflects a path of ascendancy through the church. Garvie was born in Minnesota on August 10, 1862, to a Scottish father and a Dakota mother. When his father was killed in the war, his mother fled to Canada with James and two older sons. They moved to Santee when that reservation was established and then to Sisseton, where family members already lived. Garvie began teaching at the Santee Normal Training School in 1883, where he met his future wife Anna Redwing, and in 1891 he was ordained a Congregational minister. He traveled to Washington, DC, thirteen times to represent the Santee Dakota in claims against the federal government stemming from the 1862 war.[11]

While serving the church required literacy, it did not always demand special training. In 1910, Grace Eastman, the daughter of John and Mary Jane Eastman, married Oliver Moore, a Dakota farmer and elder in the Presbyterian church in Sisseton. One day, her father, who had moved with his family from Flandreau to Sisseton in 1906, asked Oliver if he would go to Montana to serve a church there. "My husband wasn't a minister," she noted in a 1971 interview, "but he was a worker in the church, an elder, they call them in the Presbyterian Church. And [my father] wanted to know if he would go. He said there's a little church that needed somebody." The Moores took up the offer and soon set out for Poplar, Montana.[12]

Serving that church gave Oliver Moore a new job, but it also gave the couple the opportunity to live among others who traced their roots to

the Minnesota and Upper Mississippi river valleys. Situated on the Fort
Peck reservation, the church in Poplar brought the Moores to a region to
which many Dakota had fled after the 1862 war. They remained there for
several years until Grace's father died and she returned to Flandreau to
look after her mother and grandmother.[13]

The Santee and Flandreau communities themselves also provided
opportunities to serve the church. Between 1879 and 1882, seven Santee
men acted as deacons or catechists for the three Episcopalian churches
there: Our Most Merciful Savior, Holy Faith, and Our Blessed Redeemer.
For George Red Owl, these churches offered opportunities to use his
musical talents. Born in Minnesota in the 1820s, Red Owl had received
the Dakota name of Dowanna, Singer. At Santee, he led a choir of Dakota
youth that provided music for church services. He also wrote hymns for
the church, one of which, "The Missionary Carol," Episcopalian missionary Samuel Hinman included in full in his journal published in Philadelphia in 1869. Red Owl was eventually ordained an Episcopalian priest,

Our Most Merciful Savior Episcopal Church, Santee, Nebraska, 2006.

but he did not entirely leave behind his Dakota traditions: at one point, he confided in the missionary that he was writing a book about the religious customs of the Dakota.[14]

The Flandreau community also offered men leadership opportunities in the church. The First Presbyterian Church had Dakota pastors for most of its first century of existence, including John Eastman, who served for thirty years from 1876 to 1906, and Flandreau Dakota men also functioned as elders in the church. David Weston and others from the community served as lay readers for the Episcopalian church in Flandreau.[15]

For Red Owl and many other men at Santee, and Flandreau, and on other Dakota reservations, the church also provided jobs. In the words of Virginia Driving Hawk Sneve, who counts several clergymen among her Dakota forebears, "The raising up of Indian people to minister to their own race served the evangelical nature of Christianity, but it also

Tipiwakan Wakpaipaksan, Bend in the River Meeting House, built in 1871. It was used by the Flandreau Dakota until the First Presbyterian Church was built in 1873. It was then purchased by the U.S. government and used as a school for Native children that would later become Flandreau Indian School. In 1989, the structure was purchased and restored by the Moody County Museum.

provided education and employment to the Indian men and women who answered the call." The priorities of the church neatly dovetailed with the needs of Dakota men in a period when they had few other possibilities for contributing to their communities.[16]

The church also offered opportunities for Dakota women. Pilgrim Congregational Church, on the Santee reservation, gave Anna Garvie a long career as a church organist. Oliver Moore's mission in Poplar gave his wife, Grace, employment as a music teacher—and the great satisfaction of seeing her students take up their own positions in church music. Interviewed in her eighties, she took tremendous pride in pointing out that "some of the young men and young women . . . you see playing the organ in churches are my pupils."[17]

Many more women found opportunities in the auxiliaries that each reservation church organized. Originally established to cement Dakota women's loyalty to their churches and help raise funds, these Ladies' Aid Societies, first and foremost, provided an important opportunity to reconstitute the collective work groups that had characterized their lives before whites tried to transform them into Americanized Christians. Women who had worked their fields in groups, raised their children together, and sat with one another to do their fancy work could now attend meetings of the *winyan omniciye* (literally, women's society) and work collectively on behalf of their church, often side by side doing needle projects.

According to Edith Bickerstaff and Floreine Johnson, born in Santee in 1917 and 1927, respectively, church life and the winyan omniciye were at the center of their mothers' and grandmothers' lives. Women prepared and served lunches and made quilts and other items to sell at fundraisers for their church. Johnson learned from her grandmother that they raised money for a church bell for the Bazile Creek Congregational Church on the reservation by preparing meals of *wayuksapi,* or hominy, and fry bread. This was the first project undertaken by the women on the new reservation. By the time missionaries Mary and Alfred Riggs arrived in Santee in the summer of 1870, the log church built under the direction of missionaries Edward Pond and John Williamson already had its

Edith Bickerstaff and Floreine Johnson, Santee, Nebraska, 2004.

bell. "The Indians might be proud," Mary wrote in her memoir several decades later, "for they bought [the bell] with corn."[18]

"The Ladies' Aid took up most of the day," Bickerstaff recalled. She and Johnson grew up hearing this remark and much more about their mothers' and grandmothers' winyan omniciye meetings, which were always held on Wednesdays in women's homes. The women shared meals and prayers, but mostly "they did a lot of sewing." Women brought babies and young children, and women who were too aged or infirm to work were welcomed as well. They were also joined by students at the Santee Normal Training School. These gatherings, which brought together young and old to do work that Dakota women had always done together, helped to re-create bonds of kinship and friendship among women and, ultimately, rebuild Dakota communities. Looking back on her grandmothers' lives, Virginia Driving Hawk Sneve wrote, "They welcomed these social contacts, which were so like the old days when women of one family helped women of another tan hides or prepare a lodge cover, all the while gossiping, laughing, or weeping—sharing community sorrow and joy."[19]

As the wife of a prominent pastor, Mary Jane Eastman, who raised eight children, organized her life around church gatherings and meetings, as did other women married to clergy. As Mrs. John Eastman, she might have been expected to take a leadership role in her church's sewing circle and might even have embraced wholeheartedly the position of president of the Dakota Women's Board, which collected funds raised by women's groups on reservations for missionary work. At the same time, she relished the work that took place at gatherings of the women's sewing society in Flandreau. Her daughter Bessie, also married to a minister, told many stories to her children and grandchildren about growing up in her family's busy parsonage. She also recalled the quilting and beadwork that her mother did for her church.[20]

Those gatherings might have reminded Mary Jane and others of the collective work groups they had known in their communities in Minnesota. While these women no longer lived in tipis or bark lodges, they still practiced the arts they had learned as young women and then taught to their daughters. They had grown up knowing that the most prized objects they could create were decorated moccasins or garments or pouches to be given away in honor of a relative. Memories of this work and traditional responsibilities may have inspired the women who made the beadwork for Mary Jane Eastman's dress and purse, as seen in the photographs that her descendants have preserved.

The winyan omniciye also gave women the opportunity to reweave relationships with women on other reservations. When the Presbyterian Church's Dakota Missionary Society gathered every summer, women's groups were always well represented and held their own meetings. The women's meeting at the 1886 conference drew two hundred Native women as well as a dozen white missionary workers. It was at that meeting that Mary Jane Eastman was chosen president of the Dakota Women's Board.

Eastman no doubt gained visibility at these gatherings because she was married to a prominent and influential clergyman. It is also likely that as a minister's wife she attended regularly, came to know many women there, and developed many friendships. In selecting their own leaders, Dakota women exercised some of the autonomy they had always known to honor each other and their relationships.

Most winyan omniciye activity, however, took place in individual communities during the rest of the year. In 1887, Anna Garvie of Santee, secretary of the Women's Missionary Society—and the grandmother of both Edith Bickerstaff and Floreine Johnson—was unable to attend the meeting, but she sent a report that vividly sums up the nature of the work of the winyan omniciye: "We have much to detain us, so we are never all together; sometimes we are many, and sometimes only three or four, but all are ready to give when we ask for contributions. The 29th of June we had a sale in the new dining hall, some pretty quilts, moccasins, bags and pin cushions, then we had cake and lemonade. We raised in all $71.85." Although Dakota women had numerous responsibilities, the meetings took place no matter how many or how few attended. When women were able to set aside other responsibilities, they could count on the meetings of the winyan omniciye, and, in return, they gave back. Clearly, women cherished these meetings and worked hard to attend them as often as possible.[21]

Garvie's report provides a valuable glimpse at the handwork women were making to sell—quilts, moccasins, bags, and pincushions. Members of the winyan omniciye made what Dakota women had traditionally made, and they used for their own purposes the skills that missionaries had taught them. Beginning with their early efforts in Minnesota, missionaries had sought to "civilize" Dakota women by teaching them the skills they would need to approximate the lives of white women: cooking, washing as whites did, sewing, knitting, tatting, embroidering, and quilting. These activities remained in the curriculum in Santee and other missionary schools. At Santee Normal Training School, young women learned to use sewing machines to make clothes, but they also learned to make quilt squares and quilt tops by hand, using whatever scraps of muslin and other fabric were available.[22]

Of all the needle arts learned from missionaries, Dakota women and other Native women embraced quilting most fully. The cooperative work that frequently characterizes quilting, known among white women as

Julia OneElk, 12 yrs., Yankton.

Quilt block sewn by Julia One Elk at the Santee Normal Training School. J. Sterling Morton Collection, Nebraska State Historical Society.

"quilting bees," lent itself to the Dakota tradition of communal activity. In addition, like items made of hide that Dakota women created, quilts were both functional and ornamental. Not only used as blankets, they also could cover the windows, doors, and walls of log houses to keep out winter wind and cold. According to Patricia Albers and Beatrice Medicine, the "most compelling reason . . . for the widespread adoption of quilting" is that its design principles corresponded to the Dakota's own decorative tradition. Medicine, a Lakota anthropologist familiar with quilting from Standing Rock Dakota reservation in western South Dakota, and Albers, a white anthropologist who conducted research on the Dakota reservation at Spirit Lake in North Dakota, observe that pieced quilts combine varying shapes of cloth in the same way that quilled and beaded items combine different patterns and designs. In making cradleboard covers, for instance, Dakota women worked together several strips of

Cradleboard cover made of deerskin decorated with quillwork and metal jingle cones, probably created between 1780 and 1820. Artist unknown; National Museum of the American Indian, Smithsonian Institution.

decorated hide; similarly, quilts started with pieces of cloth sewn together in squares or strips that were then sewn into the larger piece.[23]

Another reason for the prominence of quilting was the easy access to the necessary materials. Flour sacks, scraps of leftover fabric, and "mission boxes" of donated clothing provided all that was needed to make a warm quilt. In creating the quilt that her grandchildren and great-grandchildren have very carefully preserved, Mary Mitchell used inexpensive remnants or pieces of fabric left from other projects. The care with which she laid out the squares, sewed them together, and tacked together the quilt top with batting and backing ensured that this quilt would make those who used it feel warm and wrapped in beauty— and in all the cultural and spiritual associations stitched into this piece of functional art.

When Mary Mitchell, who lived her whole life on the Santee reservation, made this quilt, she integrated the techniques and materials of white women's quilting with the designs favored by women of her own community. As Albers and Medicine suggest, the pieces sewn together resemble work that her mother, Emma, and her grandmother, Wicacaka,

Detail of quilt made by Mary Mitchell, in the possession of her great-granddaughter Margaret Daniels, Sioux Falls, South Dakota. Like earlier parfleches and other items, the quilt includes a red border.

would have created in earlier decades. The vine-like design of the embroidery recalls, as well, the floral patterns characteristic of Eastern Dakota women's artwork, seen of the beadwork that Mary Jane Eastman sewed on her European-style dress. For Mitchell, making this quilt helped a family member, but it also offered an opportunity to apply lessons about design and creativity she had learned from the Dakota women around her. No doubt the lessons included the importance of providing for family members and the *wakan,* sacred, nature of this work.

While Dakota women made quilts in different designs, the most characteristic became the eight-pointed star pattern. Dakota women learned it from white women, but they soon made it their own. They associated it with the morning star, known as *wicanpi tanka,* large star. According to one Dakota story, a healer on his deathbed once told his people that he would appear in the sky in the early morning after he passed into the spirit world. He told them to look for him in the eastern sky four days after his death; there he would be recognizable as a light surrounded by many different colors. The star quilt recalls this story and the many colors of the dawn.[24]

Star quilts took on special ceremonial roles in Dakota life, and to this day they are frequently used in giveaways, healing ceremonies, and life cycle events. Lucy Tuttle Redwing, Tawiyaka, Feather, was an active member of the Howe Creek Episcopal Church at Santee, as was her mother, Ellen Stone Tuttle, Winona. According to Lucy's daughter Goldie Redwing Wiley, Lucy made star quilts for the church's Ladies' Aid Society. When her granddaughter was born, probably in the 1930s or 1940s, Lucy asked the other women to make a star quilt for the baby. In doing so they adopted an art form learned from missionaries and imbued it with Dakota meanings.[25]

Lillian Moore Beane, in the star quilt given to her on the occasion of her hundredth birthday, August 25, 2011, by the Flandreau Santee Sioux Tribe. She is surrounded by her children William Beane, Sydney Beane, and Linda Olson.

Dakota women also took traditional techniques and materials and applied them to the practices and beliefs taken up from missionaries. Many beaded and quilled items incorporated Christian crosses and churches in their designs. This integration of Native art with Protestant ritual is probably seen most vividly in the quilled and beaded deerskin covers made for their Dakota-language hymnals, or *odowan*.

Many Dakota churchgoers carried their own hymnals, which were among the cherished possessions they passed along to their children. Florestine Kiyukanpi Renville, whose family attended St. Mary's Episcopal Church on the Sisseton-Wahpeton reservation at Lake Traverse, believes that Dakota people carried their hymnals to and from church because "their spirituality is a very personal and individual and continuous experience, like traditional spirituality was before white people came and forced change upon us." She inherited her mother's and grandfather's hymnals, and because she began attending Presbyterian services after her marriage, she owns both Episcopalian and Presbyterian hymnals as well.[26]

Because of the value placed on prayer books, women enhanced them with protective covers decorated with designs ranging from simple lines of beadwork or quillwork to far more elaborate patterns. One surviving hymnal cover bears a simple cross and border in quillwork, beaded edges, and strands of sinew holding several tin jingle cones with red-dyed horsehair centers. Another example is much more ornately decorated, in three different colors. The title of the Episcopalian hymnal, *Wakan Cekiye Odowan,* is prominently displayed on both front and back covers, all in quillwork. At the center of the front cover is the Niobrara cross, designed by Bishop William Hobart Hare for the Dakota members of the Episcopalian Church.[27]

Christian Dakota women on other reservations also created ornate hymnal covers, sometimes for gifts to honor special members of their community. Frank Thorburn, an Episcopalian priest who served on the Pine Ridge Lakota reservation in the 1930s and 1940s, received many gifts from parishioners, including two beaded hymnals. It is likely that women at Santee and Flandreau also made beaded and quilled prayer book covers as gifts.[28]

For many Dakota women, the *winyan omniciye* or women's societies gave shape and meaning to their new lives in unfamiliar surroundings at a time when they still felt the losses of homelands and family members. In environments that were so closely controlled by whites seeking to suppress Dakota spiritual and ritual practices, the winyan omniciye might also have offered Dakota women the opportunity to experience some of the spiritual powers that artwork traditionally embodied. The items they created, whether for selling or for giving away, helped to establish a tangible connection with their history, their homelands, and their beliefs and practices.

When Wicacaka had worked on moccasins and cradleboard covers as a young woman in Minnesota, she, like other Dakota women, stitched into them the *wakan* of the world around her. The sewing and beading in the winyan omniciye perpetuated this work and preserved for her daughter Emma and granddaughter Mary this conception of women's work and the wakan. They, in turn, would have passed along to their daughters and granddaughters knowledge of the spiritual powers of their work with beads, quills, hides, and fabric pieces arranged in intricate patterns. Church Ladies' Aid Societies, then, helped to revitalize the spiritual lives of Dakota women by encouraging them to do work that had traditionally held powerful spiritual associations.

At the same time, the winyan omniciye also opened up material possibilities for Dakota women. Before war and exile, Dakota women had begun to create garments and other items for sale to white customers. When the winyan omniciye encouraged women to make items to sell to benefit the church, it reinforced the market value of the decorated pieces they created.

Mary Mitchell, the stepdaughter of an elder (George Dowanna Red Owl) in an Episcopalian church in Santee, no doubt spent many Wednesdays as a young woman and mother at winyan omniciye meetings of her family's church. She would have worked with other women on items to sell to help support the church. In the spring of 1941, when she was seventy-eight years old, Mary traveled to the Winnebago Agency one hundred miles distant to sell dolls she had made. With this journey, she retraced the steps that her grandmothers had taken when they began selling their work to traders or when they traveled to St. Paul to sell directly to white customers. While Mary made quilts and other items for relatives, she also made some that she could sell to provide food and other necessities for her family.

Mary died just a few weeks after that trip, but the dolls acquired a life of their own. Shortly after Mary brought them to Winnebago, agency personnel received a letter from Betty J. Meggers, a doll collector who had sent similar letters to Indian agencies across the country. Meggers bought Mary's dolls for $5.00 each and eventually donated her collection to the Smithsonian Institution, where Mary's dolls and others reside to this day.[29]

For Mary and other Native women across the United States, American and European collectors provided opportunities to increase their family

Buckskin dolls made by Mary Mitchell, decorated with yarn, beads, and ink. Mitchell sold the dolls in 1943 at the Winnebago Agency, Winnebago, Nebraska, to Betty Meggers, who donated them to the Smithsonian Institution.

incomes. Indeed, historians studying Indigenous peoples in the United States in different historical periods have noted that the collapse of subsistence economies made the trade in women's fancy work increasingly important in Native economies. The proximity of tourist centers in places like Niagara Falls and New Orleans certainly expanded opportunities for Seneca and Natchez women, respectively, to sell their baskets. Similarly, the use of Blackfeet Indians to promote tourism at Glacier National Park and along the Santa Fe Railroad line created active markets for goods produced by nearby Native women. Yet even in the absence of significant tourist attractions, Native women found buyers for the goods they produced.[30]

Selling beadwork and quillwork was only one way that women helped support their families. Many women at Flandreau and Santee kept large gardens and raised chickens to supply their families; they also sold crops and eggs to neighbors or bartered for the use of tools or other necessities. Ida Tuttle, who grew up in Santee in the 1920s and 1930s, recalled that her mother sold eggs as well as her beaded and quilled creations to whites in Niobrara, Center, and other communities near the reservation. While these items might have remained in the white families, it is also likely that, in time of need, whites would have sold Ida's mother's beadwork to collectors or merchants specializing in this trade.

One such merchant, B. Y. High, established himself in Bloomfield, Nebraska, just south of the Santee reservation, in order to have direct access to the goods produced by Dakota women there. Born in Pennsylvania in 1858 and arriving in Nebraska in 1876, High began working for Niobrara merchant H. E. Bonesteel three years later. In 1903, High opened a general store in Bloomfield, which he successfully operated for more than two decades. According to his daughter, High spoke the Dakota language and earned the Dakota name Zitka Ska, White Bird. Many Dakota women came to Bloomfield to trade with High because they wanted to work with someone who spoke their language. High bought outright some of the goods these women brought to him and took others in trade for supplies from his store. Among High's customers for items made by Santee women was the Nebraska State Historical Society. It boasted in 1907 of its acquisition of the B. Y. High Collection of Santee beaded items in which "all the pieces are all very superior." The collection reportedly "was selected as the best out of the quantity sold there by the Santees." Upon High's death, his daughter donated the remainder of his inventory—over two hundred items—to the Nebraska Historical Society.[31]

Artwork in the High Collection represents a vast array of objects created in a range of styles. It includes knife sheaths, moccasins, pipe bags, and parfleches as well as pillows, pincushions, purses, and wall hangings. The items are decorated with beadwork and quillwork that re-creates older designs and with designs that show little or no resemblance to earlier artwork. Sometimes artists added new design elements to otherwise older patterns. One pouch in the collection is decorated with fringes and tin cone jingles that have tufts of dyed horsehair in their centers, as many older items did. Some of its floral beadwork resembles designs characteristic of Eastern Dakota work in the early years of production for sale in the 1840s and 1850s. A third grouping of flowers, however, uses beads of different colors randomly distributed in the design, which appears to be an innovation among the women who sold their wares to High.

This use of different colors of beads appears on both traditional objects and new creations. A turtle amulet is among the objects in the High Collection that are traditional objects decorated in new ways. Such an amulet, historically, would have been a *cekpa* bag, the ornament containing a baby's umbilical cord that was attached to a child's first ceremonial garment. Here, the turtle was created more as a toy or *tchotchke,* like the horse and rabbit in the High Collection. The turtle is decorated in the scattered color design sometimes referred to as "grandmother's mix." The randomly arranged colored beads were applied to many different pieces, including the flowers on this bag, a horn pincushion, and a velvet fish.[32]

Finally, some items in the High Collection applied more traditional designs to commercially made objects and to objects reproducing items

Pouch. Artist unknown; B.Y. High Collection, Nebraska State Historical Society.

that already existed in middle-class women's homes. The woman who created a velveteen wall hanging applied a Dakota floral pattern and a beaded
fringe to a decoration for a parlor wall, surrounded perhaps by other
knickknacks from "exotic" cultures. The creator of the beaded purse took
a leather wallet and covered it with glass beads in a floral design and the
date. The "cut beads" used on the purse were, and continue to be, especially prized by beadwork artists because their facets catch the light and
add sparkle to the beaded object.[33]

Purse, 1911. Artist unknown, B.Y. High Collection, Nebraska State Historical Society.

The High Collection holds only a few items decorated with quillwork. Easier access to beads than to porcupine quills, the possibility of completing more items with beadwork than quillwork, and the need for cash no doubt all combined to reduce the number of quillwork items made for sale. One pair of moccasins boasts bands with quillwork and beads, and one item identified as a holster is, perhaps incongruously, ornamented with delicate quill flowers. The quillwork lavished on prayer books, in contrast, suggests that this art form might have been reserved more for items that had greater value to the artists themselves or for items that were made as gifts.

High's business might have received a boost from one of the most visible customers for Santee women's artwork, John F. Lenger, a Bohemian immigrant who established himself in Niobrara in the 1870s as a music teacher and band director. Approached by a group of leaders from the Santee community to teach music on the reservation, he learned the Dakota language and soon established the Santee Sioux Band. It was made up of young men from the reservation who performed throughout the area and beyond. The band made an appearance at the Sioux City Corn Palace in 1888, the Chicago World Fair in 1893,

Horn pincushion. Artist unknown; B.Y. High Collection, Nebraska State Historical Society.

and the Trans-Mississippi Exposition in Omaha in 1898. They also gave a command performance for President Benjamin Harrison. For all Lenger's appearances with the band, he wore a costume of elaborately ornamented hide made by women on the Santee reservation.[34]

For Native peoples across the Great Lakes and Plains regions of the United States, the nineteenth century brought the devastation of war, removal, or both. In many of these communities, making and selling decorated hide objects gave women an opportunity to contribute to their families' subsistence under difficult new economic conditions. Through their artwork, women were able to express and retain traditional values within these drastically transformed circumstances. In an essay discussing the dresses that Lakota women and other Northern Plains women made for the Ghost Dances of the 1880s, Colleen Cutschall, herself a Lakota artist, notes that women painted symbols of supernatural power on these dresses as a way to call upon those powers to rescue their people from "cultural genocide." In the context of the destruction of Dakota communities in Minnesota and the Dakota's efforts to reconstitute them in new lands, it seems appropriate to view Santee and Flandreau women's artwork similarly—as a way to rescue their people from cultural annihilation.[35]

The wrenching experiences of war and internment destroyed the resistance that the Dakota had posed to missionary efforts in Minnesota for more than two decades. Conversions at Fort Snelling, Mankato, Crow Creek, and Davenport brought many women and men into the folds of the church. When finally allowed to reestablish their own communities, the Dakota adopted lifestyles that missionaries and government officials had long tried to impose upon them. Yet, as families found it impossible to live fully as farmers and farmers' wives, they returned to some of their own practices and lived a material life that blended white and Dakota ways. In a parallel manner, Dakota and white spiritual and cultural life blended as well.

The production of intricately decorated items of everyday life occupied a central place in the work that Dakota women had traditionally performed in their *tiospayes* and villages in Minnesota. These pieces of art had served functional, ceremonial, and spiritual purposes. With the end of the fur trade, sale of these pieces of art made it possible for women to make economic contributions to the survival of their communities. When missionaries and Indian agents arrived on the scene, women's activities played a powerful role in resisting the alienation of the Dakota from their culture and practices.

In the Dakota exile communities in Santee and in Flandreau, women's creative work once again played a multifaceted role in survival. Benefitting from the growing demand for Indian art, women found a ready market for their beadwork and quillwork that allowed them to contribute to the material subsistence of their families. Under the umbrella of the church's winyan omniciye, women similarly produced items whose sale helped support the church. Women also made these items as gifts for family members on ceremonial and celebratory occasions. These endeavors gave renewed energy to activities that had been central to their role as women and to community life. Finally, as women sat together in work groups that recalled those of earlier times, they could reestablish connections with their environment, with the spirits of their ancestors, and with the wakan. Spiritual survival was woven into women's creative work in Santee and Flandreau, as it had been for their mothers and grandmothers in Minnesota.

Indian Renaissance
and Dakota Women's Art

EACH YEAR SINCE 2004, the city of Winona, Minnesota, located where Wabasha's band of Mdewakantunwan Dakota once had its summer encampment, has hosted a Dakota Homecoming—in the Dakota language, *Hdihunipi*, They Return Home. The event was originally planned as a rebuttal to a much-publicized series of activities commemorating the sesquicentennial of the Grand Excursion, a visit up the river undertaken by President Millard C. Fillmore in 1854 to promote development of newly acquired territories. The Dakota Homecoming became an annual effort to speak truths about the effects of European American conquest on the Dakota people and to celebrate Dakota culture. Central to this occasion is an education tent showcasing Dakota arts and history. Ramona Kitto Stately, the great-great-granddaughter of Mazaadidi and Pazahiyayewin, survivors of the exile at Crow Creek and Davenport, coordinates the demonstrations and presentations. Myrna Weston-Louis, a descendant of Crow Creek survivors Wicacaka, Emma Red Owl, and Mary Mitchell, displays her quillwork and demonstrates the techniques of wrapping and weaving porcupine quills she uses in making jewelry and other items.[1]

The Dakota Homecoming is one of a growing number of events around the United States organized to educate and bring attention to the atrocities perpetrated by military, civilian, and religious institutions against Native peoples. These events also memorialize the victims and take steps

Myrna Weston-Louis
demonstrating
quillwork at Dakota
Gathering, Winona,
Minnesota, 2006.

toward grieving and healing for their descendants. In December 2010, for instance, the twenty-third annual Si Tanka Oyate Wokiksuye, Big Foot Memorial Ride, set out in remembrance of the 1890 massacre at Wounded Knee Creek when Big Foot and hundreds of Mniconjou and Hunkpapa Lakota men, women, and children were slaughtered by the U.S. Cavalry.[2]

The Eastern Dakota have organized specific events that publicize and reclaim their history. These occasions allow the descendants of victims interned at Fort Snelling, Mankato, Davenport, and Crow Creek to mourn the grandmothers and grandfathers who were never given proper burials and to assert the survival of the Dakota nation and people. In 1972, Dakota spiritual leader Amos Owen, chairman of the Prairie Island Sioux Community, and two white men, (Louis) Bud Lawrence and Jim

Buckley, organized the first powwow in Mankato, a city which now holds annual powwows focusing on education and reconciliation. Since 1997, runners have completed a ninety-mile overnight relay leaving Fort Snelling and arriving in Mankato on December 26 in honor of the thirty-eight Dakota warriors hanged at the end of the 1862 U.S.–Dakota War. In June 2002, representatives from several Dakota reservations gathered at Fort Thompson on the Crow Creek reservation to mark creation of a memorial park in honor of the women and children who perished during their internment there between 1863 and 1866. That November, Dakota women led a group of Natives and other allies on the first of a series of biennial Dakota commemorative marches retracing the forced march of women, children, and elders from the Lower Sioux Agency to Fort Snelling in November 1862. Also in 2002, a memorial was established at Fort Snelling State Park on the site where they were incarcerated through the spring of 1863. In 2005, Lindsay Park in Davenport, where Dakota men were held from 1863 until reunited with their families in 1866, hosted the first of several Dakota Prisoner Memorial and Descendant Wacipi (powwow).[3]

Efforts by Dakota women including Ramona Stately, Iyupseyusewin, She Who Holds the Reins, and Myrna Weston-Louis, Zitkanadutawaśtewin, Pretty Red Bird Woman, have helped revitalize the culture that genocide, conversion to Christianity, and reservation life threatened to extinguish. Stately and Weston-Louis focus on teaching Dakota arts and traditions to Dakota and other Native peoples. Like their grandmothers in the decades after the 1862 war and internment, these women are using the traditional arts of their nation to rebuild a culture after genocidal policies and other assaults on their communities.

While their grandmothers defied official policies designed to exterminate their people, Stately and Weston-Louis are part of the political and cultural "Indian Renaissance" that began in the last decades of the twentieth century. Unlike their grandmothers, they work without the guidance and teachings of elders who remembered life in the Dakota communities of Minnesota. Mary Mitchell, born at Crow Creek and raised by a mother and grandmother and other women who grew up in Minnesota, died in 1943, more than a decade before her great-granddaughter Myrna was born.

The twentieth century, which saw the passing of Mary's generation and the birth of her great-granddaughter's, posed new challenges that again threatened the Dakota communities at Santee and Flandreau. The depression of the 1930s added to persistent economic insecurity on reservations and forced many who had been able to retain their land allotments to sell or forfeit them. Native men and families left in search of work, weakening already vulnerable communities. During World War II, Native towns and reservations continued to bleed, as men and women moved to cities for well-paying war jobs. Native American communities in fact contributed a larger proportion of their young men to the military effort than all other communities in the United States.

In 1944, Congress passed the Pick-Sloan Flood Control Act, which funded the damming of the Missouri River for hydroelectricity and flood control, a move which flooded thousands of arable acres of reservation lands across the Northern Plains. A decade later, a new federal policy of "terminating" Indian reservations and relocating thousands of people to urban centers increased Natives' fears of losing their culture.[4]

Although the federal government ceased termination proceedings in the 1960s, conditions on reservations and in urban communities continued to deteriorate. In this second decade of the twenty-first century, they remain close to genocidal. Unemployment rates of more than 50 percent—even 80 percent in some places—prevail. So do very high rates of substance abuse, chronic illness, suicide, especially among young people, and violence. Native women are at particular risk of violence, according to a 2006 study by Amnesty International. Women interviewed on some reservations said they did not know any women in their community who had not suffered sexual violence.[5]

All these circumstances would have achieved the nineteenth-century goal of eradicating Dakota culture were it not for the extraordinary upsurge in Native political activism and a dramatic reversal in U.S. Indian policy. In large cities militant pan-Indian political organizing emerged in the 1960s, inspired in part by the African American civil rights and Black Power movements. The American Indian Movement (AIM), which supported sovereignty, treaty rights, and direct action, brought a new visibility to conditions on reservations and in urban communities and articulated demands for self-governance, religious freedom, and economic development.[6]

The same years witnessed the establishment of anti-poverty programs across the United States and a shift among policymakers toward allowing greater self-determination for reservations. Native peoples benefitted from War on Poverty programs, some of which were specifically designed to address their needs, and subsequent legislation targeted improving conditions on reservations. The Indian Self-Determination and Education Assistance Act of 1975 stands as a landmark shift in federal policy toward encouraging Native peoples to set the direction of educational and other services provided by the federal government. Federal policy has supported the development of tribal colleges with vocational orientation in hopes of addressing high reservation unemployment rates and providing services. The American Indian Religious Freedom Act of 1978 reversed the century-old ban on Native religious practices, and the Indian Gaming Regulatory Act of 1988 promoted opportunities for economic development through casino gambling on reservations.[7]

Despite very challenging conditions on reservations and in urban communities, the last thirty years have brought significant changes that help Native peoples reclaim their histories, reestablish their traditions, and return to their ancestors' spiritual beliefs and practices. Increased tribal self-government and tribal government funding through U.S. policy and casino earnings have facilitated educational and cultural programs on reservations. Most prominently, large powwows celebrate Native cultures and help revitalize Native arts. Dance regalia, like jingle dresses, moccasins, leggings, roaches, and bustles, have created a demand for traditional beading and other types of decoration and have encouraged new techniques for making and adorning these outfits. In addition, powwow food vendors, an integral part of these gatherings, offer traditional foods (as well as snow cones and hotdogs). Other vendors display Native beadwork, quillwork, pottery, weavings, and other art for sale to Natives and non-Natives attending, thus renewing the practice of creating merchandise for sale.

Tribal colleges have contributed to this revitalization, working with reservation health programs to train staff in chemical-dependency treatment and recovery programs, including the Red Road, which integrates Native teachings and spiritual observances. Colleges have also increasingly promoted traditional arts. Finally, at the state level, numerous initiatives have supported and expanded federal policies, particularly in education. Several states now offer Native-language instruction in public schools and mandate programs for Native students in elementary and secondary curricula.[8]

All these developments have left particular marks on the Dakota communities of Santee and Flandreau. Families who lost their lands and livelihoods during the Depression started an exodus from Santee to Sioux City and from Flandreau to Minneapolis and Chicago that continued into the 1940s. Few, if any, returned until decades later. Many who remained at Santee on their own land lost it to flooding created by Pick-Sloan Act dams. No longer able to grow grain and vegetables or raise chickens and livestock, they were displaced without any financial compensation for their losses. While neither the Flandreau nor the Santee reservations were threatened with imminent dissolution, official termination of the Ponca reservation just a few miles west of Santee no doubt caused great distress. Expectations of eventual termination caused numerous families to leave reservations in search of stability in large cities like Minneapolis and Chicago, which had growing urban Indian communities.[9]

The new directions of the 1960s and subsequent decades also affected Dakota communities. Casinos have brought employment opportunities to both Santee and Flandreau. The Nebraska Indian Community College maintains a branch campus in Santee. Both communities operate health clinics and provide housing and services for the elderly and disabled. Finally, both Santee and Flandreau hold annual powwows that provide opportunities for family reunions, honoring, feasts, and giveaways.

⤴

The Indian Renaissance of these last decades has also made possible, in many ways, the work of Myrna Weston-Louis and Ramona Stately. Weston-Louis and her husband, David Louis, have been teaching quillwork at Sisseton Wahpeton College, the tribal college on the Lake Traverse reservation. Stately is the coordinator of the Secondary Indian Education Program for the Osseo area schools near Minneapolis, which, like other Minnesota school districts with 10 percent or more Native students, is mandated to provide programming for those students in Native culture, history, and language. Both women teach traditional women's arts at Winona's annual Dakota Homecoming, organized by the Winona–Dakota Unity Alliance that grew out of the awareness among white Minnesotans of the need for greater understanding and recognition of the state's Indigenous peoples.

Weston-Louis and Stately each see themselves not only as continuing Dakota traditions but as perpetuating their own family's lineages of women's creative work. Weston-Louis's mother, Violet, was known for her ability as a seamstress and needleworker; she created beautiful beaded items and clothing, as did her grandmother Lavara. Her great-grandmother Mary Mitchell made quilts for family members and dolls to sell at church gatherings where women eagerly made the kind of art they had learned from mothers and grandmothers. Stately's great-great-grandmother Pazahiyayewin was a gifted and prolific creator of quilts, beadwork, and clothing for her children and her *tiospaye*.[10]

The work of these generations of women was central to the material life of Dakota communities. The functional pieces of art they created allowed them to store and transport food and equipment, to carry and protect their babies, and to shelter their families. Starting in the last decades of life in their Minnesota homelands and increasing in the decades following war and internment, Dakota women also made items specifically for sale. By the time Mary Mitchell brought her dolls to sell at the Winnebago Agency in 1943, producing handcrafts for sale had been a part of Dakota women's lives for many decades. It enabled them to help feed, clothe, and protect their families, just as making garments, footwear, containers, and tipi covers had enabled earlier generations to feed, clothe, and shelter theirs.

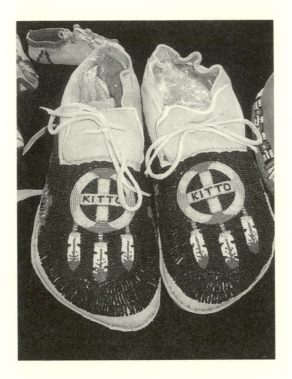

Moccasins by Ramona
Kitto Stately, on display
in the Education Tent,
Dakota Gathering,
Winona, Minnesota, 2011.

Native women artists today continue to produce items for sale to customers outside their communities as well as items for family members
and others within their communities. In both cases, they are highly conscious of the deep historical, cultural, and spiritual dimensions of this
work. Myrna Weston-Louis adds different patterns and designs to artwork
that she makes for sale mostly to white clients and to the quilled pieces
she makes for relatives and friends celebrating births, graduations, and
professional or military accomplishments. In this way, she perpetuates
the traditions of Dakota women who did the same. Weston-Louis and her
husband also maintain the understanding of creative work as thoroughly
woven into everyday life. "As multimedia artists," she says, "we have chosen porcupine quillwork as a lifestyle and are deeply committed to the
preservation of this exquisite art form." She is also conscious of sustaining the history of her people as she does quillwork. When she selects a
design and colors that reflect a sunset, for instance, she weaves into the

object not only the visual experience of that sunset but also her awareness of the spiritual powers dwelling in the sky, the clouds, and the wind.[11]

Ramona Stately focuses on members of her family and community when she makes moccasins and other beaded items. The work, she says, connects her to her grandmothers and the spiritual traditions surrounding Dakota women's creative work. For Stately, "Every stitch is a prayer." Through beadwork, she deeply experiences her relationships with the spirit of her grandmothers as well as with the beauty of the world around her and the awe she feels for creation. When she teaches about beadwork to her Native students and to visitors at the Dakota Homecoming, she articulates the place of this work within the history, traditions, and spiritual life of the Dakota: "The more we learn about culture and history and the more we listen to our ancestors, who speak to our spirits, the easier it is to find the meaning of each piece. It is then that we are able to create pieces of art that also speak to others."[12]

Like Myrna Weston-Louis, Stately comes from a multigenerational lineage of very talented women. Her great-great-grandmother Pazahiyayewin, She Shall Radiate in Her Path Like the Sun, was born in Minnesota in 1838 and learned to sew from her mother, herself very skilled in handiwork. Pazahiyayewin sewed and quilted and did beadwork and quillwork, and she taught all her daughters these skills. "No one at Santee could make a better moccasin than she," wrote her daughter Eunice Kitto Baskin in her mother's obituary.[13]

Pazahiyayewin lived through the hardest times endured by the Dakota. She was expecting her fourth child when the war broke out in 1862. Her husband, Mazaadidi, Walks on Iron, was taken from his family by U.S. soldiers, and their dwelling and belongings were destroyed the night she delivered her baby. Carrying her infant while looking after her three other children and aging mother, she walked 150 miles from the Lower Sioux Agency to Crow Creek with other women, children, and elders. There, she kept her mother and children alive and even went on hunts, when the authorities allowed them, to help supply her family and others with meat.

Years later, when Pazahiyayewin taught her daughters beadwork and quillwork, when she taught them to make moccasins—and when she

made her unsurpassed moccasins—she wove together surviving frag-
ments of the culture crushed by war and internment. Perhaps, as she
created these pieces of art and taught them to others, she kept with her
the women who had taught her and the rich environment they created.
Perhaps, for Pazahiyayewin, as for her great-great-granddaughter, every
stitch was a prayer.

The spiritual dimensions of functional work appeared most power-
fully to Stately when she made her first pair of moccasins for a young
nephew who had decided to dance at the annual Santee powwow. Her
role as "auntie" was to provide an outfit. She undertook to make the moccasins herself, although she had never made any before. To her great
surprise, she found that she had a gift for this work. "I did not know,"
she wrote, "that I was guided by a spirit who gave me this talent. I knew
for sure who had guided me when I read Pazahiyayewin's obituary, written by her daughter Eunice Baskin." This realization made her understand the obligation that she has to this grandmother. Making moccasins
reinforces her ties with her grandmother and gives her a deep sense of
responsibility to continue the work they share.[14]

This responsibility to her grandmother, however, seems inseparable
from Stately's commitment to her people. She says, "As a Dakota woman,
I believe in carrying on the art and culture of my nation." In doing so,
she honors all the women who lived through the decades of fiercest dispossession and cultural extermination. As it did for earlier generations,
beadwork, quillwork, and other art forms sustain her relationships with
and obligations to those who came before and those who follow.

The history of the Dakota people and its ongoing consequences remain
open questions both for the people and for the state of Minnesota, the
Dakota's homeland. While biennial Dakota Commemorative marches
continue to seek dialogue with local communities where fighting and violence occurred during the U.S.–Dakota War, white Minnesotans continue
to resist learning about Dakota perspectives on these historical events.
The ongoing struggle over this history was vividly evident in discussions
and events organized around the 2008 sesquicentennial of Minnesota's

statehood. Questions regarding European Americans' actions toward Native peoples were largely sidestepped by officials, and open confrontations occurred when groups of Dakota individuals challenged dominant narratives about this shared history.[15]

One hundred and fifty years after the U.S.–Dakota War, these issues remain contentious and painful. At the same time, however, Dakota women continue to sustain and nurture their families, communities, and culture, just as generations did before them.

ACKNOWLEDGMENTS

Dakota Women's Work stands as a testimony to the many Dakota women and men who have provided much assistance and guidance for this project, starting with Edith Bickerstaff at Santee and William Beane at Flandreau, who spent many long days introducing me to friends and relatives, helping arrange interviews, and participating in many themselves. In addition, William Beane most generously shared with me vast amounts of materials that he has gathered on the history of his family and the Flandreau Santee Sioux Tribe.

Many other Dakota men and women contributed time, knowledge, and insights to this project, including Wyatt Thomas, Thelma Thomas, Jim James, Mary Johnson, Bernice Medina, and Virginia Mackey at Santee; Roberta Williamson, Beverly Wakeman, Sidney H. Byrd, Myrna Weston-Louis and David Louis, and J. C. Wade at Flandreau; Jerry and Brenda Lytle, Hester and Lorenzo Fleury, Hilda Longcrow, and Rose Ducheneaux at Fort Thompson, South Dakota; Dorothy Thomas, Elaine Provost, and Ramona Frazier at Sioux City, Iowa; Emily L. Smith at Winnebago, Nebraska; Joe Campbell at Prairie Island, Minnesota; Teresa Peterson at the Upper Sioux Community, Minnesota; and Janice Bad Moccasin, Virginia Bad Moccasin, Reuben Kitto, Rod Steiner, and Vernell Wabasha. I am very grateful to Kenneth James, Sr., and to Margaret Daniels for displaying and allowing me to photograph the quilt made by their great-grandmother, Mary Mitchell. Waziyatawin and Diane Wilson read early portions of this work and made valuable suggestions to which I returned repeatedly. Ramona Kitto Stately and William Beane, in addition to all their other contributions, read through a complete draft of this manuscript and helped me fill in many gaps.

Studying the Dakota language became integral to this project. Cantemaza Neil McKay and Glen Wasicuna made every single lesson about Dakota language a lesson in history and survival. Lisa Elbert's years as a teacher were far too few, but she nevertheless inspired many of us through her full embrace of learning and teaching.

Numerous scholars generously shared research materials, knowledge, and insight gathered over many years. I am particularly grateful to Patricia Albers, Carolyn Anderson, Annette Atkins, Raymond Demallie, Donald Fixico, and Bruce White. Over ten years of research and writing, Herbert Hoover provided unstinting encouragement as well as access to his encyclopedic knowledge and vast collection of research materials and photographs. The positive response to my *Minnesota History* article, "Survival at Crow Creek," was very energizing and helpful; I want to thank in particular Leonard Wabasha, Chris Mato Numpa, and Marybeth Faimon for their comments.

Curators at many different museums made possible a focus on material culture in this research, including Marcia Anderson at the Minnesota Historical Society, Tilly Laskey at the Science Museum of Minnesota, Laura Mooney at the Nebraska State Historical Society, Susan Kennedy Zeller and Nancy Rosoff at the Brooklyn Museum of Art, Felicia Pickering at the National Museum of Natural History, and Katerina Klapstova at the Naprstek Museum in Prague. They were very gracious in educating and accommodating a scholar more used to dealing with books and letters.

Archivists provided thoughtful and insightful guidance through innumerable collections of documents and photographs in a dozen libraries and historical societies, including the Nebraska State Historical Society, the New-York Historical Society, the South Dakota State Archives, the National Archives, the Smithsonian Anthropological Archives, the New

York Academy of Medicine Library, the Center for Western Studies at Augustana College (Sioux Falls, South Dakota), the University of Minnesota Library Special Collections, the Sioux City (Iowa) Public Museum, the American Museum of Natural History, the National Museum of the American Indian, and the Moody County Historical Museum. Debbie Miller and all the librarians and archivists at the Minnesota Historical Society continue to make MHS one of the most welcoming libraries for researchers.

Colleagues at Winona State University have been completely integral to this project. Librarians Russ Denison, Kathy Sullivan, Vernon Leighton, Joe Mount, Joe Jackson, Mark Eriksen, Kendall Larson, and Allison Quam have been invaluable partners in scholarship, as has Susan Byom in chasing down materials through interlibrary loan. The staff of Teaching Learning & Technology Services has provided essential assistance with numerous technological dimensions of this project. I would particularly like to thank Ken Graetz, Joan Bernard, John Stafford, Margaret Welshons, Chad Kjorlien, and Elissa Hall. Cindy Killion organized the Native Studies discussion group that allowed me to work through some of the ideas I was developing in my research. Linda D'Amico read drafts of several chapters and generously shared her knowledge of gender and Native issues, and she and Andrea Wood each read a complete draft of my manuscript and made many valuable suggestions for sharpening my analysis. My colleagues in the History Department—Seymour Byman, Marianna Byman, Cynthia Fuerstneau, Peter Henderson, Kurt Hohenstein, Matthew Lindaman, Matthew Lungerhausen, Gregory Schmidt, Tomas Tolvaisas, and the late Alex Yard—have provided a stimulating environment for balancing the demands of teaching and research. Several of the department's office administrators lent their talents and skills to this project in numerous and essential ways: Lisa Hessel, Barb Nascak, Ann Kohner, and Alisha Syrmopoulos. Jacqueline Gessner Mathers, a WSU graduate and social studies teacher at Houston (Minnesota) High School, compiled the data and created the charts representing changes in the fur trade in the middle of the nineteenth century.

None of this would have been possible without support from the people of Minnesota and the funding provided by the State of Minnesota to Winona State University and to the Minnesota Historical Society. Winona State University has awarded this project several Professional Improvement Fund grants, and College of Liberal Arts deans Joe Gow and Troy Paino helped create an environment that supported and affirmed faculty in all their professional endeavors. The American Philosophical Society, the Minnesota Humanities Commission, and the Minnesota Historical and Cultural Grants Program of the Minnesota Historical Society also awarded generous grants that supported research and writing.

Friends in both related and completely unrelated fields—Joy Lintelman, Rick Chapman, Diane Lichtenstein, Frederica Adelman, Miriam Frank, Lisa Heldke, Susanna Short, Susanne Smith, Beth Cherne, and June Reineke—shared the intellectual excitement and the practical knowledge that keep a scholar energized and productive. Friends outside the academy have made very special contributions to this work as well, among them Joe Morse and Carol Jensen; Jo Ann Thomas and Joan Schnabel read a draft of the manuscript and made numerous practical suggestions; and Barbara Davis shared the joys and frustrations of writing and rewriting. Elizabeth Nagy, Chris Masters, and Alex Masters provided warm hospitality during each research trip to Washington, DC.

Over many years, the editors at MHS Press have worked tirelessly to sharpen my analysis and my writing. I thank Anne Kaplan, Marilyn Ziebarth, Shannon Pennefeather, and, above all, Ann Regan, who never ceases to amaze me with her sharp insight and spot-on suggestions. In addition, production manager Daniel Leary worked closely with mapmaker Tim Campbell, who graciously made all the changes I requested throughout the process.

As I neared the end of this project, I realized that much of my understanding of genocide was shaped by my life as a Jew. I particularly want to thank Yvette K. Hyman, my mother, and Rabbi Michelle Werner for all they have taught me about honoring the memory of the victims and the lives of the survivors of the Holocaust.

Hyman and Campbell family members have, for nearly ten years, allowed me to combine research trips with family visits: Eileen and Hank Campbell in New Ulm; Sarah Campbell and Mark Gustafson in Minneapolis; Ruth and Henry Campbell in Ames; Cynthia Gray and Alain Hyman, Marc Hyman, and Yvette and Robert Hyman in New York; and Laurel Robinson in Prague. Two Campbells have lived very closely with this book: John D. and Raizl Ambler. John has contributed more than I could ever have imagined with probing questions, careful reading of many drafts (including of these acknowledgments!), and really useful practical suggestions as well as reassurance, patience, and, above all, humor whenever panic or despair threatened to set in. Raizl asked questions that were wise beyond her years and kept me focused on the importance of passing on knowledge from generation to generation. *Ldor v'dor.*

NOTES

Notes to Introduction

1. Bean, *Eastman, Cloud Man, Many Lightnings;* Diedrich, "'A Good Man' in a Changing World"; author's interview with Lillian Beane and William Beane, Mar. 10, 2003, Flandreau, SD.

2. Meyer, *History of the Santee Sioux,* vii; Wilson and Taylor, *Remember This!,* 277, 4–5; Hoover, *Sioux Country,* 40–41. The Lakota Council Fires are the Oglala, They Scatter Their Own; the Sicangu, Burnt Thighs; the Mnikowaju, Planters Beside the Water; the Itazipco, Those With Bows; the Oohe Numpa, Two Kettle; and the Sihasapa, Black Feet.

3. Flute, *Dakota Iapi,* viii; Dakota historian Waziyatawin Angela Wilson, for instance, draws on Lakota sources to describe and explain Dakota practices and beliefs, as does Dakota anthropologist Barbara Feezor. See Wilson and Taylor, *Remember This!,* 277, and Feezor, "Mdewakanton Dakota Women."

4. See McCrady, *Living with Strangers,* 168, and Meyer, *History of the Santee Sioux,* 10.

5. Richard W. Hill, Sr., "Epilogue: Art through Indian Eyes," in Grimes, *Uncommon Legacies,* 235.

6. Viviane Gray quoted in Richard W. Hill, Sr., "Art of the Northeast Woodlands and Great Lakes," in Grimes, *Uncommon Legacies,* 191. Berlo and Phillips maintain that no North American Native languages have a word for art: *Native North American Art,* 9.

7. Carol Berry, "Museum Focuses on Art Rather Than Artifacts," *Indian Country Today,* Feb. 23, 2011, 40; see Rosoff, *Tipi,* for an example of this practice. For a summary of discussions surrounding Native arts, see Berlo and Phillips, *Native North American Art,* Chapter 1.

8. This phrase is borrowed from the title of an anthology of essays about collectors and the market for Native American art: Krech, *Collecting Native America*. On debates about tourist art, see David Wooley, "Contemporary Native American Traditional Arts: Comments on Traditional vs. Tourist Art and Gender Roles," in *On the Border*; and Nancy Parezo, "Indigenous Art: Creating Value and Sharing Beauty," in Deloria, *A Companion to American Indian History*, Ch. 12.

9. See Dippie, *The Vanishing American*; Dippie, *Catlin and His Contemporaries*.

10. For a discussion of oral tradition and Native American history, see Denetdale, *Reclaiming Diné History*, 34–40, and Wilson and Taylor, *Remember This!*, 277, 23–36. Material culture as a source for Native American history will be discussed in Chapter 1. Rebecca Kugel and Lucy Eldersveld Murphy, "Searching for Cornfields—and Sugar Groves," in Kugel and Murphy, *Native Women's History in Eastern North America*, xxxi.

Notes to Chapter 1

1. Author's interview with Illa Mackey, Nancy Mackey, and Edith Bickerstaff, Aug. 6, 2006, Niobrara, NE, and with Kenneth James, Sr., June 16, 2007, Flandreau, SD.

2. On cradleboards, see Hail and Ahtone, *Gifts of Pride and Love*; on spirit beings, see Philander Prescott, "The Dacotahs or Sioux of the Upper Mississippi," in Schoolcraft, et al., *Historical and Statistical Information* (1847), 3:232–33.

3. Therese Thau Heyman, "George Catlin and the Smithsonian," in Catlin, *George Catlin and His Indian Gallery*, 249–71. Catlin discusses how he came to own this object in his account of his travels across the continent, *Letters and Notes*, 132. The cradle is now in the National Museum of Natural History.

4. The portrayal of Dakota and other Native women by European and European American explorers, ethnographers, and others, and their marginalization by scholars are discussed in Rayna Green, "The Pocahontas Perplex: The Image of Indian Women in American Culture," and David D. Smits, "The 'Squaw Drudge': A Prime Example of Savagism," in Kugel and Murphy, *Native Women's History in Eastern North America*, 7–49; Patricia C. Albers, "Introduction: New Perspectives on Plains Indian Women," in Albers and Medicine, *The Hidden Half*, 280, 3–8; and Laura F. Klein and Lillian Ackerman, "Introduction," in Klein and Ackerman, *Women and Power in Native North America*, 294, 3–9.

5. Johnson, "Notes on the Mdewakanton Bark House"; Raymond J. DeMallie, "Sioux Until 1850," 724–25, and Patricia C. Albers, "Santee," 763–67, in Sturtevant, *Handbook of North American Indians*.

6. Babcock, "Sioux Villages in Minnesota." On Wabasha's village, see Nilles, *A History of Wapasha's Prairie*. On the yearly cycle of Dakota encampments, see Spector, *What this Awl Means*, 161, 67–77.

7. Pond, *The Dakota or Sioux in Minnesota*, 37–39, 45–48.

8. Pond, *The Dakota or Sioux in Minnesota*, 53–54.

9. Pond, *The Dakota or Sioux in Minnesota*, 26–27; Albers, "Santee," 764.

10. McLaughlin, *Myths and Legends of the Sioux*, 200, 64.

11. Wilson, "A Day in the Life of Maza Okiye Win," 200.

12. McLaughlin, *Myths and Legends of the Sioux*, 200, 64; and Pond, *The Dakota or Sioux in Minnesota*, 27. The wild artichoke, *Heianthus tuberosus*, was the original of the cultivated Jerusalem artichoke. Densmore, *How Indians Use Wild Plants*, 319.

13. "The Fruits and Roots of Minnesota Valley," *The Dakota Friend*, Jan. 1851, n.p.

14. Louis B. Casagrande and Orrin C. Shane III, "The Historical Tribes of the Upper Mississippi River Valley," in George Bates, *Historic Lifestyles in the Upper Mississippi River Valley*, 276; Elden Johnson, "The Seventeenth-Century Mdewakantunwan Dakota Subsistence Mode," in Spector, et al., *Archaeology, Ecology, and Ethno- history*, 203, 160.

15. "The Fruits and Roots of the Minnesota Valley"; Pond, *The Dakota or Sioux in Minnesota*, 58; Woolworth and Woolworth, "Eastern Dakota Settlement and Subsistence Patterns," 87; Deloria, *Some Notes on the Santee*, 12; Gilmore, *Uses of Plants*, 40.

16. Pond, *The Dakota or Sioux in Minnesota*, 29; Deloria, *Some Notes on the Santee*, 10–12.

17. Penney, *Art of the American Indian Frontier*, 167; Torrence, *The American Indian Parfleche*. Deloria, *Speaking of Indians*, 27.

18. Author's interview with Ramona Kitto Stately, June 4, 2011, Winona, MN.

19. Philander Prescott, "Manners, Customs, and Opinions of the Dacotahs," in Schoolcraft, et al., *Historical and Statistical Information* (1847), 4:60–61.

20. Sarah E. Boehme, "An Officer and An Illustrator: On the Indian Frontier," in Boehme, *Seth Eastman*, 2–35; for a discussion of *The Tanner*, see 18–19.

21. Red Shirt, *Bead on an Anthill*, 4–5. On quillwork technique, see Lyford and Beatty, *Quill and Beadwork of the Western Sioux*, 116.

22. Lyford and Beatty, *Quill and Beadwork of the Western Sioux*, 64.

23. Gilman, *Where Two Worlds Meet*; Dean L. Anderson, "The Flow of European Trade Goods into the Western Great Lakes Region, 1715–1760," in Brown, *The Fur Trade Revisited*, 93–113; Quimby, *Indian Culture and European Trade Goods*. For women's participation in exchanges with traders, see Chapter 2.

24. Pond, *The Dakota or Sioux in Minnesota*, 39–41.

25. On awls and awl handles, see Spector, *What this Awl Means*, 161, 18–31. Deloria, *Waterlily*, 145–47. This novel is based on ethnographic material that Deloria gathered between the 1920s and the 1940s while working with Franz Boas of Columbia University. Her research included materials from Lakota reservations, the Yankton reservation (where she was enrolled), and the Eastern Dakota in Nebraska and Minnesota. In much of her work, she sought to "demonstrate the oneness of the Dakota way of life," although she also occasionally emphasized distinctions between Lakota,

Nakota, and Dakota: Raymond J. DeMallie, "Introduction to the Bison Books Edition," Deloria, *Dakota Texts*. A recent book about descendants of Minnesota Dakota peoples in the twenty-first century draws its central premise from a description in this novel: Wilson, *Beloved Child*.

26. Deloria, *The Dakota Way of Life*, 147, 53, 31. The term appears variously as "fancywork" and "fancy work" in Deloria's writings.

27. Deloria, *Some Notes on the Santee*, 7–8; Pond, *The Dakota or Sioux in Minnesota*, 137–40.

28. Deloria, *The Dakota Way of Life*, 123; author's interview with Myrna Weston-Louis, David Louis, and Sandy Weston, June 15, 2007, Flandreau, SD.

29. Prescott, "The Dacotahs or Sioux of the Upper Mississippi," 3:233; Thomas Tyon, "Spirits," in Walker, *Lakota Belief and Ritual*, 120. Ramona Kitto Stately interview. The curvilinear floral design that has become characteristic of Eastern Dakota beadwork and quillwork emerged in the nineteenth century, although the evolution of Eastern Dakota patterns from geometric and geomorphic to floral remains unexplained. Howard, *The Dakota or Sioux Indians*, 7.

30. Ella Deloria, "Santee Ethnographic Notes," in Dakota Ethnography, Box 3, 61, Ella Deloria Archives, Dakota Indian Foundation, Chamberlain, SD, available: zia .aisri.indiana.edu/deloria_archive/. Berlo, "Dreaming of Double Woman"; Howard, *The Dakota or Sioux Indians*, 9; Myrna Weston-Louis, Sandy Weston, and David Louis interview.

31. Little Wound, "Wakan," 68–70, and George Sword, "*Kan* and Its Derivatives," 96–98, both in Walker, *Lakota Belief and Ritual*.

32. "American Indian Women: Spirituality and Status," in Medicine, *Learning to be an Anthropologist*, 193–94. Deloria, *The Dakota Way of Life*, 146–47.

33. This is a widely collected tale, with versions in Deloria, *Dakota Texts*; Eastman and Blumenschein, *Indian Boyhood*, 289; Zitkala-Sa, *Dreams and Thunder*, 171.

34. "Cantektewin: Ill-Fated Woman," in Woolworth, *Santee Dakota Indian Legends*, 76–82.

35. "Wechah the Provider," in Woolworth, *Santee Dakota Indian Legends*, 66–88.

36. M. Renville, "Tasinta Yukikipi," in Riggs and Dorsey, *Dakota Grammar*, 115–23.

Notes to Chapter 2

1. Indian Credit Books 19:31, Henry Hastings Sibley Papers, Roll 18.

2. Van Kirk, *Many Tender Ties*. Bad Hail's name appears in Dakota as Wasson-wee-chastish-nee, The Bad Hail, on the list of Mdewakantunwan signers of the 1837 treaty: Kappler, *Indian Treaties*, 2:493–94. His daughter appears as Ta-sina-sa-win in Sibley's accounts books, Indian Credit Books 19, Sibley Papers, Roll 18.

3. The records of fur trader Henry Sibley will be examined for these trends later in the chapter. The secondary literature on women in fur trade societies makes little

or no mention of women making their own purchases from traders. See Van Kirk, *Many Tender Ties;* Brown, *Strangers in Blood;* Podruchny, *Making the Voyageur World;* Bourgeault, "Class, Race and Gender."

4. *The Dakota Friend,* Jan. 1851, n.p. On the growth of Minneapolis and St. Paul, see Wills, *Boosters, Hustlers, and Speculators.* Christian F. Feest, "Collectors, Collections, and Collectibles: Early Native American Collections in Europe and North America," in Grimes, *Uncommon Legacies,* 35.

5. Kappler, *Indian Treaties,* 2:1031. For further discussion of this treaty, see p. 52 below. Meyer, *History of the Santee Sioux,* 24–25.

6. Woolworth and Woolworth, "Eastern Dakota Settlement and Subsistence Patterns," 70–89.

7. On the Dakota trade fairs, see Ewers, "The Indian Trade of the Upper Missouri," 431, and map, 441.

8. Gilman, "Last Days of the Upper Mississippi Fur Trade," 124–25; Wozniak, *Contact, Negotiation and Conflict,* ch. 2; Whelan, "Archaeological Analysis," 52–56; Anderson, "The Flow of European Trade Goods."

9. The fur trade cycle is described in a number of scholarly works, including Anderson, "The Flow of European Trade Goods"; Whelan, "Archaeological Analysis;" and Little, "People of the Red Path."

10. This is the most researched aspect of women's participation in the fur trade. See Van Kirk, *Many Tender Ties;* Brown, *Strangers in Blood;* Sleeper-Smith, *Indian Women and French Men;* Bourgeault, "Class, Race and Gender," and Podruchny, *Making the Voyageur World.*

11. Gilman, *Henry Hastings Sibley,* 74–76; Anderson, *Kinsmen of Another Kind,* 93, 180, 195.

12. For the use of the term *complementary* to describe men's and women's roles, see Klein and Ackerman, "Introduction," 3. See also Lillian Ackerman, "Complementary but Equal: Gender Status in The Plateau," in Klein and Ackerman, *Women and Power in Native North America,* 75–100.

13. Van Kirk, *Many Tender Ties,* 78–82.

14. Wingerd, *North Country,* 147, 145; Folwell, "A Visit to Farther-and-Gay Castle," 127.

15. Denial, "Pelagie Faribault's Island," 59.

16. The author seeks to use a standard orthography for Dakota names and terms. When a name appears in published form, this spelling of the name is used. *Marpiya Mase* therefore appears here with this spelling rather than *Mahpiya Maza* because it appears as such in Wilson, *Spirit Car.* Wilson, *Spirit Car,* 16–29, 49.

17. The St. Peter's River was renamed the Minnesota River in 1852, when, in response to a request from the territorial legislature, Congress changed it to the name used by the local population, the Dakota. Upham, *Minnesota Place Names,* 3.

18. The following account of Pelagie Faribault's life and her title to Pike Island is based on Denial, "A Proper Light before the Country"; and Denial, "Pelagie Faribault's Island," 59.

19. Denial, "A Proper Light before the Country," 50–56, 67–73.

20. The marriage of David Faribault, Sr., and Nancy McClure received a great deal of attention as it occurred at Traverse des Sioux at the time of the signing of the 1851 treaty through which the United States took over most of the remaining Dakota lands. See Chapter 4 for a discussion of the treaty. McClure tells the story of her wedding in Nancy Huggan, "Captivity among the Sioux," 460, 446–47. Through a previous marriage, David Faribault had a son, David Faribault, Jr., who would marry John Eastman's sister, Mary, who made the moccasins for Lillian Beane. See Chapter 5 for further discussion of this family. In recognition of her many contributions to the community, the Flandreau Santee Sioux Tribe named the senior center it operates Grace Moore Senior Citizens Center: see http://fsst.org

21. On the gender division of labor among the Dakota, see previous chapter. On hunting for both subsistence and trade, see Beltrami, *A Pilgrimage in America*, 297; Podruchny, *Making the Voyageur World*, 258; W. L. Morton, "The North West Company: Pedlars Extraordinary," in Morgan, *Aspects of the Fur Trade*, 11.

22. Bourgeault, "Class, Race and Gender," 14–15; Podruchny, *Making the Voyageur World*, 258–59.

23. Anderson, "The Flow of European Trade Goods," 109. For a list of the goods that Anderson assigned to each category, see 105. The Lake Pepin post actually received far less in the "Clothing" category than the other posts: only 45 percent of the goods shipped there were in that category, in contrast to over 70 percent for the Detroit post. The Pepin location was, at that time, the most recently established ongoing post. See also Nute, "Posts in the Minnesota Fur-Trading Area," for list and location of fur trade posts.

24. Anderson, "The Flow of European Trade Goods," 111. On Dakota warfare with Ojibwe, Sac and Fox, and other nations, see Anderson, *Kinsmen of Another Kind*.

25. Podruchny, *Making the Voyageur World*, 258; for the Ojibwe in Minnesota, see Priscilla K. Buffalohead, "Farmers, Warriors, Traders: A Fresh Look at Ojibway Women," in Aby, *The North Star State*, 119–212. Thomas Connor in Charles Gates, *Five Fur Traders of the Northwest*, 271. The "rats" that the woman brought in might very well have been animals she had trapped herself; the "oats" are wild rice, called *folle avoine*, wild oats, by the French: Charles M. Gates, "Introductory Note," 246. The diary was subsequently identified as Sayer's (Birk and White, "Who Wrote the Diary of Thomas Connor?")

26. Dolin, *Fur, Fortune, and Empire*, 282–84; Wingerd, *North Country*, 96–100.

27. Kappler, *Indian Treaties*, 2:493–94.

28. Meyer, *History of the Santee Sioux*, 25–26, 31; Anderson, *Kinsmen of Another Kind*, 82–83; Kappler, *Indian Treaties*, 2:1031, 305–10, 493–94. The 1805 treaty was never finalized, but the U.S. government still took possession of the land.

29. Anderson, *Kinsmen of Another Kind*, 159–60.

30. Lawrence Taliaferro, the first Indian agent among the Dakota, worked hard to police the whiskey trade throughout his tenure, but all efforts proved futile. His resignation was prompted in part by the rapid arrival of whiskey traders on the east bank of the Mississippi following the signing of the 1837 treaty: Meyer, *History of the Santee Sioux*, 41–42, 60–62.

31. White, *The Middle Ground*, 96–97; Dolin, *Fur, Fortune, and Empire*, 83; Meyer, *History of the Santee Sioux*, 41–42; Anderson, *Little Crow*, 259, 32, 34, 43, 51–52; Wingerd, *North Country*, 138; Anderson, *Kinsmen of Another Kind*, 128. For a fuller treatment of the place of alcohol in relations between whites and Native peoples, see Mancall, *Deadly Medicine*.

32. Gilman, *Henry Hastings Sibley*, ch. 6, 7; Wingerd, *North Country*, 92–93, 147–48.

33. Gilman, "Last Days of the Upper Mississippi Fur Trade." Steele and others financed some of these ventures with the purchase, for negligible sums, of mixed-blood Dakotas' certificates of ownership of allotments on the "Half-Breed Tract," inserted for their benefit in the 1851 Mendota treaty, and selling them for many times their value; the majority of these purchases were made from the mixed-bloods while they were interned at Fort Snelling and therefore in no position to bargain for better terms. See Millikan, "The Great Treasure of the Fort Snelling Prison Camp." Noting the accelerating demand for lumber, Ojibwe and Dakota leaders had tried to establish their own lumber mills on the Chippewa River in the years preceding the 1837 treaty; although they were unsuccessful, the possibility of adding such enterprises to their own business portfolio added to white businessmen's lobbying for the U.S. acquisition of lands between the St. Croix and the Mississippi rivers: Ronnander, "Many Paths to the Pine."

34. Anderson, *Kinsmen of Another Kind*.

35. Sibley Papers, Rolls 17, 18.

36. Mary Riggs to My Dear Parents, June 27, 1839, Riggs and Family Papers, box 3.

37. McLeod, "The Diary of Martin McLeod," 400; Jane S. Williamson to Dear Sister Aiton, Nov. 19, 1852, Williamson Papers, box 1.

38. Mary Riggs to Henrietta Longley, Apr. 4, 1842, Riggs and Family Papers, box 3.

39. Letter No. 50, Catlin, *Letters and Notes*, 133–34.

40. Andrew W. Williamson, "The American Indians," unpublished, undated manuscript, 14, Williamson Papers, box 2.

41. For an overview of scholarship on this topic and discussion of specific forms of tourist art, see Phillips, *Unpacking Culture*.

Notes to Chapter 3

1. Kerlinger Reminiscences, Huggins Papers, box 1, 132.

2. Riggs, *Tah-Koo Wah-Kan*, 105–15. See also Scrapbooks, Vol. 2, Pond Family Papers; and Lois Glewwe, "Soul Sisters: Jane Williamson and the Women of the Dakota Mission," paper delivered at the Pond Heritage Society, Aug. 17, 2009, in author's possession.

3. Prucha, *The Great Father*, 1:146–49.

4. Diedrich, *Dakota Oratory*, 50.

5. Prucha, *The Great Father*, 1:135–51.

6. Higham, *Noble, Wretched and Redeemable*, 20, 24.

7. Thomas Jefferson, First Annual Message to Congress, quoted in Spring, *Deculturalization and the Struggle for Equality*, 13. Prucha, *The Great Father*, 1:151.

8. Spring, *Deculturalization and the Struggle for Equality*, 19–20; Higham, *Noble, Wretched and Redeemable*, 111. Prucha, *The Great Father*, 1:512–27.

9. Luke Lea, "Report of Commissioner of Indian Affairs," U.S. Office of Indian Affairs, *Annual Reports* (1850), 8. Schreiber, "Education for Empire," 12–14.

10. Grimshaw, *Paths of Duty*, 189–93.

11. Meyer, *History of the Santee Sioux*, 35–36.

12. Philander Prescott, U.S. Patent Office, *Farming among the Sioux Indians*, 451–55, 126.

13. Diedrich, "'A Good Man' in a Changing World"; Wingerd, *North Country*, 146–47, 150.

14. Meyer, *History of the Santee Sioux*, 52, 63n32. See also Riggs, "Protestant Missions in the Northwest," 188, 126–27, and Riggs, "The Dakota Mission," 115–17. For the 1830 treaty, see Kappler, *Indian Treaties*, 2:305–10. "Report of Lawrence Taliaferro," U.S. Office of Indian Affairs, *Annual Reports* (1838), 495. On early American attitudes toward civilization and Christianization, see Calloway, *The World Turned Upside Down*, 43–45; and Trafzer, *As Long as the Grass Shall Grow*, 71–73.

15. See ABCFM, *Annual Report* (1837–62). The 1848 report of the "Mission to the Sioux," for instance, listed "5 stations; 5 missionaries (one a physician), 2 licentiates, 4 male and 11 female assistant missionaries;—total, 22" (261).

16. Porterfield, *Mary Lyon and the Mount Holyoke Missionaries*, 11. See Kerber, *Women of the Republic*, for the germinal discussion of the "Republican Mother" ideology.

17. Porterfield, *Mary Lyon and the Mount Holyoke Missionaries*, 5. Riggs, *A Small Bit of Bread and Butter*, iii–iv.

18. Simonsen, *Making Home Work*, 72. Grimshaw, *Paths of Duty*, 101–3. ABCFM Prudential Committee quoted in Schreiber, "Education for Empire," 33.

19. Berkhofer, *Salvation and the Savage*, 74; see also Clemmons, "Satisfied to Walk in the Ways of Their Fathers."

20. Riggs, "The Dakota Mission," 119; Riggs, "Protestant Missions in the Northwest," 188, 133.

21. Riggs, *A Small Bit of Bread and Butter,* 107; "Report of Lawrence Taliaferro," 496. "Mission to the Sioux," ABCFM, *Annual Report* (1841), 187.

22. J. W. Hancock to N. McLean, Aug. 30, 1851, U.S. Office of Indian Affairs, *Annual Reports* (1851), 181.

23. Anderson, "The Flow of European Trade Goods." Pond, *The Dakota or Sioux in Minnesota,* 31–34; Trayte, "The Role of Dress in Eastern Dakota and White Interaction," 77–78.

24. Anderson, *Little Crow,* 259, 60, 62.

25. Joseph R. Brown to W. J. Cullen, Sept. 10, 1859, U.S. Office of Indian Affairs, *Annual Reports* (1859), 87. W. J. Cullen to Hon. A. B. Greenwood, Aug. 15, 1859, U.S. Office of Indian Affairs, *Annual Reports* (1859), 59.

26. U.S. Office of Indian Affairs, *Annual Reports* (1859, 1860); W. J. Cullen to Hon. A. Greenwood, Feb. 29, 1860, Office of Indian Affairs, Letters Received by St. Peter's Agency, photocopy in Woolworth Papers.

27. Prucha, *American Indian Policy in Crisis,* 228–31.

28. Clemmons, "Satisfied to Walk in the Ways of Their Fathers," 116, 117.

29. Riggs, "The Dakota Mission," 124; Meyer, *History of the Santee Sioux,* 102, 107.

30. Stephen R. Riggs to Col. A. J. Bruce, July 15, 1845, U.S. Office of Indian Affairs, *Annual Reports* (1845), 117.

31. Joseph R. Brown to W. J. Cullen, Sept. 10, 1859, U.S. Office of Indian Affairs, *Annual Reports* (1859), 87. For a discussion of Brown's acculturation policy, see Wingerd, *North Country,* 270–72. Feezor, "Mdewakanton Dakota Women," 39.

32. Quoted in Clemmons, "Satisfied to Walk in the Ways of Their Fathers," 117.

33. P. Prescott to Major N. McLean, Aug. 30, 1851, U.S. Office of Indian Affairs, *Annual Reports* (1851), 174.

34. Jarvis, *An Army Surgeon's Notes of Frontier Service,* 6–7; Schoolcraft, et al., *Historical and Statistical Information* (1847), 1:250–52.

35. Demallie, "Sioux Until 1850," 735. For a fuller discussion of leadership among the Dakota, see Stipe, "Eastern Dakota Acculturation," 214–35. Anderson, *Little Crow,* 259, 34. Robert Hopkins and Alex. G. Huggins to Col. A. J. Bruce, July 1847, U.S. Office of Indian Affairs, *Annual Reports* (1847), 203; G. H. Pond, to Maj. Murphy, Aug. 27, 1849, U.S. Office of Indian Affairs, *Annual Reports* (1849), 122–23.

36. Amos W. Huggins to Stephen Riggs, Feb. 1, 1862, Riggs and Family Papers, box 1.

37. Clemmons, "Satisfied to Walk in the Ways of Their Fathers," 162–65. Eastman and Blumenschein, *Indian Boyhood,* 289, 43.

38. Eastman and Blumenschein, *Indian Boyhood,* 289, 6.

39. Eastman and Blumenschein, *Indian Boyhood,* 4–28.

40. P. Prescott to Major N. McLean, Sept. 23, 1850, U.S. Office of Indian Affairs, *Annual Reports* (1850), 87.

41. Quoted in Clemmons, "Satisfied to Walk in the Ways of Their Fathers," 168, 269–70.

42. Clemmons, "Satisfied to Walk in the Ways of Their Fathers," 268–72.

43. Stephen R. Riggs, "Annual Report of the Dakota School at Traverse des Sioux, under the care of the A.B.C.F.M, for the year ending July 1845," ABCFM, *Annual Report* (1845–46), 116.

44. Mary Riggs to "My Dear Henrietta," July 25, 1838; also Riggs to My dear sister Henrietta, July 19, 1838, both Riggs and Family Papers, box 3.

45. Mary Riggs to My Dear Parents, June 27, 1839, Riggs and Family Papers, box 3.

46. Riggs, *Mary and I*, 76; on Indian visits, see White, "Indian Visits."

47. Anderson, *Little Crow*, 259, 108–9.

48. Anderson, *Little Crow*, 106–12;

49. Anderson, *Little Crow*, 107, 259; Wingerd, *North Country*, 272–80, 293–94.

50. Robertson, "A Reminiscence of Thomas A. Robertson," 559. Anderson, *Little Crow*, 259, 111.

51. The following account of developments leading up to the war draws on Anderson, *Little Crow*, 116–36, and Wingerd, *North Country*, 290–305.

52. Anderson, *Little Crow*, 259, 130.

Notes to Chapter 4

1. Wingerd, *North Country*, 315, 329; Meyer, *History of the Santee Sioux*, 120n16; "Prevention and Punishment of the Crime of Genocide," www.un.org/ga/ (accessed Apr. 5, 2011).

2. Carley, *The Sioux Uprising of 1862*, 67; Meyer, *History of the Santee Sioux*, 153–57. The majority of the Dakota who were removed to Santee were Mdewakantunwan, but the group also included some Wahpekute, Sisitunwan, and Wahpetunwan Dakota. The majority of Sisitunwan and Wahpetunwan had fled Minnesota at the end of the war, some, including Taoyateduta, toward Canada, and others toward the Missouri River and beyond. In 1867, the U.S. government established a reservation for the Sisitunwan and Wahpetunwan at Lake Traverse, just over the Minnesota border in the Dakota Territory. Several hundred Sisitunwan settled on the south shore of Spirit Lake in North Dakota, where, in 1870, an Indian agent was appointed to distribute supplies and agricultural equipment: Meyer, *History of the Santee Sioux*, 198–202, 220–23. In Canada, reserves for the Dakota were established in Manitoba and Saskatchewan: Howard, *The Canadian Sioux*. On the internment of the Dakota and genocide, see Chris Mato Numpa, "Dakota Commemorative March: Thoughts and Reactions," in Wilson, *In the Footsteps of Our Ancestors*, 67–83.

3. Author's interview with Cora Jones, June 19, 2007, Santee, NE; Sneve, *Completing the Circle*, 37, 58. For more on the life of Pazahiyayewin, see Ramona Stately, "Pazahiyayewin and the Importance of Remembering Dakota Women," in Wilson, *In the Footsteps of Our Ancestors*, 192–96.

4. Waziyatawin Angela Wilson, "Manipi Hena Owas'in Wicunkiksuyapi (We Remember All Those Who Walked)," in Wilson, *In the Footsteps of Our Ancestors*, 1–21.

5. On the trials, see Chomsky, "The United States–Dakota War Trials," Meyer, *History of the Santee Sioux*, 123–24, and Wingerd, *North Country*, 312–14; on the removal to Mankato, see Meyer, *History of the Santee Sioux*, 127–29, and Wingerd, *North Country*, 320–22.

6. Quoted in Wingerd, *North Country*, 326.

7. S. R. Riggs to S. B. Treat, Jan. 21, 1863, Nute, Northwest Missions manuscripts, box 21. See also Wilson, *In the Footsteps of Our Ancestors*, and Monjeau-Marz, *The Dakota Indian Internment at Fort Snelling*. For accounts of the march to Fort Snelling and the internment during the winter of 1863, see Wilson, *In the Footsteps of Our Ancestors*; for a discussion of the route of the forced march, see Lisa Elbert, "Tracing Their Footsteps," in Wilson, *In the Footsteps of Our Ancestors*, 196–211. On the internment at Fort Snelling, see Monjeau-Marz, *The Dakota Indian Internment at Fort Snelling*.

8. Meyer, *History of the Santee Sioux*, 140–41. According to Meyer, this action "constituted something of an innovation in United States Indian policy," in that it abandoned the concept of Indian participation in decision-making: "Now a precedent had been set for the unilateral abrogation of treaties and the management of Indian affairs by Congress, without event the illusion of the Indians' consent" (141). In 1994, the Winnebago at Black River Falls, Wisconsin, officially adopted a new constitution which changed their name to the Ho-Chunk Sovereign Nation. *Ho-Chunk*, the name they historically called themselves, means "People with the Big Voice." The Winnebago Tribe of Nebraska, in Winnebago, Nebraska, retains the name *Winnebago*; it uses the nation's historic name for its economic development agency, Ho-Chunk, Inc., and is considering changing its name to *Ho-Chunk* as well. This work will use the name *Ho-Chunk*.

9. Temple, *Camp McClellan during the Civil War*, 31. Meyer, *History of the Santee Sioux*, 143–44; Carlson, "They Tell Their Story," 278, 260–261.

10. Green, *A Peculiar Imbalance*, 129–39. I am indebted to John Campbell for this reference.

11. For a fuller discussion of the removal of the Dakota to Crow Creek, see Hyman, "Survival at Crow Creek," 161.

12. Meyer, *History of the Santee Sioux*, 146; "The Winnebago at Their New Reservation," *Mankato Weekly Record*, July 11, 1863, 1. For white Minnesotans' responses to the U.S.–Dakota War, see Wingerd, *North Country*, 315–30.

13. William Beane, e-mail message to author, July 20, 2004.

14. John P. Williamson to My Dear Father, May 9, 1863, Williamson Papers, box 1. John P. Williamson to My Friends The Riggs, May 25, 1863, Riggs and Family Papers, box 1. John P. Williamson testimony, Sept. 9, 1865, Congress Joint Special Committee, *Condition of the Indian Tribes: Report of the Joint Special Committee, Appointed Under Joint Resolution of March 3, 1865: With an Appendix* (Washington, DC: GPO, 1867), 413–15.

15. William Beane, e-mail to author.

16. For a late-twentieth-century discussion of the land's lack of suitability to crops, see Lawson, *Dammed Indians Revisited.*

17. Smith, *Ho-Chunk Tribal History,* 56. Little Hill testimony, Oct. 3, 1865, Congress Joint Special Committee, *Condition of the Indian Tribes,* 417. Author's interview with David Smith, Dec. 11, 2009, Winnebago, NE.

18. Peter Tapetatanka to S. R. Riggs, c. 1865, Riggs and Family Papers, box 2, translated by Sid Byrd. This letter and others used in this chapter were translated by Dakota elders Clifford Canku, Agnes Ross, Ellen Weston, Elmer Weston, Margaret Weston Sherman, Sid Byrd, and Mona Wakeman Miyasato in Flandreau, SD, with assistance from a federal grant. When the grant was completed, Sid Byrd translated several more letters. These translations are part of the Dakota Archives, housed at the Moody County Museum, Flandreau, SD. William Beane of Flandreau, SD, generously provided me with copies of these translations. For a discussion of the problems with provisions at Crow Creek, see Lass, "The "Moscow Expedition.'"

19. Sneve, *Completing the Circle,* 58–59; Jeanette and Virgil Weston, interview conducted by Herbert Hoover, July 17, 1971, Flandreau, SD, American Indian Research Institute [hereafter AIRP], University of South Dakota, tape 726. I am grateful to Beverly Wakeman for sharing with me the Redwing family tree.

20. St. A. D. Balcombe to Col. C. W. Thompson, Sept. 3, 1864, U.S. Office of Indian Affairs, *Annual Reports* (1864), 410–11; Williamson testimony, 414; John P. Williamson to My Dear Father, Dec. 24, 1863, Williamson Papers, box 1; Barton, *John P. Williamson, a Brother to the Sioux,* 80–84.

21. John P. Williamson to Dear Bro. Riggs, July 26, 1864, and John P. Williamson to Rev. S. R. Riggs, July 5, 1864, both Riggs and Family Papers, box 2. Ida Allen, interview conducted by Vince Pratt, July 26, 1971, Flandreau, SD, AIRP tape 752.

22. Quoted in "Dakota Sacrifice Honored," *Indian Country Today,* June 19, 2002; also in videotape of event. Mr. Steiner generously provided a copy of this tape.

23. J. M. Stone to Hon. N. Edmunds, Oct. 3, 1865, U.S. Office of Indian Affairs, *Annual Reports* (1865), 228. Meyer, *History of the Santee Sioux,* 153. Mae Eastman, interview conducted by Vince Pratt, Flandreau, SD, July 28, 1971, AIRP tape 754.

24. Quoted in "Dakota Sacrifice Honored."

25. Belden, Furnas, and Pierce, *The Second Nebraska's Campaign Against the Sioux*, 16. I am most grateful to Rod Steiner for this citation. Furnas was appointed Indian agent for the Omaha, Winnebago, and Ponca tribes shortly after his service leading the Second Nebraska. He then served as second governor of Nebraska. His successful political career underscores just how mainstream his attitudes toward Indians were. See Robert C. Farb, "Robert W. Furnas as Omaha Indian Agent, 1864–1866," *Nebraska History* 32 (Sept. 1951).

26. For a discussion of the centrality of sexual violence against Indigenous women in the colonization of North America, see Smith, *Conquest*, 10 and *passim*. See also Berkhofer, *The White Man's Indian*, part 1. The Amnesty International report *Maze of Injustice* confirms that these attitudes persist in the present, leading to the extremely high proportion of Native women experiencing rape today.

27. David Faribault testimony, Congress Joint Special Committee, *Condition of the Indian Tribes*.

28. Amnesty International USA, *Maze of Injustice*. J. M. Stone to Hon. N. Edmunds, Oct. 3, 1865, U.S. Office of Indian Affairs, *Annual Reports* (1865), 228.

29. U.S. Office of Indian Affairs, *Annual Reports* (1864, 1865, 1866).

30. Temple, *Camp McClellan during the Civil War*, 29; Carlson, "They Tell Their Story," 278, 261.

31. Robert Hopkins to S. R. R. Riggs, Aug. 20, 1864, Riggs and Family Papers, box 2.

32. Thomas Williamson to Hon. W. P. Dole, July 25, 1863, U.S. Office of Indian Affairs, *Letters Sent*, St. Peter's Agency, roll 764. Carlson, "They Tell Their Story," 278, 262; Wagoner, "Camp McClellan and the Redskins," 20; author's telephone interview with Ramona Kitto Stately, Apr. 10, 2011.

33. John Campbell, "As 'A kind of freeman'?: Slaves' Market-related Activities in the South Carolina Upcountry, 1800–1860," in Berlin, *The Slaves' Economy*. Folwell, *A History of Minnesota*, 2:262. On conditions at the Rock Island prison, see Wright, "Rock Island Prison, 1864–1865"; I am indebted to William Beane for this citation. See also McAdams, *Rebels at Rock Island*. To this day, the U.S. Army maintains a cemetery at the Rock Island Arsenal that includes the graves of Confederate soldiers: see Baselt, "Rock Island National Cemetery." No burial marker of any sort exists anywhere in the area for the Dakota men and women who perished at Camp McClellan.

34. Hewanke to Stephen R. Riggs, c. 1864–65, Riggs and Family Papers, box 1.

35. Author's interview with Beverly Wakeman and Ellen Weston, Mar. 19, 2003, Flandreau, SD. Riggs, *Tah-Koo Wah-Kan*, 371; Temple, *Camp McClellan during the Civil War*, 38.

36. Riggs, *Tah-Koo Wah-Kan*, 372.

37. Illa Mackey, Nancy Mackey, and Edith Bickerstaff interview. Henry "Jim" James, Jr., of Santee, NE, a great-grandson of Mary Hoffman's, generously shared

with me family papers related to Hoffman and her father, including letters Wheeler Hoffman wrote to Mary and to Mary's daughter Anna Lavara St. Clair James.

38. Riggs, *Tah-Koo Wah-Kan*, 349. Gideon Pond quoted in ABCFM, *Annual Report* (1863), 144.

39. Thomas Williamson and Stephen Riggs quoted in ABCFM, *Annual Report* (1863), 144. Riggs, *Tah-Koo Wah-Kan*, 162.

40. ABCFM, *Annual Report* (1863), 148; Meyer, *History of the Santee Sioux*, 137.

41. Hinman to Whipple, Jan. 6, 1864, Whipple Papers, box 3. Williamson testimony, 416.

42. John P. Williamson to St. A. D. Balcombe, Aug. 2, 1864, U.S. Office of Indian Affairs, *Annual Reports* (1864), 415.

43. John P. Williamson to St. A. D. Balcombe, Aug. 2, 1864, U.S. Office of Indian Affairs, *Annual Reports* (1864), 343–44.

44. Riggs, *Tah-Koo Wah-Kan*, 345–46.

45. "The Indian Prisoners" *Mankato Weekly Record*, Mar. 7, 1863, 2. John P. Williamson to Thomas Williamson, June 9, 1863, and Aug. 27, 1863, both Williamson Papers, box 1.

46. Elias Ruban to Stephen R. Riggs, Nov. 14, 1864, Riggs and Family Papers, box 2.

47. Wasteste to Stephen R. Riggs, c. 1864, Riggs and Family Papers, box 2. Joseph Napesniduta to Stephen R. Riggs, c. 1864, Riggs and Family Papers, box 2, translated by Sid Byrd.

48. John P. Williamson to Thomas Williamson, July 21, 1863, Williamson Papers, box 1.

49. John P. Williamson to Stephen R. Riggs, July 5, 1864, Riggs and Family Papers, box 2. Sarah F. Marpihdagawin to H. B. Whipple, Dec. 4, 1863, Whipple Papers, box 3. Wambditanka to Stephen R. Riggs, c. 1864–65, Riggs and Family Papers, box 1. Wakanojanjan was among the Dakota leaders who fled to Canada at the end of the war. He and Shakpe (Shakopee) were taken prisoners there and brought back to Fort Snelling. They were hanged on Nov. 11, 1865, after a brief pretense of a trial. Carley, *The Dakota War of 1862*, 75.

50. Zenas Mazakinyanhiyaye to Stephen R. Riggs, c. 1864, Riggs and Family Papers, box 1. Light to Stephen R. Riggs, c. 1863–66, Riggs and Family Papers, box 1.

51. Augustin Frenier to Stephen R. Riggs, c. 1864–65, Riggs and Family Papers, box 2.

52. Carlson, "They Tell Their Story," 278, 271–73.

53. "Petition of Sioux Prisoners Confined in Camp Kearney near Davenport, Iowa," Mar. 6, 1865, photocopy in author's possession. William Beane provided me with access to this document.

54. Levi, *Survival in Auschwitz*.

Notes to Chapter 5

1. Meyer, "The Establishment of the Santee Reservation."

2. The name *Isanti* derives from *Isantamde*, Knife Lake, in Minnesota, where many Mdewakantunwan had lived: Riggs and Dorsey, *Dakota Grammar*, 159.

3. James Garvie, "Brief History of the Santee Sioux Indians of Nebraska and the Flandreau Sioux Indians of South Dakota," *U.S. Congressional Serial Set* (1817), 5.

4. Pond, *The Dakota or Sioux in Minnesota*, 139.

5. Sneve, *Completing the Circle*, 64; author's telephone interview with Virginia Driving Hawk Sneve, Apr. 12, 2011.

6. Sneve, *Completing the Circle*, 61.

7. John P. Williamson to Alfred Riggs, Apr. 3, 1872, and Jan. 11, 1871, and Thomas Williamson to Alfred Riggs, July 2, 1872, Oahe Mission Collection.

8. John P. Williamson to J. M. Stone, Aug. 12, 1867, and Samuel D. Hinman to J. M. Stone, Aug. 15, 1867, U.S. Office of Indian Affairs, *Annual Reports* (1867), 283–84. A. L. Riggs to Asa Janney, Aug. 30, 1870, U.S. Office of Indian Affairs, *Annual Reports* (1870), 240. Anne Beiser Allen, "The Controversial Career of Rev. Samuel D. Hinman," *Nebraska History* (Fall 2009): 120. I am grateful to Jim James for this citation.

9. H. B. Denman to Charles E. Mix, Nov. 1, 1867, U.S. Office of Indian Affairs, *Annual Reports* (1867), 267; J. M. Stone to N. G. Taylor, Aug. 15, 1867, U.S. Office of Indian Affairs, *Annual Reports* (1867), 281–83; Asa Janney to Samuel M. Janney, Sept. 10, 1870, U.S. Office of Indian Affairs, *Annual Reports* (1870), 234–35.

10. Crow Creek Census, May 1, 1864, in Brown and Family Papers, roll 3.

11. J. M. Stone to N. G. Taylor, Aug. 15, 1867, U.S. Office of Indian Affairs, *Annual Reports* (1867), 281–83; J. M. Stone to H. B. Denman, Sept. 1, 1868, U.S. Office of Indian Affairs, *Annual Reports* (1868), 245–48; Asa M. Janney to Samuel M. Janney, Sept. 8, 1869, U.S. Office of Indian Affairs, *Annual Reports* (1869), 340–41. Mae Eastman interview, AIRP tape 754, 9. Meyer, *History of the Santee Sioux*, 242–57; *An Experiment of Faith.*

12. Meyer, *History of the Santee Sioux*, 162, 242–43; Kappler, *Indian Treaties*, 2:998–1003; *An Experiment of Faith.*

13. This structure would remain in place until the Wheeler-Howard Act of 1934, which allowed tribes on reservations to elect their own leadership and practice some limited self-government, though still requiring rigid adherence to parameters set by the U.S. government. See Deloria, *The Nations Within*.

14. John P. Williamson to E. P. Smith, Sept. 22, 1874, U.S. Office of Indian Affairs, *Annual Reports* (1874), 242; Williamson to Smith, Aug. 10, 1878, U.S. Office of Indian Affairs, *Annual Reports* (1878), 30–31; Isaiah Lightner to Commissioner of Indian Affairs, Ninthmonth [Sept.] 1, 1880, U.S. Office of Indian Affairs, *Annual Reports* (1880), 122.

15. "Extract from a letter by Rev. H. D. Hinman, Jan. 25, 1868," Hinman Papers. Barclay White, "Report of the Northern Superintendent," U.S. Office of Indian Affairs, *Annual Reports* (1875), 312.

16. *Niobrara Pioneer*, Dec. 30, 1875, 2, and Feb. 15, 1889, 2.

17. Isaiah Lightner to Commissioner of Indian Affairs, Ninthmonth [Sept.] 1, 1880, U.S. Office of Indian Affairs, *Annual Reports* (1880), 122. James E. Helms, "Report of the Commissioner of Indian Affairs," Aug. 19, 1891, U.S. Office of Indian Affairs, *Annual Reports* (1891), 293.

18. Brown and Janney, *Minutes of Convention*, 33.

19. Ross, *Keeper of the Female Medicine Bundle*, 97.

20. Author's interview with Floreine Johnson and Edith Bickerstaff, May 14, 2003, Santee, NE; Mae Eastman interview, 13; Louise Wolfe, interview conducted by Jean Neeley, Dec. 3, 1973, Santee, NE, AIRP tape 614.

21. Isaiah Lightner to Commissioner of Indian Affairs, Ninthmonth [Sept.] 1, 1880, U.S. Office of Indian Affairs, *Annual Reports* (1880), 121. Ella Worden, "Our Cooking School," *Word Carrier*, Feb. 1891, 5. Cochran, *Dakota Cross-Bearer*, 34–35. Lillian Beane and William Beane interview; "Christmas Feast at Rev. John Eastman's House," *Moody County Enterprise*, Dec. 29, 1892; on barbecue, see *Moody County Enterprise*, July 12, 1888. Typescripts of the two articles courtesy of William Beane.

22. For a review of literature on the emotional and social significance of food, see Locher, "Comfort Foods"; on the place of food in developing national and ethnic identity, see Williams-Forson, *Building Houses Out of Chicken Legs*, Pilcher, *Food in World History*, and Pilcher, *Que Vivan Los Tamales!*

23. Cora Jones interview; Anna Wolfe, interview conducted by Jean Neeley, Nov. 28, 1973, Santee, NE, AIRP tape 613; Louise Wolfe interview; Gilmore, *Uses of Plants*, 17–18, 20.

24. Penman, *Honor the Grandmothers*, 117.

25. Trayte, "The Role of Dress in Eastern Dakota and White Interaction," 130–31.

26. Floreine Johnson and Edith Bickerstaff interview. Anna and Jim were divorced just a few years after the photo was taken, and he was ordained after the divorce. Don Allan, "James W. Garvie: Man of The West," in Huseboe, *Papers of the Twenty-Second Annual Dakota History Conference*, 13–31. I am indebted to Beverly Wakeman, who shared with me the Redwing family tree, where I located Anna's mother and grandmother. [Isaiah] Lightner, report, Eightmonth [Aug.] 25, 1877, U.S. Office of Indian Affairs, *Annual Reports* (1877), 147.

27. Photo courtesy of William Beane. Mary Jane's mother married David Faribault, Sr.; Mary Jane's sister-in-law, Mary Eastman, married David Faribault, Jr.; Bean, *Eastman, Cloud Man, Many Lightnings*, 57.

28. For examples, see Moore, "Negotiated Identities," on Canadian Athabaskan peoples and Anderson, "Proper Names, Naming, and Labeling in Saami," on the

Indigenous Saami in Finland. Riggs and Dorsey, *Dakota Grammar*, 208; Deloria, *The Dakota Way of Life*, 122.

29. Census of the Santee Indian Tribe, 1869, Records of the Bureau of Indian Affairs, Winnebago Agency, Record Group 75, roll 78. I am most grateful to Carolyn Anderson for providing me with a photocopy of this document.

30. Register of Santee Indian Families, ca. 1902, Winnebago Agency, National Archives, Lenexa, KS. I am most grateful to Carolyn Anderson for providing me with a photocopy of this document. Descendants know Wicacaka's daughter and grand-daughter by the English names Emma and Mary.

31. "Report of the number of Indians in Camp at Fort Snelling Minnesota," Mar. 14, 1863; "List of Indian Prisoners Confined at Camp Kearney, Davenport, Iowa, January 20, 1866," *Letters Received by the Office of Indian Affairs*, St. Peter's Agency, 1866–1867, microfilm roll 765. I am grateful to William Beane for providing me with photocopies of these documents. "List of families at Santee Agency on the Santee Reservation," National Anthropological Archives, MS 3167.

32. Ida Allen, interview conducted by Joseph F. Rockboy, Mar. 1, 1973, Flandreau, SD, AIRP tape 890; Jess Wakeman, interview conducted by Vince Pratt, July 26, 1971, Flandreau, SD, AIRP tape 755; Floreine Johnson and Edith Bickerstaff interview.

33. Gary Bevington, "Protestant Proselytizing and Native Language Education Among the Sioux," in Tyler, *The Artist and the Missionary*, 33–46; Charles Kurtzleb, "Educating the Dakota Sioux, 1876–1890," *North Dakota History* 32 (Oct. 1965): 202.

34. "Iapi Oaye," and "The Word Carrier of the Santee Normal Training School," in Littlefield, *American Indian and Alaska Native Newspapers and Periodicals*, 151–57, 403–7.

35. Floreine Johnson and Edith Bickerstaff interview.

36. Sneve, *That They May Have Life*, 69–73.

37. "'Speaking Indian': Parameters of Language Use among American Indians," in Medicine, *Learning to be an Anthropologist*, 22.

38. Talbot, "Spiritual Genocide."

39. *Niobrara Pioneer*, June 14, 1877, n.p. Charles Hill to Commissioner of Indian Affairs, Aug. 25, 1887, U.S. Office of Indian Affairs, *Annual Reports* (1887), 156. Joseph Clements to Commissioner of Indian Affairs, Aug. 31, 1895, U.S. Office of Indian Affairs, *Annual Reports* (1895), 205.

40. Interview with Mrs. Harry Lawrence, Apr. 27, 1965, Woolworth Papers, box 7. For the Dakota in Minnesota in the late nineteenth century, see Meyer, *History of the Santee Sioux*, 273–93, and Feezor, "Mdewakanton Dakota Women."

41. Deloria, *Speaking of Indians*, 58. Myrna Weston-Louis, David Louis, and Everett Weston interview.

42. Sneve, *Completing the Circle*, 54.

43. Author's interview with Judith Peterson, May 21, 2003, Flandreau, SD.

44. Ross, *Keeper of the Female Medicine Bundle*, 129–33.

45. Deloria, *Speaking of Indians*, 58; Anna Wolfe interview.

46. Wilson, *Spirit Car*, 164. The Santee population declined from 974 in 1870 to 791 in 1874 and 736 in 1879. According to Roy Meyer, "the Santee population was considerably reduced both through the deaths themselves and through the panic-stricken flight of many who did not catch the disease": *History of the Santee Sioux*, 166–67. Author's interview with Goldie Redwing Wiley and Edith Bickerstaff, Aug. 8, 2004, Santee, NE.

47. Nellie R. De Cory, interview conducted by Jean Neeley, Nov. 7, 1973, Santee, NE, AIRP tape 941; Illa Mackey, Nancy Mackey, and Edith Bickerstaff interview. "Mackey-Frazier Family History," typescript. I am grateful to Clement Mackey for making a copy of his family history for me.

48. Author's interview with Bernice Blakney and Edith Bickerstaff, Aug. 9, 2004, Santee, NE; Riggs, *Early Days at Santee*, 11; author's interview with Clement Mackey, Aug. 3, 2006, Santee, NE.

Notes to Chapter 6

1. Barclay White, "Summary of the Status of the Tribes, 1868–1904," Barclay White Journals (c. 1904), 3:354, Nebraska State Historical Society.

2. See Deloria, *Custer Died for Your Sins*, 101–24. On the internalized oppression and historical trauma resulting from colonization, see Duran, *Healing the Soul Wound*.

3. Eastman, *The Soul of the Indian*, 105–6. Pond, *The Dakota or Sioux in Minnesota*, 60–65; Anderson, *Little Crow*, 259, 19–20.

4. Irwin, "Freedom, Law, and Prophecy," 35–37. See Pond, *The Dakota or Sioux in Minnesota*, 90–93; Schoolcraft, et al., *Historical and Statistical Information* (1847), 2:198–99.

5. Talbot, "Spiritual Genocide"; Prucha, *The Great Father*, 2:646–48, 953–54. Deloria, *God Is Red*, 240–41.

6. Meyer, *History of the Santee Sioux*, 153–54.

7. Kappler, *Indian Treaties*, 2:1000. While federal law made all Native Americans citizens in 1924, individual states retained authority over suffrage qualifications and recognition of their right to vote: Prucha, *The Great Father*, 2:793–94.

8. Anderson, *Kinsmen of Another Kind*, 277; Meyer, *History of the Santee Sioux*, 159, 242–53.

9. See Deloria, *Singing for a Spirit*, and Cochran, *Dakota Cross-Bearer*, about the lives of two Dakota men in the Protestant ministry. On the training of Native missionaries at the Santee Normal School, see Bevington, "Protestant Proselytizing and Native Language Education," 36–37.

10. *An Experiment of Faith*; Allen, *History of the Flandreau Santee Sioux Tribe*.

11. Rogel, *"Mastering the Secret of White Man's Power,"* 37–38; Allan, "James W. Garvie."

12. Grace Moore, interview conducted by Vince Pratt, Aug. 20, 1971, Flandreau, SD, AIRP tape 803.

13. For a history of the Dakota on the Fort Peck reservation, see Dennis J. Smith, "Convergence: Fort Peck Assiniboines and Sioux Arrive in the Fort Peck Region, 1800–1871," in Miller, *The History of the Fort Peck Assiniboine and Sioux Tribes*, 41–64.

14. "Report of the Santee Mission for the Year Ending June 31, 1879"; "Report of the Santee Mission for the Year Ending September 17, 1880"; "Report of the Santee Mission for the Year Ending June 30, 1881"; "Report of the Santee Mission for the Year Ending June 30, 1882," Bishop Hare Collection, box 5, folder 56. Samuel Hinman, "Journal Written at Santee Mission," Hinman Papers, 39; Welsh, *Journal of the Rev. S. D. Hinman*, 25, 45–46. George Red Owl married Emma Anpetuomani after the Dakota were removed to Santee.

15. *An Experiment of Faith*, 27.

16. Sneve, *Completing the Circle*, 98.

17. Grace Moore interview.

18. Floreine Johnson and Edith Bickerstaff interview; Riggs, *Early Days at Santee*, 15.

19. Ella Worden, "Mrs. Walking Hawk's Sewing Society," *Word Carrier*, Jan. 1886, 1; student essay, Santee Normal Training School Papers, box 1, folder 2; Sneve, *Completing the Circle*, 67.

20. Author's interview with Judy Jones, Dec. 12, 2009, Flandreau, SD.

21. "Indian Women's Missionary Society," *Word Carrier*, Jan. 1887, 3.

22. Clement Mackey interview.

23. Patricia Albers and Beatrice Medicine, "The Role of Sioux Women in the Production of Ceremonial Objects: The Case of the Star Quilts," Albers and Medicine, *The Hidden Half*, 280, 129; "Lakota Star Quilts: Commodity, Ceremony, and Economic Development," in Medicine, *Learning to be an Anthropologist*, 166–71.

24. "Lakota Star Quilts," 166–71; Wallis, *Beliefs and Tales of the Canadian Dakota*, 22–23. On quilting and missionaries, see Laurie N. Anderson, "Learning the Threads: Sioux Quiltmaking in South Dakota," in MacDowell and Dewhurst, *To Honor and Comfort*, 95–101.

25. Goldie Redwing Wiley and Edith Bickerstaff interview; author's interview with Ida Tuttle and Edith Bickerstaff, Aug. 9, 2004, Santee, NE; "Lakota Star Quilts," 168–69. When Lillian Beane turned one hundred in Aug. 2011, the Flandreau Santee Sioux Tribe gave her a star quilt made especially for this occasion. See http://fsst.org.

26. Lee, et al., *Shaping Survival*, 98–99.

27. Sneve, *That They May Have Life*, 83.

28. Barbara A. Hail, "Beaded Bibles and Victory Pouches: Twentieth Century Honoring Gifts," *American Indian Art Magazine* (Summer 1988): 40–47.

29. Betty Jane Meggers to Gabe E. Parker, and Hermina S. Neumann to Betty Jane Meggers, undated letters, 1941, National Anthropological Archives. Meggers

was herself a noted anthropologist; her book *Amazonia* has been described by one author as "maybe the most influential book" on the subject: Mann, *1491*, 288.

30. Nancy Shoemaker, "The Rise and Fall of Iroquois Women," and Jean M. O'Brien, "'Divorced from the Land:' Resistance and Survival of Indian Women in Eighteenth-Century New England," in Kugel and Murphy, *Native Women's History in Eastern North America*, 313, 342; Usner, *Indian Work*, ch. 4, 5; Davies, "Frontier Merchants and Native Craftsmen." See also Meyer, *Selling the Indian*.

31. "Report of Archeologist," Nebraska State Historical Society *Proceedings* (1907), 325; for biographical material on High, see B. Y. High Collection, Nebraska State Historical Society.

32. On *cekpa* amulets, see Chapter 1.

33. Monture, *The Complete Guide to Traditional Native American Beadwork*, 23.

34. "Santee Indian Band," *Niobrara Pioneer*, Dec. 28, 1888, 3; James H. Howard, "John F. Lenger: Music Man among the Santee," *Nebraska History* 53 (1972): 195–215. George Red Owl and James Garvie were members of this band, as was Oliver LaCroix.

35. Penney, *Art of the American Indian Frontier*, 34–35. Colleen Cutschall, "Dresses, Designers, and the Dance of Life," in Her Many Horses, *Identity by Design*, 89.

Notes to Epilogue

1. Sarah Elmquist, "Winona-Dakota Connection at Unity Park June 4," *Winona Post*, May 29, 2011, and Amanda Romaine, "Dakota Homecoming and Reconciliation Prompt Reflection," *Winona Post*, June 13, 2004; Nick Coleman, "Journey Toward Reconciliation," *Minneapolis Star Tribune*, June 27, 2004, www.startribune.com (accessed July 26, 2011). On the history of the Dakota in the Winona area, see Nilles, *A History of Wapasha's Prairie;* on the Grand Excursion, see Keillor, *Grand Excursion*. For more on the Dakota Homecoming, see www.dakotahomecoming.org.

2. Roseanna Renaud, "Big Foot Memorial Ride—23 Years," *Lakota Country Times*, Jan. 5, 2010, www.lakotacountrytimes.com (accessed July 26, 2011).

3. Melodie Andrews, "The U.S.–Dakota War in Public Memory and Public Space: Mankato's Journey Toward Reconciliation," Atkins, *The State We're In*, 51–60. On the Mankato Powwow, see www.mahkatowacipi.org. Wilson, *In the Footsteps of Our Ancestors;* "Dakota Sacrifice Honored," *Indian Country Today*, June 19, 2002, www.indiancountry.com (accessed July 26, 2011); Reuben Kitto to author, Mar. 24, 2011.

4. Trafzer, *As Long as the Grass Shall Grow*, 370–87; Lawson, *Dammed Indians Revisited;* Deloria, *The Nations Within*, 190–95.

5. Amnesty International USA, *Maze of Injustice*, 2.

6. Deloria, *The Nations Within*, 232–43; Johnson, *American Indian Activism;* Josephy, *Red Power*.

7. Deloria, *The Nations Within*, 197–231; Prucha, *The Great Father*, 2:1157–63, 1165; Sharon O'Brien, "A History of the American Indian Religious Freedom Act and Its Implementation," *Indian Affairs* (Summer 1988): ii–iii.

8. Baird-Olson and Ward, "Recovery and Resistance," 28–29.

9. Author's interview with Carolyn White, Aug. 27, 2008, Sioux City, IA; Meyer, *History of the Santee Sioux*, 307–8, 339–41. Lawson, *Dammed Indians Revisited;* Floreine Johnson and Edith Bickerstaff interview; Allen, *History of the Flandreau Santee Sioux Tribe*, 124–30; Myrna Weston-Louis, David Louis, and Sandy Weston interview. On Ponca termination, see Ritter, "The Politics of Retribalization," http://digitalcom mons.unl.edu/greatplainsresearch/233/ (accessed Oct. 31, 2011).

10. Myrna Weston-Louis, David Louis, and Sandy Weston interview; Ramona Kitto Stately interview; Stately, "Pazahiyayewin and the Importance of Remembering Dakota Women," 194–95.

11. 2011 Educational Learning Tent—Artist and Presenter Biographies, Winona-Dakota Connection 2011, June 4, 2011, Winona, MN, in author's possession.

12. Ramona Kitto Stately interview. Learning Tent Presenters, Winona-Dakota Connection 2011.

13. Quoted in Stately "Pazahiyayewin and the Importance of Remembering Dakota Women," 195.

14. Stately, "Pazahiyayewin and the Importance of Remembering Dakota Women," 195.

15. Tom Meersman, "Protesters Decry 'Shameful History': A Group Halted the Sesquicentennial Wagon Train at Fort Snelling, Protesting the State's Treatment of Indians," *Minneapolis Star Tribune*, May 11, 2008, B9; Kara McGuire, "Minnesota's Sesquicentennial at the Capitol: Celebration, Somber Protest," *Minneapolis Star Tribune*, May 12, 2008, B3.

BIBLIOGRAPHY

Manuscript Collections

Bishop Hare Collection. Center for Western Studies, Augustana College, Sioux Falls, SD.

Brown, Joseph R. and Samuel J., and Family Papers. Minnesota Historical Society, St. Paul.

Hinman, Samuel, Papers. Center for Western Studies, Augustana College, Sioux Falls, SD.

Huggins, Alexander, Papers. Minnesota Historical Society, St. Paul.

National Anthropological Archives, American Museum of Natural History. Smithsonian Institution, Washington, DC.

Nute, Grace Lee. Northwest Missions Manuscripts and Index. Minnesota Historical Society, St. Paul.

Oahe Mission Collection. Center for Western Studies, Augustana College, Sioux Falls, SD.

Pond Family Papers. Minnesota Historical Society, St. Paul.

Riggs, Stephen R., and Family Papers. Minnesota Historical Society, St. Paul.

Santee Normal Training School Papers. Center for Western Studies, Augustana College, Sioux Falls, SD.

Sibley, Henry Hastings, Papers. Minnesota Historical Society, St. Paul.

Whipple, Henry B., Papers. Minnesota Historical Society, St. Paul.

White, Barclay, Journals. Nebraska State Historical Society, Lincoln.

Williamson, Thomas S., Papers. Minnesota Historical Society, St. Paul.

Woolworth, Alan, Papers. Minnesota Historical Society, St. Paul.

Interviews

Allen, Ida. Flandreau, SD. July 26, 1971. Interview with Vince Pratt. American Indian
   Research Project, University of South Dakota, Vermilion.
Allen, Ida. Flandreau, SD. March 1, 1973. Interview with Joseph F. Rockboy. American
   Indian Research Project, University of South Dakota, Vermilion.
Beane, Lillian. Flandreau, SD. March 10, 2003. Interview with author.
Beane, William. Flandreau, SD. March 10, 2003. Interview with author.
Bickerstaff, Edith. Santee, NE. May 14, 2003; August 8, 9, 2004; August 6, 2006.
   Interviews with author.
Blakney, Bernice. Santee, NE. August 9, 2004. Interview with author.
De Cory, Nellie R. Santee, NE. November 7, 1973. Interview with Jean Neeley. Amer-
   ican Indian Research Project, University of South Dakota, Vermilion.
Eastman, Mae. Flandreau, SD. July 17, 1971. Interview with Vince Pratt. American
   Indian Research Project, University of South Dakota, Vermilion.
James, Kenneth, Sr. Flandreau, SD. June 16, 2007. Interview with author.
Jones, Cora. Santee, NE. June 19, 2007. Interview with author.
Jones, Judy C. Flandreau, SD. December 12, 2009. Interview with author.
Johnson, Floreine. Santee, NE. May 14, 2003. Interview with author.
Lawrence, Elizabeth (Mrs. Harry). April 27, 1965. Alan Woolworth Papers. Minne-
   sota Historical Society, St. Paul.
Louis, David. Flandreau, SD. June 15, 2007. Interview with author.
Mackey, Clement. Santee, NE. August 3, 2006. Interview with author.
Mackey, Illa. Santee, NE. August 6, 2006. Interview with author.
Mackey, Nancy. Santee, NE. August 6, 2006. Interview with author.
Moore, Grace. Flandreau, SD. August 20, 1971. Interview with Vince Pratt. American
   Indian Research Project, University of South Dakota, Vermilion.
Peterson, Judith. Flandreau, SD. May 21, 2003. Interview with author.
Smith, David. Winnebago, NE. December 11, 2009. Interview with author.
Sneve, Virginia Driving Hawk. April 12, 2011. Telephone interview with author.
Stately, Ramona Kitto. Winona, MN. June 4, 2011. Interview with author.
Tuttle, Ida. Santee, NE. August 9, 2004. Interview with author.
Wakeman, Jess. Flandreau, SD. July 26, 1971. Interview with Vince Pratt. American
   Indian Research Project, University of South Dakota, Vermilion.
Weston, Everett (Sandy). Flandreau, SD. June 15, 2007. Interview with author.
Weston, Jeanette. Flandreau, SD. July 17, 1971. Interview with Herbert Hoover.
   American Indian Research Project, University of South Dakota, Vermilion.
Weston, Virgil. Flandreau, SD. July 17, 1971. Interview with Herbert Hoover. Amer-
   ican Indian Research Project, University of South Dakota, Vermilion.
Weston-Louis, Myrna. Flandreau, SD. June 15, 2007. Interview with author.

White, Carolyn. Sioux City, IA. August 27, 2008. Interview with author.

Wiley, Goldie Redwing. Santee, NE. August 8, 2004. Interview with author.

Wolfe, Anna. Santee, NE. November 28, 1973. Interview with Jean Neeley. American Indian Research Project, University of South Dakota, Vermilion.

Wolfe, Louise. Santee, NE. December 3, 1973. Interview with Jean Neeley. American Indian Research Project, University of South Dakota, Vermilion.

Published Works

Aby, Anne. *The North Star State: A Minnesota History Reader*. St. Paul: Minnesota Historical Society Press, 2002.

Albers, Patricia, and Beatrice Medicine. *The Hidden Half: Studies of Plains Indian Women*. Washington, DC: University Press of America, 1983.

Allen, Clifford. *History of the Flandreau Santee Sioux Tribe*. Flandreau, SD: Tribal History Program, Flandreau Santee Sioux Tribe, 1971.

American Board of Commissioners for Foreign Missions. *Annual Report*. http://cata log.hathitrust.org/api/volumes/oclc/29653983.html.

Amnesty International USA. *Maze of Injustice: The Failure to Protect Indigenous Women from Sexual Violence in the USA*. New York: Amnesty International USA, 2007.

An Experiment of Faith: The Journey of the Mdewakanton Dakota Who Settled on the Bend in the River: A Brief History of the Organization and Construction of the First Presbyterian Church, Flandreau. South Dakota: privately printed, 2003.

Anderson, Gary Clayton. *Kinsmen of Another Kind: Dakota-White Relations in the Upper Mississippi Valley, 1650–1862*. Lincoln: University of Nebraska Press, 1984.

———. *Little Crow, Spokesman for the Sioux*. St. Paul: Minnesota Historical Society Press, 1986.

Anderson, Myrdene. "Proper Names, Naming, and Labeling in Saami." *Anthropological Linguistics* 26.2 (Summer 1984): 186–201.

Atkins, Annette. *The State We're In: Reflections on Minnesota History*. St. Paul: Minnesota Historical Society Press, 2010.

Babcock, Willoughby M., Jr. "Sioux Villages in Minnesota Prior to 1837." *Minnesota Archaeologist* 11 (1945): 126–46.

Baird-Olson, Karren, and Carol Ward. "Recovery and Resistance: The Renewal of Traditional Spirituality among American Indian Women." *American Indian Culture and Research Journal* 24.4 (2000): 1–35.

Barton, Winifred W. *John P. Williamson, a Brother to the Sioux*. New York: Fleming H. Revell Co., 1919.

Baselt, Fonda. "Rock Island National Cemetery." *Illinois State Genealogical Society Quarterly* 24 (1992): 24–26.

Bates, George. *Historic Lifestyles in the Upper Mississippi River Valley*. Lanham, MD: University Press of America, 1983.

Bean, William. *Eastman, Cloud Man, Many Lightnings: An Anglo-Dakota Family*. Lincoln, NE: W. L. Bean, 1989.

Belden, George P., Robert W. Furnas, and Henry W. Pierce. *The Second Nebraska's Campaign Against the Sioux*. Lincoln: Nebraska State Historical Society, 1963.

Beltrami, Giacomo. *A Pilgrimage in America, Leading to the Discovery of the Sources of the Mississippi and Bloody River with a Description of the Whole Course of the Former and of the Ohio*. 1828. Reprint, Chicago: Quadrangle Books, 1962.

Berkhofer, Robert. *Salvation and the Savage: An Analysis of Protestant Missions and American Indian Response, 1787–1862*. Lexington: University of Kentucky Press, 1965.

Berkhofer, Robert F. *The White Man's Indian: Images of the American Indian, from Columbus to the Present*. New York: Vintage Books, 1979.

Berlin, Ira. *The Slaves' Economy: Independent Production by Slaves in the Americas*. London: Frank Cass, 1991.

Berlo, Janet C., and Ruth B. Phillips. *Native North American Art*. Oxford: Oxford University Press, 1998.

Berlo, Janet Catherine. "Dreaming of Double Woman." *American Indian Quarterly* 17.1 (Winter 1993): 31.

Birk, Douglas M., and Bruce M. White. "Who Wrote the Diary of Thomas Connor?" *Minnesota History* 46 (Spring 1979): 170–88.

Boehme, Sarah. *Seth Eastman: A Portfolio of North American Indians*. Afton, MN: Afton Historical Society Press, 1995.

Bourgeault, Ron. "Class, Race and Gender: Political Economy and the Canadian Fur Trade 1670s to 1820s." Ph.D. diss., University of Regina, 1986.

Brown, Jennifer. *The Fur Trade Revisited*. East Lansing: Michigan State University Press/Mackinac State Historic Parks, 1994.

———. *Strangers in Blood: Fur Trade Company Families in Indian Country*. Vancouver: University of British Columbia Press, 1980.

Brown, Levi K., and Joseph J. Janney. *Minutes of Convention and Report of a Visit to the Santee and Ponca Indians in Nebraska and Dakota*. Oxford, PA: [privately printed,] 1886.

Calloway, Colin. *The World Turned Upside Down: Indian Voices from Early America*. Boston: St. Martin's Press, 1994.

Carley, Kenneth. *The Dakota War of 1862*. 1976. Reprint, St. Paul: Minnesota Historical Society Press, 2001.

———. *The Sioux Uprising of 1862*. St. Paul: Minnesota Historical Society, 1976.

Carlson, Sarah-Eva. "They Tell Their Story: The Dakota Internment at Camp McClellan in Davenport, 1862–1866." *The Annals of Iowa* 63 (Summer 2004): 278.

Catlin, George. *George Catlin and His Indian Gallery*. New York and Washington, DC: W. W. Norton/Smithsonian American Art Museum, 2002.

———. *Letters and Notes on the Manners, Customs, and Conditions of the North American Indians; Written during Eight Years' Travel (1832–1839) Amongst the Wildest Tribes of Indians in North America.* 1841. Reprint, New York: Dover Publications, 1973.

Chomsky, Carol. "The United States–Dakota War Trials: A Study in Military Injustice." *Stanford Law Review* (1990): 98.

Clemmons, Linda. "Satisfied to Walk in the Ways of Their Fathers: Dakotas and Protestant Missionaries, 1835–1862." Ph.D. diss., University of Illinois Champaign-Urbana, 1998.

Cochran, Mary. *Dakota Cross-Bearer: The Life and World of a Native American Bishop.* Lincoln: University of Nebraska Press, 2000.

Davies, Cynthia. "Frontier Merchants and Native Craftsmen: The Fred Harvey Company Collects Indian Art." *Journal of the West* 21.1 (1982): 120–25.

Deloria, Ella. *The Dakota Way of Life.* Sioux Falls, SD: Mariah Press, 2007.

———. *Some Notes on the Santee.* Vermillion: W. H. Over Dakota Museum, University of South Dakota, 1967.

———. *Speaking of Indians.* Vermillion, SD: Dakota Press, 1979.

Deloria, Ella Cara. *Dakota Texts.* Lincoln: University of Nebraska Press, 2006.

———. *Waterlily.* Lincoln: University of Nebraska Press, 1988.

Deloria, Philip. *A Companion to American Indian History.* Malden, MA: Blackwell Publishers, 2002.

Deloria, Vine. *Custer Died for Your Sins: An Indian Manifesto.* Norman: University of Oklahoma Press, 1988.

———. *God is Red: A Native View of Religion.* New York: Fulcrum Publishing, 2003.

———. *The Nations Within: The Past and Future of American Indian Sovereignty.* New York: Pantheon Books, 1984.

———. *Singing for a Spirit: A Portrait of the Dakota Sioux.* Santa Fe, NM: Clear Light Publishers, 1999.

Denetdale, Jennifer. *Reclaiming Diné History: The Legacies of Navajo Chief Manuelito and Juanita.* Tucson: University of Arizona Press, 2007.

Denial, Catherine. "Pelagie Faribault's Island: Property, Kinship, and the Meaning of Marriage in Dakota Country." *Minnesota History* 62 (Summer 2010): 48–59.

———. "'A Proper Light before the Country': The Shifting Politics of Gender and Kinship among the Dakota, Ojibwe and Non-Native Communities of the Upper Midwest, 1825–1845." Ph.D. diss., University of Iowa, 2005.

Densmore, Frances. *How Indians Use Wild Plants for Food, Medicine, and Crafts.* New York: Dover, 1974.

Diedrich, Mark. *Dakota Oratory: Great Moments in the Recorded Speech of the Eastern Sioux, 1695–1874.* Rochester, MN: Coyote Books, 1989.

———. "'A Good Man' in a Changing World: Cloud Man, the Dakota Leader, and His Life and Times." *Ramsey County History* 36 (Spring 2001): 4–14.

Dippie, Brian. *The Vanishing American: White Attitudes and U.S. Indian Policy.* Middletown, CT: Wesleyan University Press, 1982.

Dippie, Brian W. *Catlin and His Contemporaries: The Politics of Patronage.* Lincoln: University of Nebraska Press, 1990.

Dolin, Eric. *Fur, Fortune, and Empire: The Epic History of the Fur Trade in America.* New York: W. W. Norton Co., 2010.

Duran, Eduardo. *Healing the Soul Wound.* New York: Teachers College Press, 2006.

Eastman, Charles. *The Soul of the Indian: An Interpretation.* Lincoln: University of Nebraska Press, 1980.

Eastman, Charles Alexander, and Ernest L. Blumenschein. *Indian Boyhood.* Lincoln: University of Nebraska Press, 1991.

Ewers, John C. "The Indian Trade of the Upper Missouri before Lewis and Clark: An Interpretation." *Bulletin of the Missouri Historical Society* 10 (1954): 429–46.

Feezor, Barbara. "Mdewakanton Dakota Women: Active Participants in Mdewakantonwan Cultural Transformations, 1860–1900." Ph.D. diss., University of California Los Angeles, 1994.

Flute, Rebecca. *Dakota Iapi,* ed. and rev. by Neil McKay and Lisa Elbert. Third ed., Minneapolis, MN: American Indian Studies Program, University of Minnesota, 2002.

Folwell, William. *A History of Minnesota.* St. Paul: Minnesota Historical Society, 1956.

Folwell, William W. "A Visit to Farther-and-Gay Castle." *Minnesota History* 12 (June 1931): 110–33.

Gates, Charles. *Five Fur Traders of the Northwest: Being the Narrative of Peter Pond and the Diaries of John Macdonell, Archibald N. McLeod, Hugh Faries, and Thomas Connor.* St. Paul: Minnesota Historical Society, 1965.

Gilman, Carolyn. *Where Two Worlds Meet: The Great Lakes Fur Trade.* St. Paul: Minnesota Historical Society, 1982.

Gilman, Rhoda. *Henry Hastings Sibley: Divided Heart.* St. Paul: Minnesota Historical Society Press, 2004.

———. "Last Days of the Upper Mississippi Fur Trade." *Minnesota History* 42 (Winter 1970): 122–40.

Gilmore, Melvin R. *Uses of Plants by the Indians of the Missouri River Region.* Lincoln: University of Nebraska Press, 1977.

Green, William. *A Peculiar Imbalance: The Fall and Rise of Racial Equality in Early Minnesota.* St. Paul: Minnesota Historical Society Press, 2007.

Grimes, John. *Uncommon Legacies: Native American Art from the Peabody Essex Museum.* New York: American Federation of Arts with University of Washington Press, 2002.

Grimshaw, Patricia. *Paths of Duty: American Missionary Wives in Nineteenth-Century Hawaii.* Honolulu: University of Hawaii Press, 1989.

Hail, Barbara A., and Jacob Ahtone. *Gifts of Pride and Love: Kiowa and Comanche Cradles.* Bristol, RI: Haffenreffer Museum of Anthropology, Brown University, 2000.

Her Many Horses, Emil. *Identity by Design: Tradition, Change, and Celebration in Native Women's Dresses.* New York: Collins with National Museum of the American Indian, Smithsonian Institution, 2007.

Higham, C. L. *Noble, Wretched and Redeemable: Protestant Missionaries to the Indians in Canada and the United States, 1820–1900.* Albuquerque: University of New Mexico Press, 2000.

Hoover, Herbert. *Sioux Country: A History of Indian-White Relations.* Sioux Falls, SD: Center for Western Studies, Augustana College, 2000.

Howard, James. *The Canadian Sioux.* Lincoln: University of Nebraska Press, 1984.

———. *The Dakota or Sioux Indians: A Study in Human Ecology.* Lincoln, NE: J. L. Reprint Co., 1980.

———. "John F. Lenger: Music Man among the Santee." *Nebraska History* 53 (1972): 195–215.

Huggan, Nancy. "Captivity among the Sioux: The Story of Nancy McClure." *Collections of the Minnesota Historical Society* 6 (1894): 438–60.

Huseboe, Arthur. *Papers of the Twenty-Second Annual Dakota History Conference Held at Augustana College, Sioux Falls, South Dakota, May 31–June 2, 1990.* Sioux Falls, SD: Augustana College, 1990.

Hyman, Colette. "Survival at Crow Creek, 1863–1866." *Minnesota History* 61 (Winter 2008–9): 148–61.

Irwin, Lee. "Freedom, Law, and Prophecy: A Brief History of Native American Religious Resistance." *American Indian Quarterly* 21 (Winter 1997): 35.

Jarvis, Nathan. *An Army Surgeon's Notes of Frontier Service, 1833–48.* N.p.

Johnson, Elden. "Notes on the Mdewakanton Bark House." *Minnesota Archeologist* 24 (1962): 48–52.

Johnson, Troy. *American Indian Activism: Alcatraz to the Longest Walk.* Urbana: University of Illinois Press, 1997.

Josephy, Alvin M. *Red Power: The American Indians' Fight for Freedom.* Lincoln: University of Nebraska Press, 1999.

Kappler, Charles. *Indian Treaties, 1778–1883.* New York: Interland Publications, 1972.

Keillor, Steven. *Grand Excursion: Antebellum America Discovers the Upper Mississippi.* Afton, MN: Afton Historical Society Press, 2004.

Kerber, Linda. *Women of the Republic: Intellect and Ideology in Revolutionary America.* Chapel Hill: University of North Carolina Press, 1980.

Klein, Laura F., and Lillian A. Ackerman. *Women and Power in Native North America.* Norman: University of Oklahoma Press, 1995.

Krech, Shepard. *Collecting Native America, 1870–1960.* Washington, DC: Smithsonian Institution Press, 1999.

Kugel, Rebecca, and Lucy Eldersveld Murphy, eds. *Native Women's History in Eastern North America before 1900: A Guide to Research and Writing.* Lincoln: University of Nebraska Press, 2007.

Lass, William. "The 'Moscow Expedition.'" *Minnesota History* 39 (Summer 1965): 227–40.

Lawson, Michael. *Dammed Indians Revisited: The Continuing History of the Pick-Sloan Plan and the Missouri River Sioux.* Pierre: South Dakota State Historical Society Press, 2009.

Lee, Lanniko, Florestine Kiyukanpi Renville, Karen Lone Hill, and Lydia Whirlwind Soldier. *Shaping Survival: Essays by Four American Indian Tribal Women,* ed. by Jack W. Marken and Charles L. Woodard. Lanham, MD: Scarecrow Press, 2001.

Levi, Primo. *Survival in Auschwitz: The Nazi Assault on Humanity.* New York: Simon and Schuster, 1996.

Little, Bryce. "People of the Red Path: An Ethnohistory of the Dakota Fur Trade, 1760–1851." Ph.D. diss., University of Pennsylvania, 1984.

Littlefield, Daniel. *American Indian and Alaska Native Newspapers and Periodicals.* Westport, CT: Greenwood Press, 1984.

Locher, Julie. "Comfort Foods: An Exploratory Journey into the Social and Emotional Significance of Food." *Food & Foodways* 13 (2005): 273–97.

Lyford, Carrie A., and Willard W. Beatty. *Quill and Beadwork of the Western Sioux.* U.S. Office of Indian Affairs. Lawrence, KS: Printing Dept., Haskell Institute, 1940.

MacDowell, Marsha, and C. Kent Dewhurst, eds. *To Honor and Comfort: Native Quilting Traditions.* Santa Fe: Museum of New Mexico Press with Michigan State University Museum, 1997.

Mancall, Peter. *Deadly Medicine: Indians and Alcohol in Early America.* Ithaca, NY: Cornell University Press, 1995.

Mann, Charles. *1491: New Revelations of the Americas Before Columbus.* New York: Knopf, 2005.

McAdams, Benton. *Rebels at Rock Island: The Story of a Civil War Prison.* DeKalb: Northern Illinois University Press, 2000.

McCrady, David G. *Living with Strangers: The Nineteenth-Century Sioux and the Canadian-American Borderlands.* Lincoln: University of Nebraska Press, 2006.

McLaughlin, Marie L. *Myths and Legends of the Sioux.* 1916. Reprint, Lincoln: University of Nebraska Press, 1990.

McLeod, Martin. "The Diary of Martin McLeod." *Minnesota History* 4 (August–November 1924): 351–439.

Medicine, Beatrice. *Learning to be an Anthropologist and Remaining "Native": Selected Writings.* Urbana: University of Illinois Press, 2001.

Meggers, Betty. *Amazonia: Man and Culture in a Counterfeit Paradise.* Chicago: Aldine Atherton, 1971.

Meyer, Carter. *Selling the Indian: Commercializing and Appropriating American Indian Cultures.* Tucson: University of Arizona Press, 2001.

Meyer, Roy W. "The Establishment of the Santee Reservation, 1866–1869." *Nebraska History* 45 (March 1964): 59–97.

———. *History of the Santee Sioux: United States Indian Policy on Trial.* Lincoln: University of Nebraska Press, 1968.

Miller, David. *The History of the Fort Peck Assiniboine and Sioux Tribes, 1800–2000.* Helena: Montana Historical Society Press and Fort Peck Community College, 2008.

Millikan, William. "The Great Treasure of the Fort Snelling Prison Camp." *Minnesota History* 62 (Spring 2010): 4–17.

Monjeau-Marz, Corinne. *The Dakota Indian Internment at Fort Snelling, 1862–1864.* St. Paul, MN: Prairie Smoke Press, 2005.

Monture, Joel. *The Complete Guide to Traditional Native American Beadwork: A Definitive Study of Authentic Tools, Materials, Techniques, and Styles.* New York: Wiley Publishing, 1993.

Moore, Patrick. "Negotiated Identities: The Evolution of Dene Tha and Kaska Personal Naming Systems." *Anthropological Linguistics* 49 (Fall–Winter 2007): 283–307.

Morgan, Dale. *Aspects of the Fur Trade: Selected Papers of the 1965 North American Fur Trade Conference.* St. Paul: Minnesota Historical Society, 1967.

Nilles, Myron. *A History of Wapasha's Prairie, 1660–1853: First Called Keoxa, Later Winona, Minnesota.* 1978. Reprint, Winona, MN: Winona County Historical Society, 2005.

Nute, Grace Lee. "Posts in the Minnesota Fur-Trading Area, 1660–1855." *Minnesota History* 11 (December 1930): 353–85.

On the Border: Native American Weaving Traditions of the Great Lakes and Prairie—Plains Art Museum, March 15–May 27, 1990. Moorhead, MN: Plains Art Museum, 1990.

Penman, Sarah, ed. *Honor the Grandmothers: Dakota and Lakota Women Tell their Stories.* St. Paul: Minnesota Historical Society Press, 2000.

Penney, David. *Art of the American Indian Frontier: The Chandler-Pohrt Collection.* Detroit, MI: Detroit Institute of Arts, University of Washington Press, 1992.

Phillips, Ruth. *Unpacking Culture: Art and Commodity in Colonial and Postcolonial Worlds.* Berkeley: University of California Press, 1999.

Pilcher, Jeffrey. *Food in World History.* Hoboken, NJ: Taylor Francis Ltd., 2006.

————. *Que Vivan Los Tamales! Food and the Making of Mexican Identity*. Albuquerque: University of New Mexico Press, 1998.

Podruchny, Carolyn. *Making the Voyageur World*. Lincoln: University of Nebraska Press, 2006.

Pond, Samuel W. *The Dakota or Sioux in Minnesota as They Were in 1834*. 1908. Reprint, St. Paul: Minnesota Historical Society Press, 1986.

Porterfield, Amanda. *Mary Lyon and the Mount Holyoke Missionaries*. New York: Oxford University Press, 1997.

Power, Samantha. *A Problem from Hell: America and the Age of Genocide*. New York: Harper Perennial, 2007.

Prescott, Philander. *Farming Among the Sioux Indians*. 31st Cong., 1st Sess., House Executive Doc. 20. Washington, DC: Government Printing Office, 1850.

Prucha, Francis. *American Indian Policy in Crisis: Christian Reformers and the Indian, 1865–1900*. Norman: University of Oklahoma Press, 1976.

————. *The Great Father: The United States Government and the American Indians*. 2 vols. Lincoln: University of Nebraska Press, 1984.

Quimby, George. *Indian Culture and European Trade Goods: The Archaeology of the Historic Period in the Western Great Lakes Region*. Madison: University of Wisconsin Press, 1966.

Red Shirt, Delphine. *Bead on an Anthill: A Lakota Childhood*. Lincoln: University of Nebraska Press, 1998.

Riggs, Mary. *Early Days at Santee: The Beginnings of Santee Normal Training School, Founded by Dr. and Mrs. A. L. Riggs in 1870*. Santee, NE: Santee N.T.S. Press, 1928.

————. *A Small Bit of Bread and Butter: Letters from the Dakota Territory, 1832–1869*. South Deerfield, MA: Ash Grove Press, 1996.

Riggs, Stephen R. "The Dakota Mission." *Collections of the Minnesota Historical Society* 3 (1870–80): 115–128.

————. *Mary and I: Forty Years with the Sioux*. 1880. Reprint, Williamstown, MA: Corner House, 1971.

————. "Protestant Missions in the Northwest." *Collections of the Minnesota Historical Society* 6 (1894): 117–88.

————. *Tah-Koo Wah-Kan or, the Gospel among the Dakotas*. 1869[?]. Reprint, New York: Arno Press, 1972.

Riggs, Stephen R., and James Owen Dorsey. *Dakota Grammar: With Texts and Ethnography*. 1893. Reprint, St. Paul: Minnesota Historical Society Press, 2004.

Ritter, Beth. "The Politics of Retribalization: The Northern Ponca Case." *Great Plains Review* (1994), http://digitalcommons.unl.edu/greatplainsresearch/233.

Robertson, Thomas. "A Reminiscence of Thomas A. Robertson." *South Dakota Historical Collections* 20 (1940).

Rogel, Amy. *"Mastering the Secret of White Man's Power": Indian Students at Beloit College, 1871 to 1874.* Beloit, WI: Beloit College, 1990.

Ronnander, Chad. *"Many Paths to the Pine: Mdewakanton Dakotas, Fur Traders, Ojibwes, and the United States in Wisconsin's Chippewa Valley, 1815–1837."* Ph.D. diss., University of Minnesota, 2003.

Rosoff, Nancy. *Tipi: Heritage of the Great Plains.* Brooklyn, NY, and Seattle: Brooklyn Museum and University of Washington Press, 2011.

Ross, A. C. *Keeper of the Female Medicine Bundle: Biography of Wihopa.* Denver, CO: Wiconi Waste Publishing, 1998.

Schoolcraft, Henry Rowe, and Seth Eastman. *Historical and Statistical Information Respecting the History, Condition, and Prospects of the Indian Tribes of the United States; Collected and Prepared Under the Direction of the Bureau of Indian Affairs Per Act of Congress of March 3rd, 1847.* Philadelphia: Lippincott, Grambo, 1851–57.

Schreiber, Rebecca. "Education for Empire: Manual Labor, Civilization, and the Family in Nineteenth-Century American Missionary Education." Ph.D. diss., University of Illinois–Champaign-Urbana, 2007.

Simonsen, Jane. *Making Home Work: Domesticity and Native American Assimilation in the American West, 1860–1919.* Chapel Hill: University of North Carolina Press, 2006.

Sleeper-Smith, Susan. *Indian Women and French Men: Rethinking Cultural Encounter in the Western Great Lakes.* Amherst: University of Massachusetts Press, 2001.

Smith, Andrea. *Conquest: Sexual Violence and American Indian Genocide.* Cambridge, MA: South End Press, 2005.

Smith, David Lee. *Ho-Chunk Tribal History: The History of the Ho-Chunk People from the Mound Building Era to the Present Day.* 1996.

Sneve, Virginia Driving Hawk. *Completing the Circle.* Lincoln: University of Nebraska Press, 1995.

———. *That They May Have Life: The Episcopal Church in South Dakota, 1859–1976.* New York: Seabury Press, 1977.

Spector, Janet. *What this Awl Means: Feminist Archaeology at a Wahpeton Dakota Village.* St. Paul: Minnesota Historical Society Press, 1993.

Spector, Janet, Elden Johnson, Eric Christopher Grimm, University of Minnesota, and Department of Anthropology. *Archaeology, Ecology, and Ethnohistory of the Prairie-Forest Border Zone of Minnesota and Manitoba.* UNIC Anthropology Conference. *Reprints in Anthropology* 31. Lincoln, NE: J & L Reprint Co., 1985.

Spring, Joel. *Deculturalization and the Struggle for Equality: A Brief History of the Education of Dominated Cultures in the United States.* Boston: McGraw-Hill, 2001.

Stipe, Claude. "Eastern Dakota Acculturation: The Role of Agents of Culture Change." Ph.D. diss., University of Minnesota, 1968.

Sturtevant, William, general editor. *Handbook of North American Indians*. 13: "The Plains." Washington: Smithsonian Institution, 2001.

Talbot, Steve. "Spiritual Genocide: The Denial of American Indian Religious Freedom, from Conquest to 1934." *Wicazo Sa Review* 21 (Autumn 2006): 7–39.

Temple, Seth. *Camp McClellan during the Civil War*. Davenport, IA: Contemporary Club, 1928.

Torrence, Gaylord. *The American Indian Parfleche: A Tradition of Abstract Painting*. Seattle: University of Washington Press with Des Moines Art Center, 1994.

Trafzer, Clifford E. *As Long as the Grass Shall Grow and Rivers Flow: A History of Native Americans*. Fort Worth, TX: Harcourt College Publishers, 2000.

Trayte, David. "The Role of Dress in Eastern Dakota and White Interaction, 1834–1862: A Symbol in Contending Cultures." Ph.D. diss., University of Minnesota, 1993.

Tyler, Suzanne, ed. *The Artist and the Missionary: A Native-American Euro-American Cultural Exchange: Proceedings of the 1992 Plains Indian Seminar*. Cody, WY: Buffalo Bill Historical Center, 1994.

U.S. Congress. *Condition of the Indian Tribes: Report of the Joint Special Committee, Appointed Under Joint Resolution of March 3, 1865: With an Appendix*. Report, 39th Cong., 2d Sess., Senate, no. 156. Washington, DC: Government Printing Office, 1867.

U.S. Office of Indian Affairs. *Letters Sent by the Office of Indian Affairs, 1824–1881*. Washington, DC: National Archives, 1963.

———. *Annual Reports of the Office of Indian Affairs*.

Upham, Warren. *Minnesota Place Names: A Geographical Encyclopedia*. 3rd ed. St. Paul: Minnesota Historical Society Press, 2001.

Usner, Daniel. *Indian Work: Language and Livelihood in Native American History*. Cambridge, MA: Harvard University Press, 2009.

Van Kirk, Sylvia. *Many Tender Ties: Women in Fur-Trade Society, 1670–1870*. Norman: University of Oklahoma Press, 1983.

Wagoner, Levi. "Camp McClellan and the Redskins." *Annals of Jackson County, Iowa* 5 (1908): 19–22.

Walker, J. R. *Lakota Belief and Ritual*. Lincoln: University of Nebraska Press with Colorado Historical Society, 1991.

Wallis, Wilson D. *Beliefs and Tales of the Canadian Dakota. Tales of the Santee (Eastern) Dakota Nation*. Vol. 1. St. Paul, MN: Sisseton-Wahpeton Sioux Tribe with Prairie Smoke Press, 1999.

Welsh, William. *Journal of the Rev. S. D. Hinman, Missionary to the Santee Sioux Indians*. Philadelphia: McCalla Stavely Printers, 1869.

Whelan, Mary K. "The Archaeological Analysis of a Nineteenth Century Dakota Economy." Ph.D. diss., University of Minnesota, 1987.

White, Bruce M. "Indian Visits: Stereotypes of Minnesota's Native People." *Minnesota History* 53 (Fall 1992): 99–111.

White, Richard. *The Middle Ground: Indians, Empires, and Republics in the Great Lakes Region, 1650–1815*. New York: Cambridge University Press, 1991.

Williams-Forson, Psyche A. *Building Houses Out of Chicken Legs*. Chapel Hill: University of North Carolina Press, 2006.

Wills, Jocelyn. *Boosters, Hustlers, and Speculators: Entrepreneurial Culture and the Rise of Minneapolis and St. Paul, 1849–1883*. St. Paul: Minnesota Historical Society Press, 2005.

Wilson, Angela Cavender. "A Day in the Life of Maza Okiye Win." *Minnesota History* 56 (Winter 1998–99): 200–201.

———. *In the Footsteps of our Ancestors: The Dakota Commemorative Marches of the 21st Century*. St. Paul, MN: Living Justice Press, 2006.

Wilson, Angela Cavender, and Eli Taylor. *Remember This! Dakota Decolonization and the Eli Taylor Narratives*. Lincoln: University of Nebraska Press, 2005.

Wilson, Diane. *Beloved Child: A Dakota Way of Life*. St. Paul, MN: Borealis Books, 2011.

———. *Spirit Car: Journey to a Dakota Past*. St. Paul, MN: Borealis Books, 2006.

Wingerd, Mary. *North Country: The Making of Minnesota*. Minneapolis: University of Minnesota Press, 2010.

Woolworth, Alan R. *Santee Dakota Indian Legends. Tales of the Santee (Eastern) Dakota Nation*. Vol. 2. St. Paul, MN: Sisseton-Wahpeton Sioux Tribe with Prairie Smoke Press, 2003.

Woolworth, Alan R., and Nancy L. Woolworth. "Eastern Dakota Settlement and Subsistence Patterns Prior to 1851." *Minnesota Archeologist* 39 (1980): 70–89.

Wozniak, John S. *Contact, Negotiation and Conflict: An Ethnohistory of the Eastern Dakota, 1819–1839*. Washington, DC: University Press of America, 1978.

Wright, Charles. "Rock Island Prison, 1864–1865." *Southern Historical Society Papers* I (April 1876): 281–92.

Zitkala-Sa (Gertrude Simmons Bonnin). *Dreams and Thunder: Stories, Poems, and the Sun Dance Opera*. Lincoln: University of Nebraska Press, 2001.

INDEX

Page numbers in *italic* refer to illustrations.

ILLUSTRATION CREDITS

pages 3, 120, 132   Photos courtesy of William Beane

pages 6–9   Timothy D. Campbell, based on map "Locations of the Santee Sioux," in Roy W. Meyer, *History of the Santee Sioux: United States Indian Policy on Trial*, opposite p. 42

page 17   National Museum of Natural History, Smithsonian Institution, catalogue # E 73311-0

pages 23, 151, 152, 154, 159, 160, 178   Photos by author

page 24   Science Museum of Minnesota, catalogue # 61-12

page 27   Rockwell Museum of Western Art

page 29   Minnesota Historical Society collections, 1998.163.831.43

page 32   Peabody Essex Museum, catalogue # E6641

page 33   Bern Historical Museum

page 36   Brooklyn Museum of Art, catalogue # 506759 a-b

pages 56–59   Jacqueline Gessner Mathers

page 131   Photo courtesy of the Center for Western Studies, Augustana College

page 144   Nebraska State Historical Society, catalogue # 8634-254

page 145   National Museum of the American Indian, Smithsonian Institution, catalogue # 253885

page 157   Nebraska State Historical Society, catalogue # 11055-2914; photo by author

page 158   National Museum of the American Indian, Smithsonian Institution, catalogue # 28516 page 163   National Museum of Natural History, Smithsonian Institution, catalogue # 424906, 424907

page 166   Nebraska State Historical Society, catalogue # 8634-219

page 167   Nebraska State Historical Society, catalogue # 8634-131

page 168   Nebraska State Historical Society, catalogue # 8634-114

page 172   Photo by Carol Slade